THE EDITORS

Lee S. Shulman is Associate Professor of Educational Psychology at Michigan State University. He is engaged in research on cognitive behavior in adults and in cognitive development of children. He received his M.A. and Ph.D. at the University of Chicago. His articles have appeared in the *American Educational Research Journal, Personnel and Guidance Journal,* and *School Review.*

Evan R. Keislar is Professor of Educational Psychology at the University of California, Los Angeles. He is primarily interested in the psychology of instructing the young child, and is carrying out research at the kindergarten-primary level to study principles of learning underlying instruction in various fields. He received his M.A. at the Pacific School of Religion, his Ph.D. at the University of California. He is Consulting Editor of the *American Educational Research Journal.*

Learning by Discovery

JEROME S. BRUNER
Harvard University

LEE J. CRONBACH
Stanford University

ROBERT B. DAVIS
Madison Project, Webster College

ROBERT M. GAGNÉ
University of California, Berkeley

ROBERT GLASER
University of Pittsburgh

DAVID HAWKINS
University of Colorado

JEROME KAGAN
Harvard University

EVAN R. KEISLAR
University of California, Los Angeles

HOWARD H. KENDLER
University of California, Santa Barbara

LLOYD N. MORRISETT
Carnegie Corporation of New York

LEE S. SHULMAN
Michigan State University

M. C. WITTROCK
University of California, Los Angeles

LEARNING BY DISCOVERY:

A CRITICAL APPRAISAL

Lee S. Shulman
Evan R. Keislar
Editors

Proceedings of a conference on Learning by Discovery under the sponsorship of Stanford University and the Committee on Learning and the Educational Process of the Social Science Research Council. The conference was conducted and reported pursuant to a contract with the United States Department of Health, Education, and Welfare, Office of Education, under the provisions of the Cooperative Research Program.

RAND MCNALLY & COMPANY   CHICAGO

RAND McNALLY EDUCATION SERIES

B. Othanel Smith *Advisory Editor*

Broudy and Palmer, *Exemplars of Teaching Method*
Broudy, Smith, and Burnett, *Democracy and Excellence in American Secondary Education*
Burns and Lowe, *The Language Arts in Childhood Education*
Dupuis, *Philosophy of Education in Historical Perspective*
Farwell and Peters, eds., *Guidance Readings for Counselors*
Foshay, ed., *Rand McNally Handbook of Education*
Hains, *Guiding the Student Teaching Process in Elementary Education*
Kaplan and Steiner, *Musicianship for the Classroom Teacher*
Kimbrough, *Political Power and Educational Decision-Making*
Krumboltz, ed., *Learning and the Educational Process*
Lewenstein, *Teaching Social Studies in Junior and Senior High Schools*
Lieberman and Moskow, *Collective Negotiations for Teachers*
Litwack, Holmes, and O'Hern, *Critical Issues in Student Personnel Work*
Michaelis, ed., *Teaching Units in the Social Sciences*, 3 volumes
Norris, Zeran, and Hatch, *The Information Service in Guidance*, 2nd edition
Parker, ed., *Rand McNally Curriculum Series*
    Ford and Pugno, eds., *The Structure of Knowledge and the Curriculum*
    Parker and Rubin, *Process as Content*
    Wellington and Wellington, *The Underachiever*
Perrodin, ed., *The Student Teacher's Reader*
Peters and Farwell, *Guidance: A Developmental Approach*
Peters, Shertzer, and Van Hoose, *Guidance in Elementary Schools*
Phi Delta Kappa, *Education and the Structure of Knowledge*
Phi Delta Kappa, *Improving Experimental Design and Statistical Analysis*
Rollins and Unruh, *Introduction to Secondary Education*
Shulman and Keislar, eds., *Learning by Discovery*
Smith, ed., *Aesthetics and Criticism in Art Education*
Smith and Ennis, eds., *Language and Concepts in Education*
Taba and Elkins, *Teaching Strategies for the Culturally Disadvantaged*
Trump and Baynham, *Focus on Change: Guide to Better Schools*
Vassar, ed., *Social History of American Education*, 2 volumes
Wolf and Loomer, *The Elementary School: A Perspective*
Zeran and Riccio, *Organization and Administration of Guidance Services*

Also published by Rand McNally,
    Gage, ed., *Handbook of Research on Teaching*—A Project of the American Educational
        Research Association

Preface

SINCE ITS ORGANIZATION IN 1962, THE COMMITTEE ON LEARNING AND the Educational Process of the Social Science Research Council has been active in fostering research in the area of the application of psychology to education. It has arranged a conference on the perceptual and linguistic aspects of reading, and two six-week summer conferences (one in 1964 and one in 1965) for the training of educational research workers, largely at the postdoctoral level.

In February of 1964 the committee decided to initiate a conference on the topic of *learning by discovery*, the proceedings of which are reported in the present volume. The conference, held in New York City, January 28 and 29, 1965, was sponsored by the U.S. Office of Education in cooperation with Stanford University. It was held in order to (1) clarify some of the issues involved; (2) review what is now known about this subject; and (3) suggest ways of extending knowledge in this field.

The members of the committee during 1964 and 1965 included Lee J. Cronbach, Stanford University, chairman; Eleanor J. Gibson, Cornell University; Richard Atkinson, Stanford University; Evan R. Keislar, University of California, Los Angeles; George A. Miller, Harvard University; Lloyd N. Morrisett, Carnegie Corporation of New York, and Judson C. Shaplin, Washington University, St. Louis. Ben Willerman served as staff for the committee until his death in 1965, when he was replaced by Rowland L. Mitchell, Jr.

The subcommittee delegated to plan the conference included Evan Keislar, chairman; Robert Gagné, American Institute for Research, Pittsburgh; and Jerome Kagan, Harvard University. Lee S. Shulman, Michigan State University, was appointed recorder for the conference.

In addition to the members of the committee and subcommittee, the following individuals participated in the conference: Jerome Bruner, Harvard University; Robert Davis, The Madison Project, Webster College, St. Louis, Missouri; Robert Glaser, University of Pittsburgh; David Hawkins, University of Colorado; Robert Karplus, University of California, Berkeley; Howard H. Kendler, University of California, Santa Barbara; Bert Y. Kersh, Center for Teaching Research, Monmouth, Oregon; Sonia Osler, The Johns Hopkins Hospital; Walter R. Reitman, University of Michigan; Lee S. Shulman, Michigan State University; Michael Wallach, Duke University; Sheldon H. White, University of Chicago; David Wiley, University of California, Los Angeles; Merlin C. Wittrock, University of California, Los Angeles; Rowland L. Mitchell, Jr., Social Science Research Council. Observers included J. Richard Suchman, U.S. Office of Education; Charles Whitmer, National Science Foundation; Rosslyn Suchman, Office of Naval Research and Gallaudet College, Washington, D.C.

Appreciation is expressed to the U.S. Office of Education for its sponsorship of the conference, under Project No. F-064, in cooperation with Stanford University as contracting agent, and to the staff of the Social Science Research Council, who made the physical arrangements for the conference. We are also indebted to Roslyn Blum and Carolyn Stern for helpful suggestions with respect to revisions in the manuscript, to Joyce Stewart for her transcriptions of the many audio-tapes of conference discussions and her typing of the final manuscript, and to Joan Lynas for her assistance in the preparation of the bibliography and index. We also thank Clara Hahne for her administrative services before, during, and after the conference.

Lee S. Shulman
Evan R. Keislar

East Lansing, Michigan
Los Angeles, California
March, 1966

Contents

Introduction

THIS VOLUME IS DIVIDED INTO FIVE MAJOR SECTIONS. THE FIRST SECTION deals with the dimensions of the issue of *learning by discovery*. In his paper, David Hawkins takes the position that there are certain kinds of things that can be learned only by discovery. Among them are those experiences which constitute the preparation process in any learning sequence. He also argues that in education, as in many other practical sciences, the art of the practitioner is often capable of producing effects which the theoretician is still at a loss to explain. Robert Glaser looks at the question of discovery in the direct terms of the psychologist concerned with problems of training. His implication, vis-a-vis Hawkins, is that when an objective is described in behavioral terms, the behavior is clearly teachable.

The second section of the volume deals with the educational and psychological research pertaining to discovery. M. C. Wittrock reviews the literature of research in "The Learning by Discovery Hypothesis." By so doing, he attempts to clarify some of the confusion which has pervaded the field. In "The Logic of Experiments on Discovery," Lee Cronbach presents a critical analysis of research, not only on learning by discovery, but in the general field of education itself. He is especially critical of the constricted range of dependent variables typically utilized in learning experiments and suggests a dramatic increase in their number and scope.

The third section focusses upon attempts to utilize ideas generated by the concept of learning by discovery in curricular innovations. In his article, Jerome Bruner describes the activities of classes engaged in some unique approaches to the social sciences. He presents a number of vivid examples of children making discoveries and attempts to enumerate a list of elements which account for what takes place in the classroom. "Discovery in the Teaching of Mathematics" finds Robert Davis discussing the way in which notions of learning by discovery have influenced the objectives and execution of the Madison project, one of the 'new mathematics' curricula. Both papers in this section focus on what teachers do.

The fourth section deals with psychological research and theory and their implications for the practice of education. In "Varieties of Learning and the Concept of Discovery," Robert M. Gagné utilizes his hierarchical model of kinds of learning as a tool for analyzing the relevance of the concept of discovery in learning. "Learning, Attention, and the Issue of Discovery" is Jerome Kagan's analysis of the personological or, as he prefers to call them, parapsychological variables in learning by discovery. Kagan emphasizes the developmental and individual-difference variables which must be taken into consideration before evaluation of any principle of learning can take place.

The final section of the volume is composed of reflections, further reflections, and a retrospective analysis. In their papers, Howard Kendler and Lloyd Morrisett review and analyze the preceding papers in an on-the-spot operation which took place in the final session. In "The Problem of Discovery: Conference in Retrospect," Evan Keislar and Lee Shulman utilize the advantages of time and their editorial opportunity to study the papers to present a retrospective analysis of the conference and a prospectus for future research in this area. Since the same sources were so frequently cited by different authors, a common bibliography for all the papers is presented at the end of the book.

At the end of each of the first four sections is a summary of the discussions which took place immediately following the presentation of each paper. Summarizing discussions by a group of psychologists, physical scientists, philosophers, and educators, carried on over a two-day period, is a task which admits of a number of strategies. Reporting verbatim the words of the discussants has the distinct advantage of preserving the dramatic impact of assertion and confrontation; however, it has the concomitant disadvantage of discontinuity and disorganization invariably present when any group of individuals is engaged in active debate.

An alternative strategy is to ignore the actual sequence of positions taken and simply to present, in most distilled form, the gist of statements made by members of the group in any discussion as these are appropriate to a specified topic.

In this volume a compromise procedure was adopted. We decided to preserve, whenever possible, the dramatic and dialectical advantages of reporting the confrontation between ideas, while introducing greater order and homogeneity of content into the summarized discussions. To do this required modifying the order in which various conversations occurred, while maintaining the feeling of dialogue in the interchanges. It is hoped that, in this form, the volume will serve the needs of its readers more adequately, just as a history is more valuable than a simple chronicle. The various positions taken by the participants on the topic of, for example, language and discovery, may have spanned all five sessions of the conference. For purposes of this volume, however, all these statements and rebuttals are gathered together in a single session, as if they had occurred contiguously. Whenever this procedure might have produced a distortion, the original context was retained. Hence, the discussion sections represent a mating of academic responsibility and editorial license. The license, however, is taken only with sequence, never with content.

PART ONE

THE ISSUE

Chapter I

Learning the Unteachable

DAVID HAWKINS

IN THIS PAPER I HAVE TWO PARALLEL INTERESTS. THE FIRST IS THE investigative art which we adults practice who are interested in the furtherance of education; here I shall try to speak partly as a philosopher of science. The second is to report, by a few small examples, a particular kind of investigation into the investigative art as practiced by children of elementary school age.

The art we are engaged in, as I see it, is a potentially fruitful combination of the practical and the scientific. We hope to contribute some real guidance to the evolution of educational systems, primarily through learning some significant things about the psychology of learning and of teaching. Our efforts are being made, I believe, in an historical situation where the best practice excels the best theory in quite essential ways; this fact defines a strategy we ought to follow.

There have often been times in the history of science when the personal knowledge of practitioners was significantly deeper than anything embedded in the beliefs and writings of the academically learned. Indeed, science has never started in a social vacuum, but has grown typically out of the interplay of *Theorizein* and those practically achieved mappings of nature embodied in the working arts. There is an amusing example in the mathematical theory of probability. It is recorded by Suetonius that the Emperor Claudius wrote a treatise on the art of dicing. The Roman and Greek form of the game, still played in England I think, involved three throws of three dice, each ranging in score from aces to boxcars ('dog' to 'Venus'). In the Middle Ages, gentlemen and ladies played vigorously, and there were schools of theory and strategy. Yet, with the exception of unimportant anticipations, we can date the beginning of combinatoric *theory* from the famous conversation of Pascal with the good Chevalier de Mérée. What every soldier of the Legion knew a good bit about from his *tesserai* had to

3

wait two thousand years for the literal breakthrough into the camp of the learned—a break through a wall of social insulation; and because of the relevance to the flourishing mathematics of Pascal's day, it was not long before a mathematician would know more about the subject than any mere gentleman. Part of the explanation, of course, is social onus. De Moivre had to apologize in his preface for writing about it at all.

As another example, there is the story of Gilbert, who has a deserved fame in the history of physics because he had the wit and intellectual courage to seek instruction concerning the magnet from metallurgists, mariners, and miners, rather than rest content with his tradition.

Of course the situation is never twice the same, in any detail, and our situation is more complex, but I think it justifies the analogy and thus suggests directions.

I have, and want only, to speak personally in the first instance. The good teaching I have observed, teaching by teachers who are accustomed to major success, owes little to modern theories of learning and cognition and much to apprenticeship, on-the-job inquiry, discussion, trial—ceaseless trial—within a common-sense psychological framework; a framework that is not all unsophisticated, however, and is able to accept individual insights from psychological (mostly psychotherapeutic) sources but without jargon or dogma: keeping the practice dry.

I would say also that the difference between the best teaching and the worst, or even the average, is very great. I conjure up a measure which would scale about like the distribution of billiard scores, not normal but skewed, even logarithmically skewed, and for the reasons that generally underly the logarithmico-normal distributions: something that increases its accommodation with its growth.

Under these circumstances, it seems to me the better part of wisdom to find the good school situations—not the better third but the best one per cent—and engage in close observation and intellectual resonance; then to try to recreate such situations and make them more abundant and reproducible, no holds barred. Nothing about this process is easy, but it can be done because it is done—but rarely. Nor is formal codification a first or a safe step. The essence is certainly not a simple one; more than likely it is a subtle mapping across conspicuous variations in local culture and individual style. However difficult the formulation, there are in practice many ways by which one can recognize good school situations without consulting or writing a formulary. We all know some of them, and probably none knows all of them. The best at it are likely to be those who practice the art and are articulate, can talk back to academics; so the initial role of the latter is necessarily and enjoyably a humble one. In fact, this first direction of research is co-extensive with some kinds of practical innovative work that many of us have begun to engage in, sometimes, I think, with too prompt a closure as to our goals.

This may turn out to be the kind of talk which will leave me in the position of a speaker who was constrained to finish by saying, "Now, if there is anyone I haven't insulted, I apologize." I expose my own breast, if that helps. At any rate, I want to expose my own belief, surely based on inadequate evidence, that most experimental work in the psychology of learning and teaching has not been very relevant to learning or teaching. A teacher friend of mine put it thus: "Most psychologists," she said, "have never really *looked* at children." Since of course most psychologists, and certainly all those here, *have* obviously looked at children, the remark may need some interpretation.

To interpret: Let me say something first about the concept of *preparation*, as when one talks about preparing an experiment. I do not mean the preparation which consists in getting oneself ready, but the preparation of the subject of the experiment, a light-beam, or a colony of paramoecia, or a child, or classroom of children. In physics or in chemistry of a classical sort, the preparation in this sense is what one does by arranging boundary conditions—by isolating and controlling—or in observing them; it does not matter in one sense, except the boundary conditions relevant to testing a particular hypothesis may be almost infinitely rare in the wild state. In the modern range of physics the concept gets a sharper meaning, because to get a system in an antecedently well defined state involves choice, and thus a sacrifice: To achieve definition, i.e., preparation, the experimenter must introduce discontinuities in his knowledge of the system's past, must give up information conjugate to what he has gained in the preparation. In psychological investigation this is always likewise true in principle, though we have no firm formulations of it. In atomic physics, to compensate, we are usually dealing with relatively simple systems, and the preparation requires no long history—other than that of science itself.

There are many psychological experiments, I know, which require comparatively simple preparation; and good sampling across the relevant dimensions of a universe will sometimes help to reduce uncertainty in wild or unanticipated variables. So we settle for some kind of statistical preparation. Problems of control are more or less solved if we do not demand too much, and others can get more or less similar results. What

5

I want to say, however, is that the preparation involved in pedagogical investigations goes up very sharply with the significance of their results and that an experiment which takes a half-hour or a day or a week to prepare is, in general, not worth doing.

There is a fundamental theory about experiments; it comes out of physics and is relevant here, not because we are doing physics but because whatever we are doing is done in a physical milieu and not in a world of abstractions. To call something an independent variable is not to use a name but to claim an achievement. To do experiments in the high-energy physics of very small, things, for example, one must have apparatus whose large size can be specified in advance, from purely dimensional considerations. In biology another dimension looms as crucial, that is preparation time. To put a complex system in a prepared state takes time. The good biological experiments have such a long preparation time that husbandry becomes the dominant characteristic of a lab or station; in the short run, at least, its resident prepared species determine its experiments. And let us not forget that the greatest achievements of 19th-century biology were essentially opportunistic in their methodology, exploratory rather than experimental. I know some of the exceptions and I do not want to oversimplify, but that is the general picture.

In theory there is a natural measure of *amount* of preparation and, derivatively, of preparation time. It is the logarithm of the improbability of the prepared state in the milieu from which the sample is drawn, molecule, or paramoecium, or child, or classroom, or school. Judged by this standard, situations of optimal learning require a great deal of preparation. If we do experiments in learning with only superficial preparation—instructions, 'training,' etc., of short duration—then the rare things get swamped by statistical noise, the tail of the distribution is invisible. Whatever its limitations, the work of Piaget has the relevance it has because of a relatively long preparation for the observations resulting; and I am sure an even longer preparation is needed to get past some of the limitations of such work, including possible errors of interpretation, etc. But this is the other side of the picture from the usual complaint about lack of statistical methodology. The latter *alone*, with perfunctory preparation, will bury the Piaget phenomena. This brings me back to the point that looking for optimal teaching situations 'in the wild,' and seeking to stabilize and reproduce them, is an easier start than trying to create them *de novo*. The lack of this I see as the greatest stumbling block in a 'scientific' approach, and the commitment to it as a great scientific hope. Let us take, as a practical unit, the work

6

of an optimal teacher in involving a whole class of children before he, as a teacher, is ready to harvest any impressive results. These times are automatically months at least, and for some purposes, years—lifetimes. If I am right in this, it means that the now standard image of the lab or clinic is inappropriate. It means that investigators in this area will look rather like teachers, or educational innovators, or classroom ethologists spending months watching preparations or 'doing' them and—to come back to my teacher friend's complaint—finally, "really looking at children."

Considered realistically, the preparatory art in this field will never be a simply programmed procedure, for the reason that each subject, whether four-year-old or college student, will differ in some important ways from all the others, and that there will of necessity be an artful intermixture of observation, diagnosis, treatment all along the way, tailored in some critical respects to each subject. It is of, course, most unlikely that different children will arrive at any predetermined point by the same pathway, or at the same time; on any cross section of a group, in any record of performance, there will be a large variance. It is this variance, or some part of it, which is often stereotyped and quantified as 'ability,' importing into the description of learning dubious assumptions not only of constancy but especially of linearity, without which the dispositional concept of ability becomes ill-defined.

You may have been troubled already as to what I mean by the contrast of preparation and experiment. The experiment is simply the injection of some specified material for learning, at a point when it is judged, by whatever criteria, that children have been brought to a state of preparation, or of momentary readiness, to have educationally interesting and significant interactions with it.

Let me give an example from the background of elementary school science in the middle grades. Very often in the study of physical systems, there is some real point, both literal and figurative, which has to be identified in order that sharp physical analysis can get under way. One of these is with the Archimedean balance, say a board on a stabilizing fulcrum with blocks for weights. This is a system which children can encounter, with interesting results, over a wide range of ages. But let us suppose we are in the range of the sort of result which Archimedes immortalized, the law of the unequal arm balance. I shall not even try to enumerate the learning preconditions that make this an educationally hopeful encounter. One is that children have a rule-schema already established; they are *looking for* a rule of balance. There are many interesting phenomena here, including 'wrong' rules that work very well over a variety of cases. I shall single out only one, which is that children often measure in to the blocks, from the ends of the board, rather than outward from the center of support. You can easily suppress this phenomenon of end-measuring if you want to. The point is that you *don't* want to; it is part of the definition of a prepared state. Suppose you encourage a tabulation of balanced configurations. Can a rule be extracted from this tabulation that will enable you to predict new balance configurations? Of course, since there is a simple transformation from one coordinate system into the other. Try end-measuring with equal numbers of blocks on the two sides, and you'll get a pretty obvious rule. Now try it with unequal numbers. The case is rather like that of the Ptolemaic-Copernican transformations, and for similar reasons. From our point of view there is a shadow parameter, like the Ptolemaic deferent: the half-length of the board. But from the child's point of view it is no shadow, the ends of the board are real natural markers, and he is accustomed to using their like in many other manipulations, physical and intellectual. To ask him to disregard them would be to remove a reliable conceptual tool, without replacing it. The pedagogical experiment, then, is to define empirically a set of pathways by which children will *discover* the possibilities of a fulcrum-centered coordinate system. Some children will have gotten it first, without any interest in the ends of the board. They are out of this particular game. Some will not make the transition, in spite of the preparation; those the experimenters will come back to, in another context. Some will make the transition only because 'teacher told them to.' Here the experiment is simply spoiled. But some will make it—if the preparation has been artful, and right. These we watch carefully, and listen to their discourse, perhaps taking some part in it as stabilizers and amplifiers. What were the paths? One might be some analogy to other centered systems i.e., tall block houses, or trees; preparation cannot exclude this variance, it is of the essence of experience. Another might be from accidental or contrived asymmetry of the board itself, with an extra weight to balance. A third might be from mapping the real board into the realm of tabulated numbers, then 'seeing' what we would call the linear transformation; some children have this early comfort with number-schemata. (But no one will see the world in a number line unless he has first seen the world.) A fourth will have been passive, but gotten the idea by contagion from a classmate. What has happened here? How does this differ from being told, by book or teacher?

A negative purpose in such experiments is to probe for the limits of what has been accomplished. Will the accomplishment appear to have evaporated, in a slightly altered context? Has a new schema really been laid down, a new *analogon* stored for future trial, or will there be several rediscoveries later on before the logical pathway is really cleared? One investigation commits us to many more. Do we measure the swing of a pendulum in from the extremes? Again, we can. Of a heavy bob and a light bob, will the heavy one swing out *farther* on the other side? What is a pendulum doing when it is not swinging? (Under what conditions will the balance analogy, so inappropriate by gross visual analogies, be retrieved here?)

Of course, I do not wish to limit investigation to these kinds, where we are interested in the way humans construct taxonomies or road maps or networks (conceptual nets—it would beg many questions, at this stage, to call them "nomological"). But they are among the most important investigations, not only for education, but for epistemology in general. Significant concepts, concepts which reduce gross redundancy and bring order to our perception of the world, are not communicated, in the first instance, and thus cannot be 'taught.' This is the evidence of epistemology, from the time of Plato and Aristotle. A *word* can be taught, a name that will name a concept if it stands out for naming. But concepts can be *learned*, which means evolved in the economy of individual experience. Concepts of this order are not transmitted ready-made in the pulsed code of human communication, for they belong first to the apparatus which encodes and decodes those factual messages, not to the messages themselves. No one learns a first language by being 'told' it, he rather *abstracts* it from the rich parallel redundancy of two sorts of messages coming together: these from the natural, and those from the vocal, environment of his infancy. It is so likewise, I believe, with the later beginnings of scientific conceptualization: Such concepts as I speak of do not come first, and then serve to link and order the paths of experience; they grow, rather, as stopping places and intersections along paths of experience which, relative to them, are preconceptual. The process is as with the growth of cities; their highways create them.

The special importance of such investigations as I have been discussing—and epistemologically prejudging—is to describe, and fix vividly, the distinction between the evolution of conceptual expedients and the storage and recovery of single items of information in terms of already established conceptual habits. If we are going to talk about discovery in this conference, let us not forget that the word itself suffers from ambiguity of just the kind I have been discussing. This ambiguity is treated neatly by Stephen Toulmin (1953), who wrote a book on it. Most people, when they hear about a new scientific discovery, assume that what happened is like the discovery of a lost manuscript or a new continent or planet. But as Toulmin points out, many of the great discoveries, so called, are not like that at all. Einstein, for a famous example, did not find any new previously unknown entities or facts; what he found was a new way of classifying and relating known things, and this had the virtue of leading to predictions of fact which were new, discoveries in the second sense.

Toulmin illustrates what he means by the example of geometrical optics, which gives a uniform schematic representation of certain optical phenomena by finding an isomorphism between those phenomena and corresponding geometrical elements. The optical phenomena are not new; what is new is the ability to see them as elements in a geometrical pattern.

I am sure that Toulmin overdoes the contrast, or at least under-does the rich historical interconnections between new fact and new vision, each facilitating the other. But the contrast is still essential. In the elementary school context, we have seen Toulmin's particular example enacted more than once with the varied phenomena of light and shadow. It is not true that children first have all the facts straight, so to say, and then get the geometrical counterpart. And it is most emphatically not true that they can first get the geometry, and then anticipate the optics. A dominant group do not have the 'facts' straight at all, even up to gross errors in predicting where shadows will intersect things (surprisingly, this incompetence includes not a few adults). Their usual ability to summon forth the dubious statement, Light Travels in Straight Lines helps not at all. What one sees always is the intercommunication of fact and framework, of model and modeled.

In my discussion so far my main point has been the need to create, reproduce, and describe essentially complex and metastable states of momentary readiness for learning or evolving some rudimentary but powerful conceptual tools of science and thus the need of optimal teaching as a tool of investigation. It is my contention that the serious inquirer into learning at this level is almost committed, for the sake of knowledge, to become an educational reformer malgré lui.

Let me now come to the specific claims, hypotheses, or hunches suggested by the slogan, 'Discovery Method.' I shall be quick to say I react negatively to it, partly because I have already seen it used as a defense against a lack of subject content and as a way of minimizing the importance of preparation—of plowing, sowing, cultivating, irrigating—as against harvesting. Discovery Method suggests that teachers car harvest without the long preparation; and that notion can only, I think, take us back to the food-gathering stage, with thin crops indeed. If I were free to define from scratch, intending it to be a eulogistic term, I would say it was an attempt to teach with minimum self-deception about the powers of the spoken or printed word.

The crucial theoretical issue, as I see it, is an issue of cognitive psychology. It is an issue over the way we conceptualize what goes on in educationally significant learning. It is an issue, specifically, over the inherent simplicity or complexity of such learning, its inherent dependence on the cognitive history of the learner, and the kind and degree of autonomy exhibited by such a learner when he does learn or, to use an Aristotelian expression, the autotelic character of his operation.

This issue ought to be sharply distinguished from any overall debate about better and worse ways of teaching, although it has great relevance obviously. Arguments from theory to method are likely, at this stage, to be nonsequiturs. As said above, the best arguments seem likely, for some time, to run the other way. The notion that there is a single best way of teaching, across the universe of individual differences, of histories of preparation, of age, of teachers, is highly implausible. Still, there are directions indicated. One of them is typified by an old and well-known experiment of Edward Tolman, representing a type of study which psychologists have been too quick, I believe, to dismiss: latent learning experiments with rats. I bow for the moment to their authority concerning the rat, but not concerning the man. I have seen and heard reported too much of the same kind of human learning, sometimes, to minimize its importance, called play without directors and enticers. And that minimizing is what our schools have tended to do, almost to the vanishing point. But I should also make another claim, an a priori one in relation to the psychology of learning. This has to do with the inherent structural features of the adult world of science into which we propose to induct children. The order of this world is more complex than can be represented by the topology of linear orderings, or even of branching trees. It is inherently a network, a network of experimental paths intersecting at knots or nodes of significant conceptualization. We map this network, or try to, into linear orderings when we go marching through the curriculum, the 'little racecourse.'

We ourselves do not know the multiplicity of paths—which is one of the reasons why teaching cannot be separated from the arts and heuristics of discovery. What we do know, from the theory and history of knowledge, is that in exploring and mapping such a domain the fundamental metric is not feet or miles but an informational measure in psychological space, such that a well-trodden path is in principle a short one, and the path always long to what is new. The economy of slowing down, even wandering, lies in the creation of highways. When we say that a particular curricular involvement has, for certain children, a lot of mileage, we literally mean a large reduction of redundancy, and this could properly be called 'bittage" instead of 'mileage.' But variances of personal constitution and history will never allow a teacher to lead a child by his shortest paths unless the teacher directs himself toward a reinforcement of the child's autonomy, and thus in leading well is also led.

If there is any cogency in my argument, it suggests that the most promising scientific methodology in the study of learning and teaching is not that of the compact experiment, an image from the physical sciences. Nature simply doesn't scale that way. It seems to me entirely likely, indeed, that even the investigation of complex automata will soon reach beyond the paradigm of the neatly isolated system with its independent and dependent variables clearly labeled, with a few intervening ones grudgingly conceded; we won't design them for predictability but for evolution, ours as well as theirs. Yet, surely all such systems are gross and stilted when compared to the human child.

Chapter II

Variables in Discovery Learning

THE QUESTION ASSIGNED TO MY CONSIDERATION ASKS, IS LEARNING BY DIS-
covery an important principle in curriculum development? I approach
this task as someone concerned with the design of educational practice.
I am interested in the requirements and specifications for the development of procedures and materials for discovery learning. As an educational designer, I work as a technologist, supplied with a presently
meager, but apparently increasing, body of technological principles and
practices. These are emerging from the interplay between practical attempts at education and relevant research and knowledge from the
sciences which contribute to pedagogical methods.

My design orientation provides me with the following plan of
operation: First, I must analyze the behavior with which I am concerned and specify some performance which will represent a standard of
competence to be attained at the end of a sequence of educational experiences. This performance specification establishes a model or standard
around which individual differences will be displayed. The selected performance must be specified in terms of its class properties because the
stimulus, response, and structural characteristics of the subject-matter
content and the behavioral repertoires involved will determine what I
wish to teach and, correspondingly, how it is to be taught. I should not
be too rigid, however, in sticking to an early specification of this performance because certainly the selection of my instructional goals will
be influenced by my analysis of the behavior under consideration.

Second, I need to specify the characteristics of the students I am
to teach. These characteristics need to be determined either prior to
instruction or in the process of early learning. I shall need to know the
extent to which the student has already acquired some of the things to
be learned, the extent to which he has the prerequisites for learning the
next instructional steps, the extent to which antecedent learning facilitates or interferes with new learning under the conditions I have in

13

mind, and the extent to which an individual can make the necessary sensory discriminations and exhibit motor skills required for initial learning steps.

With information about both the target performance to be attained and the existing preinstructional behavior, I can proceed from one state to the other. This sets up my third task, which is to guide the student or allow him to go from one state of development to another, and I must construct the procedures and materials that I wish to employ in this educational process. As part of this process, I must make provisions for motivational effects, by which I mean providing conditions which will result in the maintenance and extension of the competence being taught.

Finally, I must make provision for assessing and evaluating the nature of the competence achieved by the learner in relation to the performance criteria that have been established.

If this description of the educational process sounds harshly technological, perhaps some elegance has been lost in analysis. But, presumably, once the basic techniques are designed, it is time for the practitioner to apply all the artistry and sensitivity he can muster.

In this paper I will consider only the *first step* of the *first task*, i.e., the general examination of the behavior under concern prior to an experimental analysis.

I cannot emphasize enough the importance of this first task—the analysis of behavior. I believe that it has been neglected in psychological research, and I also believe that it has been the most important element in recent improvements in instruction. In the design of educational programs, analyses of the terminal objectives to be achieved have been a more influential endeavor than manipulations in methods of teaching these objectives. This is probably so because it is the first step in the sequence of tasks in instructional design. (The fascination of Piaget and the Geneva School lies, to some extent, in their keen analyses of children's behavior; but they stop short of the succeeding steps in the operational plan for instruction.)

My analysis begins with an examination of the tasks that have been labeled discovery learning. I find here that I am confronted by a confusion between two different kinds of events. One has to do with learning by discovery, that is, teaching certain objectives by a discovery method; the other has to do with learning to discover, or teaching for a terminal objective which is manifested by the ability to make discoveries.

LEARNING BY DISCOVERY

The most prevalent case, learning by discovery is defined usually as teaching an association, a concept, or rule which involves 'discovery' of the association, concept, or rule. This is contrasted with a more direct instructional sequence in which a discovery method is not employed. And there are variations between these two. When one examines the task situations and instructional sequences that have been called discovery and those that have been contrasted with discovery, what are the outstanding features? Two differences are apparent: First, a learning-by-discovery sequence involves induction. This is the procedure of giving exemplars of a more general case which permits the student to induce the general proposition involved. Assessment of attainment is accomplished by testing whether the student has indeed induced the general proposition by getting him to verbalize it, getting him to apply it to certain exemplars in a way that indicates that he knows the general proposition, or by getting the student to generate additional exemplars. Finding the structure in a body of subject-matter instances is an example of induction, and the structure eventually discovered is a general proposition characterizing or summarizing the properties of these instances.

Second, in using the discovery method, the imposition of a structured instructional sequence is minimized in order to provide a relatively unguided sequence onto which the individual imposes his own structure. This kind of sequence, of necessity, allows the student to pursue blind alleys and find negative instances; and consequently, he makes some wrong moves or incorrect responses in the process of learning. Discovering implies a low probability of making a successful response. Such being the case, errors have a high probability of occurrence.

Discovery sequences can generally be characterized by these two properties: one, inductive sequences, and, two, trial and error or errorful learning in various degrees.

We should then examine these two processes: induction and errorful learning. Depending upon the behavioral objectives these processes are to teach, that is, whether they are to result in the establishment of associations, a concept, a rule, or generalization, these processes can be considered in different ways and can have different merits. However, before considering them with respect to particular terminal behaviors, it is of some use to discuss them generally.

Induction

I begin with the contrast to induction first. This is a teaching sequence in which a rule is presented before exemplars or instances of the rule. This is expository teaching, and in early work with programmed sequences, a rule–example–incomplete example sequence, appeared to be an excellent method for the efficient introduction of a new rule

(Evans, Homme, and Glaser, 1962). The rule–example–incomplete example presentation has the student working on the example of a new rule very early in his exposure to it. In this sort of sequence, the student is given an explicitly stated rule and one or more carefully chosen examples before being asked for a response to an incomplete example. An effective prompt is then set up which minimizes incorrect responses and which provides the student with the reinforcing activity of directly using the rule. Implied here is the rationale that rather than run the risk (at least in the fixed sequence of early program formats) of having the student induce an incorrect rule, it is preferable to state the rule for him explicitly. This philosophy leads to the rejection of inductive presentation. With a rule-example sequence, the student can recognize and apply a rule with proficiency, and often it seems hazardous and slow to approach a rule through induction or through incidental learning. With rule and then example, the student adopts the expert's carefully chosen statement of a rule rather than using his own more fallible induction-derived statement. The limited range of exemplars in most teaching and textbook situations may make it possible for the student to induce what is essentially an incorrect rule but one which happens to fit all the examples presented. This is another possible source of danger in the induction process.

The rule-example expository sequence just described is very frequently used in education. A teacher will typically enunciate a principle and follow this with a series of instances of the principle. This is a prevalent procedure because it leads to quick reinforcement for the teacher and the student. They both see close-to-critrion behavior occur rapidly. It is reinforcing, perhaps for the same reason that the use of punishment is reinforcing to the teacher—because it brings quick results. Other means of influencing behavior are more laborious and their results show up only in the long run.

Presenting rules first is also very effective because it is more useful to remember a general statement that mammals are warm-blooded animals and bear their young live than it is to remember that each specific species, such as monkeys, horses, cows, cats, dogs, etc. is a mammal (Mechner, 1961). Similarly, it is more useful to remember that the square of any number ending in 5 is equal to x times (x + 1) followed by 25, than it is to remember the squares of specific numbers. In general, one is better off remembering information when it is stored in condensed abstract form rather than in many specific instances. The general statement is often the first one given in teaching because it is easiest to remember and because defining and presenting an adequate sample of instances is a difficult task. Sometimes examples of a general case have little dignity and statement of the rule is more profound. It is often easier, more dignified, and more productive of instant knowledge to state the rule before giving examples. While the words I use here suggest negative emotional loadings, nevertheless, for some purposes and for teaching certain kinds of tasks, rule-example is quite effective.

Consider now inductive teaching. Francis Mechner (1961) lucidly points out that great teachers and great writers know the principles of inductive teaching intuitively. Their writings provide us with demonstrations of the effectiveness of giving examples *before* rules. LaFontaine teaches a code of ethics through a series of allegorical fables. Shaw, in *Adventures of the Black Girl in Her Search for God*, makes a general point by providing a succession of specific instances which permit the reader to induce the general concept. Interestingly, Shaw's episodes describe noninstances of the concept being established: Moses, Freud, Pavlov, and others are instances of what God is not, and through these examples Shaw conveys his message.

Good writers ingeniously use a series of incidents to establish the concept of a character. It is hard work, at least for me, to read through the development of a Dostoevsky character so that the concept of this character emerges. C. P. Snow, with an inferior literary style, reinforces me more quickly because he tells me that Arthur Brown is this kind of a character—I get the rule first. Induction is also used by poets and composers when they develop general concepts by specific examples of images and themes.

In summary, it is a long-standing procedure, recognized in society for its excellence, that concepts and principles are learned by the presentation of specific instances which permit the learner or the recipient to generalize among specific instances of a class and to discriminate between instances and noninstances of a class. In these sequences of induction, the learner makes some false inductions, errors if you will, in the course of inducing the rule. Depending upon the subject matter, some rules can be pretty definitively learned, that is, subject to little further correction, such as inducing the concept of equality in mathematics. Other inductive sequences are subject to constant emendation or revision, such as the personality of a character in a story or such scientific concepts as force, energy, or the electron.

This inductive procedure is somewhat similar to the way we teach a concept according to the notions of Hull, Skinner, Keller and Schoenfeld, and, I suspect, Piaget. To teach a child the concept of redness, we first insure that the child has a relevant response available, in this case, that he can already say the word 'red.' However, he does not yet use it appropriately. (It is not under appropriate stimulus control.) The teaching sequence might point to a succession of pictures or objects asking each time, What color is this? Every time the child gives the right answer, he is provided with some event or context which provides confirmation or other reinforcement. The teacher or teaching sequence does not give the rule by pointing to objects and saying this is red, this is green, etc. The child is permitted to make responses by himself to the separate instances. The teaching sequence utilizes various kinds of red objects so that the student is provided with a succession of situations in which a correct response has a high probability of occurrence. Sequences of noninstances or negative instances are employed in which nonred (or possibly the color of the nonred object) is accepted as an appropriate response. The teaching procedure is careful to randomize the nonrelevant dimensions involved so that there are included large and small objects, distant and near objects, dark and light objects, and coarse and smooth objects. The child thus learns to generalize among objects in the class of redness. In the course of this process, the teaching sequence might introduce obviously different colors asking which one is blue and so on. Once the child says red only to red objects and not to nonred objects, and blue only to blue objects, he has acquired and perhaps discovered the concepts of redness and blueness.

In summary, then, the principle is that an abstraction or general case is learned by the establishment of generalizations among specific instances of a class and the discriminations between instances and noninstances of a class. In learning the concepts of triangle and quadrilateral, the student must generalize the reponse 'triangle' to any three-sided figure and the response 'quadrilateral' to any four-sided figure. He must also learn to discriminate between these two classes. In larger sequences of topics, a student learns what an operation is after he can add, subtract, multiply, etc. He learns what a proof is after he has seen a large number of different kinds of proofs. And he understands what homeostasis is after he learns about different kinds of physiological equilibria. General understanding is induced from a wealth of inexperience with specific cases (vide Mechner, 1961).

Errorful Learning

The second identifying characteristic of discovery learning is that in the course of discovering things for themselves, students will undoubtedly make mistakes as a result of exploring blind alleys and negative instances. Since it seems that the most intellectually satisfying discoveries are those which are not obvious from the data at the student's immediate disposal, there is the probability that such discoveries will not be made. To this extent, there may be a basic incompatibility between inducing discoveries and minimizing error.

To begin with a contrast again, the development of teaching machines has emphasized the minimization of errors. And while, so far as I know, completely errorless learning has not been demonstrated in a teaching machine program, it has been demonstrated in the ingenious work reported by Terrace (1963a; 1963b) in teaching pigeons a red-green discrimination, and also to discriminate between a horizontal and a vertical line. An error is defined in this work as a response to a stimulus correlated with nonreinforcement, a so-called S—. The results of these studies indicate that performance following discrimination learning without errors lacks three characteristics that were found following learning with errors. Only those birds that learned the discrimination with errors show (1) 'emotional' responses in the presence of S—, (2) occasional bursts of responses to the incorrect stimulus, and (3) less effective transfer to related discriminations. The technique Terrace used was to begin with two stimuli, widely separated on three stimulus dimensions, and then to progressively reduce the differences between two dimensions, maintaining only the difference in the third. This technique was recognized by William James in a discussion of discrimination in psychophysics in 1890.

Schlosberg and Solomon (1943) reported a study in which they trained rats on a Lashley jumping stand in a black-white discrimination. In order to equate for what they call the "negative factor" which prevents learning and increases response latency, they permitted no errors to occur which would be punished. In this way the value of the negative factor would be determined only by the distance to be jumped and hence equal for all stimulus presentations. They trained their animals very gradually in positive responses to a white stimulus so that an error was never made. As a result of this procedure, the experimenters say that "the gradient established by reward was uncomplicated by the effects of 'punishment'" (p. 26).

As Terrace points out, the demonstration of errorless learning suggests possible revision in currently accepted accounts of discrimination learning. These currently accepted accounts agree that the extinction of responding to S—, and hence the occurrence of errors, is a necessary condition for formation of a discrimination. As succinctly stated by Keller and Schoenfeld, "Extinction is the hallmark of discrimination" (1950). The accounts of Spence and Hull on discrimination learning are similarly based upon learning that occurs in the presence of S+ and extinction in the presence of S−, respectively. Harlow (1959) expressly incorporates error in his error factor theory. In general, discrimination learning without errors is excluded fom these conditioning-extinction theories where excitatory and inhibitory gradients are postulated.

The general rationale for error minimization in instruction is the following: (1) When errors occur, there is lack of control over the learning process and opportunity is provided for the intermittent reinforcement of incorrect responses; this results in interference effects highly resistant to extinction. (2) Frustration and emotional effects, difficult to control, are associated with extinction and interference. And (3) richer learning, that is, richer in associations, takes place when the associative history of the learner is employed to extend his learning; this is accomplished by mediators or thematic promptings which make positive use of existing knowledge and serve to guide learning.

There is, perhaps, another reason behind the drive to minimize errors. This is the fact that the use of errors and the possible value of incorrect responses has not been investigated much in studies of learning related to the educational process. The contingencies generally studied have been those following correct responding—a reinforcing event, a punishing event, or withholding a reinforcing event. The contingencies following an incorrect response that have been studied are primarily punishment, withholding reinforcement, and to some extent, variations of corrective feedback information. This latter contingency has not, however, been as systematically investigated as the others. Recent experimental studies like those of Suppes and Ginsberg (1962) suggest that overt correction of errors in young children results in faster learning than does just knowledge about whether or not responses were correct. Although with adults, Suppes points out, studies like that of Burke, Estes, and Hellyer (1954) show that requiring the learner to make an overt correction response after informational feedback does not increase learning rate nor asymptotic performance. (Indeed, many learning studies assume, e.g., Bower (1962), that under certain conditions, correction following an incorrect response has reinforcing value equal to confirmation following a correct response.) In general, the 'guided' aspects of studies of guided discovery attempt to make use of error, but effective use requires development of theory and data about the function of error responses.

An exception to the lack of use of error responses in the course of instruction has been the work reported by Lewis and Pask on adaptive teaching systems (1965). The adaptive teaching procedure which these men propose requires the student to reveal, by making some sort of error, the kind of instruction he should receive next. This requirement, they suggest, need not conjure up an image of an aversive and threatening situation in which the student is forced to reveal his ignorance. If adaptive control is competently designed, a student's weaknesses are revealed by his selection of response alternatives. Where no adaptive procedures are available for dealing with error, the minimization of error is forced upon a teaching procedure.

Error minimization advocates might suggest that the adaptive system could do better by preventing errors from occurring in the first place. Lewis and Pask react to this by pointing out that the presence of error is tacitly acknowledged by the error minimizers when they cue or prompt in the course of a program to adjust a program to the population of students being taught. These nonadaptive programs remove error factors without allowing them to be manifested in the form of overt mistakes. This necessarily involves working in the dark; and hence programs which forestall error often make provisions for far more error possibilities than any one student is likely to have, and, hence consist of less-than-challenging tasks.

Adaptive teaching systems, in contast to error minimization, take seriously the view that students profit from their mistakes. In addition, an instructional sequence should require that students discover things for themselves, and in the course of self-discovery the student will undoubtedly make mistakes. Thus, there is a basic incompatibility between this self-discovery process and error minimization.

At this point, I am sure of one thing: I have not resolved any issues. But I do hope that I have laid out for inspection what seem to me to be relevant variables and nuances that are involved in learning by discovery. On the basis of my review of the kind of learning situations that have been included under this label, I have pointed out that the hallmarks in this kind of learning involve two identifying characteristics: induction and errorful learning. And I have attempted to look further into these two aspects to provide some specific variables for their operational handling.

Task Properties

So far I have discussed the characteristics of learning by discovery in general. This really does not get us very far in efforts at instructional design because the characteristics of a teaching sequence interact with the properties of the terminal tasks that are being taught. Therefore, induction and errorful learning take on differential usefulness depending upon whether we are teaching response precision, simple associations, concepts, rules and principles, or higher-order strategies.

Consider first the establishment of response precision. An evident characteristic of the educational process that leads to subject-matter mastery is the increasing precision of the student's response. The student's initial performance is variable, crude, and rarely meets the criteria of subject-matter competence. An effective instructional procedure tolerates this initial state and gradually takes him toward mastery. In order to accomplish this, the teaching process involves the progressive establishment of narrower limits for correct performance. Increasing competence in performing such new skills as learning to write or learning precise timing in music is accomplished by gradually contracting performance tolerances. This can be done progressively so that each successive range of successful performance includes a major portion of the range of variations already in the student's repertoire. Over the sequence of instruction, the range of observed performance will align itself with a particular range of acceptable performance defined as subject-matter competence. I would suggest that this can be done and should be done with a minimum amount of errors, since a sudden or inappropriate constriction of performance criteria can lead to extinction and loss of motivation. The use of errors and induction for this kind of learning seems not especially appropriate.

Consider next the learning of associations: The process involved is attaching the increasingly precise responses being learned to particular subject-matter stimulus situations so that subject-matter mastery is attained because the precise responses are under the command of detailed subject-matter discriminative stimuli. In learning translation in a second language, for example, the precise expression of a word meaning already in the learner's repertoire is transferred to new subject-matter stimuli. The transfer of stimulus control is a major process in teaching students to make precise subject-matter discriminations and teaching them to use previously learned skills in response to new stimuli. This process, like the establishment of response precision, does not seem to require induction and errorful learning. Through the use of mediators, associations can be taught so that errors are minimized. As Gilbert (1958) has pointed out, in learning the correspondence between the number one and the color brown, and zero and black, in teaching the resistor color code, it is possible to teach such associations on almost one trial by the use of mediating stimuli. The student learns by means of statements such as 'one brown penny' and 'zero black nothingness.' The procedure of stimulus fading, used widely in operant conditioning and in programmed instruction, can also be used to transfer existing associations to new ones with little error.

With respect to the learning of concepts, I have already indicated that induction may be a useful procedure. Whether or not errorful learning is useful may be debated in light of the work of Terrace in discrimination learning. The question here centers around whether, in the discrimination-training aspects of concept formation, errorful learning has useful consequences.

In the learning of rules, principles, and higher-order strategies, I can be less than definitive although the use of induction and error seem indicated. At this point it is a matter of some systematization and experimental analysis along the lines of variables I have been discussing.

In summary, learning by discovery, when analyzed, appears to involve not only the properties of induction and errorful learning, but also interactive effects with task properties.

TEACHING FOR DISCOVERY

I turn now, briefly, to teaching for discovery, or learning to discover. This is much easier to talk about. Since we know so little about it, one can say anything and enjoy his own speculations without the constraints of knowledge. Again the problem is analysis of the behavior involved because it is unlikely that we can teach discovery behavior adequately until the component behavior repertoires have been analyzed. Once we specify or at least postulate relevant situational and behavioral variables, discovery behavior should be more amenable to instructional manipulation. Right off, it seems likely that discovery behavior is specific to the subject matter domain in which discovery takes place. Discovery requires different concepts and logical combinations when one is working in microbiology or botany, or breaking hieroglyphic codes. Presumably, there is some communality of behavioral repertoires, but there will be much significant specific variance.

Mechner in a recent chapter on "Science Education and Behavioral Technology" (1965) lists subdivisions of scientific method and research skills which seem to be manageable pieces of discovery in science. He lists such things as deductive reasoning skills, inferential reasoning skills, skill in generating hypotheses, skill in selecting "fruitful" hypotheses, skill in testing hypotheses and deciding which experiments to perform, skill in formulating problems that can be solved by the scientific method, and generalized traits such as patience, perseverance, and curiosity. Skill in generating hypotheses is described as a type of scanning, like free association, except that it involves statements about the world. Each statement is checked against experience until it is refuted. If it is not refuted it becomes a scientific contribution. Mechner writes:

> The terminal behavior test for this skill would require the student to generate and test, at a certain minimal rate, hypotheses about a universe with which he has had some previous experience. The behavioral technologist, in developing the terminal behavior specifications, would have to (a) make the behavior overt rather than covert, (b) circumscribe the universe for the hypotheses, and (c) circumscribe the range of data against which the successive hypotheses are tested by the student. Here, the use of a computer suggests itself. It should be possible to develop a program for the computer that would make the computer behave like a small, artificial, circumscribed universe. This universe would be described by a set of specific input-output relationships, some of them determined and others probabilistic. The student of "creativity" [discovery] would start out by learning his "subject matter," i.e., how this computer behaves under various specific conditions. At the end of this subject-matter training, there would still be a great deal about the computer-universe that would be unknown to him. Here he must begin to generate hypotheses and test them. A program could be designed to develop this skill. The program would teach the student in the standard step-by-step fashion how to generate hypotheses on the basis of some available data and then to test the hypotheses in brute force manner against other available data until the hypothesis is refuted or until the data are exhausted. At the end of the program, the student would be generating and testing hypotheses at the desired rate.

Another way of looking at discovery behavior is suggested by the work on computer simulation of information processing. The work pioneered by Simon and Newell (1964) identifies elementary information processes which combine into compound processes. The processes identified might be considered as heuristics which are teachable behaviors which can be combined by the learner to produce discovery behavior. For example, a paper by Simon and Simon (1962) identifies certain heuristics for discovering and verifying mating combinations in chess. The discovery heuristic involves a tree of move possibilities which explores branches that turn out to be false leads. This exploration tree consists of move possibilities in which the attacker has to discover a branching sequence of moves, one subtree of which leads to a checkmate. The authors write that, "The exploration tree is precisely analogous to the paths tried out by a subject in a maze-running experiment, except that it includes branches for defender's choices as well as branches for the attacker's trees" (p. 427). A heuristic program simple enough to be simulated by hand is able to discover mating combinations in about 52 of the 136 chess positions. Slight modification of the program adds 10 more mating combinations that would be discovered. Simon and Simon conclude:

> The conclusion we reach from our investigations is that the discovery of 'deep' mating combinations by expert chess players requires neither prodigious memory, ultra-rapid processing capacities, nor flashes of insight. Combinations as difficult as any that have been recorded in chess history will be discovered by the selective heuristics we have outlined. . . . The evidence strongly suggests that expert chess players discover combinations because their programs incorporate powerful selective heuristics and not because they think faster or memorize better than other people (1962, p. 429).

A third line of endeavor which is of interest for consideration as an influential variable in teaching for discovery has to do with the study of curiosity and exploration. An increasing amount of research has been directed to the study of this area in the past decade (Fowler, 1965). Research, much of it with infra-human organisms, has indicated that the strength of exploratory behavior is positively related, within limits, to the degree of change in the stimulus situation provided by novel, unfamiliar, complex, surprising, or incongruous situations introduced into the environment. Too great or too abrupt a change, however, is disrupting and may preclude exploration. In complex situations, an individual encounters change by way of his interaction with or manipulation of the elements involved. Such interaction provides the stimulus change which can elicit curiosity and exploratory behavior. Investigations have also demonstrated that behaviors are learned that lead to a change in the stimulus display. Thus, in addition to stimulus change eliciting exploratory behavior, experiments show that organisms will respond in order to secure novel, unfamiliar stimuli. In general, these findings demonstrate that stimulus change or sensory variation may be employed to selectively reinforce behaviors which result in change, and that this variation in the situation will serve concomitantly to elicit exploratory behavior. When stimulus change is used as a reinforcing stimulus, it seems reasonable to hypothesize that learning variables which influence acquisition and extinction will influence the acquisition and extinction of exploratory and curiosity behavior as they do other learned behavior. This suggests that a student's curiosity and explorations which enhance discovery may be elicited and maintained in an instructional environment which provides for appropriate variation in the stimulus characteristics of the subject materials confronting him.

In summary, interesting leads for studying 'learning to discover' come from operant analysis, cognitive simulation and studies of exploratory drive. Finally, the excursion that this paper has taken into the intricacies of 'discovery learning' brings to mind the admonition of Edward L. Thorndike who wrote the following: ". . . if we avoid thought by loose and empty terms, or if we stay lost in wonder at the extraordinary versatility and inventiveness of the higher forms of learning, we shall never understand man's progress or control his education."

Chapter III

The Meaning of Discovery In Learning

QUITE APPROPRIATELY, THE FIRST DISCUSSION BEGAN WITH A QUESTION on the nature of discovery as a method of teaching.

A participant raised the issue of whether what we call discovery teaching must always be inductive, and nondiscovery teaching, deductive. He referred to experiences of his own where the rule-example method had, in fact, elicited discovery experiences, as he suddenly discovered what the teacher had been talking about during an earlier rule-example sequence. Hence, teaching by discovery may not be synonymous with inductive teaching, but rather the discovery process can result from either inductive or deductive teaching.

Another discussant demurred. He felt that such a definition of learning by discovery fell into the box of looking at discovery as an intervening process in the learner. Instead, he maintained that in the literature we traditionally view discovery only as manipulative, that is, something teachers do. When people advocate discovery, they are advocating the withholding of answers from pupils. The teacher knows how an answer is obtained, but the students do not. Hence, the major question in the issue of learning by discovery is the extent to which you get better pedagogy by not telling the student what the teacher already knows.

This discussion brought out a theme which was to appear and reappear throughout all of the discussions of the conference. In attempting to clarify the meaning of learning by discovery for teaching, is it more valuable to focus upon what the teacher must do (the independent variable), is it more important to find out what it is the learner does when he learns by discovery, or is it best to look primarily at the end product in the form of what the learner has finally learned to do (the dependent variable)? The danger to avoid is that of assuming a necessary isomorphism between the independent and intervening variables. Just because the teaching is inductive, it does not follow that the learner is discovering. Conversely, simply because the teacher is instructing didactically, discovery experiences on the part of the learner are not precluded.

If we are to consider the possibility that discovery refers to an intervening process in the learner, what form shall our descriptions of this process take? For one participant, discovery was essentially a mediational process in the learner, and he asserted that the terms which are generally utilized to describe or distinguish among mediational processes are equally useful in discussing processes of discovery.

A slightly different attack was suggested by another participant. He maintained that in these processes a student confronted with a set of concrete experiences is led to scan through a range of stored models of different kinds and try to fit these models to the data or problem at hand. What is discovered is not something outside the learner, but an appropriate internal structure for handling the situation or problems. He must translate these experiences into his own language frames rather than learn a formal list which is already in his own language. What we need to investigate is the linkage between the complex language forms we are aware of and the kinds of experiences we control for the pupil while he is learning.

A great advantage of learning this linguistically is that the relationship is now in a form that has enormous substitution possibilities. Hence, the crux of the discovery process is recognition and understanding of the relationships among concrete experiences and the operation of putting these experiences into the compact form of language.

It was suggested that the idea of language alone was too restricting. The key point in discovery learning is that of stimulus change. The child learns concepts and abstractions by being asked to pick out the invariants. This requires not only providing for stimulus change so that the child may pick out these invariants, but more important, arranging for the child to seek to change the stimuli himself in order to discover these invariants. This ability is more than simply learning a heuristic. Heuristics can be subject-matter specific; one used for code-breaking is not likely to be the same as one used for chess-playing. One participant pointed out that learning by pure induction rarely exists. What the learner does is to scan through a range of stored models of different kinds and to try and fit these models to the data or problems at hand. The role of language represents a major means by which one codes stored models and retrieves them. Linguistic cues help tell the learner which model to bring out with respect to the kinds of data being dealt with.

A discussant now suggested that within any of these definitions of discovery, a particular way of looking at the nature of what is taught is implied. To be amenable to learning by discovery, what is taught can never be meaningless, senseless, or arbitrary. Instead, it must be somehow rational and structured. You cannot discover the irrational except by accident. You must take as your subject matter for research or pedagogy things that are amenable to rationality, such that something in your head can in fact match something 'out there.' When this happens, the resulting match is essentially a reinforcement of an important educative response. The problem for the child is to find an order out there that fits the order he has figured out in his head. This approach was dubbed the 'cultivation of rationality.'

It was suggested that, no matter what kinds of discovery you are concerned with, you must never lose sight of the importance of the antecedent explorations of the field. In Piaget's terms, we have been talking about the jump from the level of concrete perceptual experiences to abstract formulations and verbally stated conceptualizations. This is not a large single jump· it is rather a process. The finding of a language code of appropriate linguistic structure is mediated by a process one might call abstraction. This is nonverbal, or even preverbal in many ways and, most important, is a function of the richness of the antecedent crisscrossing of an exploratory field by the individual in order that patterns may begin to emerge. It is wrong for us, as it was for Poincaré, to speak of the triumphant moment of discovery without emphasizing the antecedent richness of preparation from which, and only from which, this pattern of discovery can emerge. Poincaré was not adept at introspection and so he thought that his ideas just popped into his mind, but he worked for a long time with the discoveries before the harvest was possible. The importance of language is that it is the universal vehicle of patterns. Therefore, the problem is one of finding an appropriate linguistic pattern which fits our experiences and is adequate to provide the appropriate exploration of the field.

The discussion now turned to consideration of discovery as a terminal behavior. In this sense the construct can take on two very different forms, analogous to Piaget's distinction of assimilation and accommodation. First, we have discovery within an accepted framework, and then, we have discovery which is in fact the reconstruction of an accepted framework and the development of a new one. Psychological research has traditionally looked only at the first kind, which is probably trivial, because we can understand these phenomena within frameworks we have already overlearned. The development of the revolutionary insight, which is really a totally different way of looking at things, is a much more difficult psychological phenomenon. Here, the notion that we have a process of finding structures in our own coded language system to fit what is out there does not seem to be the case, because it is very often precisely the problem of giving new meaning to our old words or even making new words, that makes this the second kind of discovery. We do not know how to set up instructional conditions which will elicit these revolutionary discoveries, but it is quite certain that the little 'coding' types of experiments that characterize the psychological literature of learning by discovery, e.g., seeing that something is spelled backwords, have absolutely nothing to do with the second kind of discovery.

This distinction between a minor discovery and a major one was sharpened even further by the suggestion that different terms should be used to describe these two phenomena. Minor, or assimilation type, discovery might be simply called *discovery*. On the other hand, major discovery should probably be called by some other name, *conceptual invention*. These two phenomena are quite different and should be treated as such.

PART TWO

THE RESEARCH

Chapter IV

The Learning By Discovery Hypothesis

M. C. WITTROCK

THE HYPOTHESIS

Introduction

MANY STRONG CLAIMS FOR LEARNING BY DISCOVERY ARE MADE IN EDU-
cational psychology. But almost none of these claims has been empirically substantiated or even clearly tested in an experiment. In this
chapter we will state the learning by discovery hypothesis; briefly look at
the many interests in the hypothesis; analyze it into the independent,
intervening, and dependent variables it denotes; review the literature
related to each of these variables; and make suggestions for future empirical research. The independent–intervening–dependent variable approach has proven useful with other problems in psychology and education. Perhaps it can help us to comprehend some of the complexities
and to avoid some of the tautologies in the research on learning by discovery. The value of this chapter rests on this assumption.

Statement of the Hypothesis

To call learning by discovery an hypothesis will come as a surprise
to some readers who accept it as a postulate supported by data, intuition, and common sense. However, one of its leading proponents also
considers it an hypothesis. In a well known article Bruner (1961) discusses four benefits said to accrue from discovery learning: greater intellectual potency, intrinsic motivation, memory processing, and the
learning of the heuristics of discovery. Concluding the section on intellectual potency, he presents the learning by discovery hypothesis:

> It is, if you will, a necessary condition for learning the variety
> of techniques of problem solving, of transforming information for
> better use, indeed for learning how to go about the very task of

33

learning. Practice in discovering for oneself teaches one to acquire information in a way that makes that information more readily viable in problem solving. So goes the hypothesis. It is still in need of testing. But it is an hypothesis of such important human implications that we cannot afford not to test it—and testing will have to be in the schools (p. 26).

In the above quote, Bruner makes several important points. He states that learning by discovery is an hypothesis, and that the solving of problems is an appropriate dependent variable to index its results. Practice at problem solving is an independent variable. As we shall see at the end of this chapter, he makes another point—the hypothesis is still in need of testing.

The Dilemma

In another article, he is apparently less convinced that learning by discovery is an unproven hypothesis. After commenting on the passivity of knowledge-getting in the classroom (peaches are grown in Georgia; New York is our largest port, etc.) which lacks thinking as a reward for learning, Bruner writes:

One experiment which I can report provides encouragement. It was devised and carried out by the research group with which I am associated at Harvard in collaboration with teachers in the fifth grade of a good public school. It is on the unpromising topic of the geography of the North Central States and is currently in progress so that I cannot give all of the results. We hit upon the happy idea of presenting this chunk of geography not as a set of knowns, but as a set of unknowns. One class was presented blank maps, containing only tracings of the rivers and lakes of the area as well as the natural resources. They were asked as a first exercise to indicate where the principal cities would be located, where the railroads, and where the main highways. Books and maps were not permitted and "looking up the facts" was cast in a sinful light. Upon completing this exercise, a class discussion was begun in which the children attempted to justify why the major city would be here, a large city there, a railroad on this line, etc.

The discussion was a hot one. After an hour, and much pleading, permission was given to consult the rolled up wall map. I will never forget one young student, as he pointed his finger at the foot of Lake Michigan, shouting, "Yipee, Chicago is at the end of the pointing-down lake." And another replying, "Well, OK: but Chicago's no good for the rivers and it should be here where there is a big city (St. Louis)." These children were thinking, and learning was an instrument for checking and improving the process. To at least a half dozen children in the class it is not a matter of indifference that no big city is to be found at the junction of Lake Huron, Lake Michigan, and Lake Ontario. They were slightly shaken up transportation theorists when the facts were in.

The children in another class taught conventionally, got their facts all right, sitting down, benchbound. And that was that. We will see in six months which group remembers more. But whichever does, one thing I will predict. One group learned geography as a set of rational acts of induction—that cities spring up where there is water, where there are natural resources, where there are things to be processed and shipped. The other group learned passively that there were arbitrary cities at arbitrary places by arbitrary bodies of water and arbitrary sources of supply. One learned geography as a form of activity. The other stored some names and positions as a passive form of registration (Bruner, 1959, pp. 187–188).

In this second quote from Bruner, some of the complexities of the learning by discovery hypothesis become apparent when one applies the independent-dependent variable framework suggested above. It is important that children be taught to discover on their own, to be able to solve problems, to transfer to related situations (including further study in the same discipline), to be motivated to continue to learn, and to increase in independence. However, the quote from Bruner includes not only ends but means. A particular way of learning is hypothesized to produce these important ends.

After observing the children's overt behavior, Bruner concludes that the children presented with the blank maps were thinking. No doubt they were. But it would be better to have empirical data to index their thought. It seems that regardless of which group performs better six months after learning, the group that received the blank maps received the better treatment. Herein lies the crux of the dilemma among educational psychologists about discovery learning. When learning and discovery are measured by one event, discovery cannot be given as a cause for learning. It does no good to say tautologically that those who discover learn. For example, the desired result is an event named *learning by discovery*. The treatment designed to produce the result is also an event named *learning by discovery*. A tautological conclusion easily follows. The discovery learners learned by discovery, therefore their treatment was the better one, regardless of the data.

The treatment and its results must be kept separate from each other. The treatment is an independent variable. It may or may not produce transfer, savings, retention, or ability to discover as well as, or better than, some other treatment.

To evaluate discovery learning, we should obtain empirical data on its consequences. These data will have common sense and intuition to complement or refute them. Many people feel that, surely, practice at discovering is the best treatment to teach children to discover information by themselves. In any event, it may be difficult to convince many that one can learn to discover best by some route other than simply practicing the terminal behavior.

The Dialectic

Any individual whose intuitions favor discovery learning, both for its results and its treatments, will find himself with many colleagues. According to many of its proponents, learning by discovery produces knowledge which transfers to new situations. Through practice at problem solving it develops problem solving ability. It is intrinsically motivating and is its own reward. By being taught to solve problems, to behave in a scientific and inductive fashion, and to go beyond the data, a student is helped to become a mature person. It is a useful conceptualization for the teaching of many subjects in schools. Left to his own resources, the student's individual history will determine the proper sequence of learning activities. It is an important end in its own right. It deserves attention, and students should have some practice at discovering answers for themselves. One must learn to produce rather than to reproduce answers and knowledge. So goes the argument for learning by discovery.

According to some people less enthusiastic about it, only those students who have already learned how to discover may learn by discovery. It assumes that every individual can best be taught by one method, learning by discovery, when individual differences may require several different approaches.

The hypothesis confuses means with ends. To produce the ability to discover (an end) may involve more than simple practice at discovering (a means). Discovery is time consuming. The essence of a culture is that everyone need not discover for himself everything anew but that he can profit from the experiences of others as summarized in language. Even the motivation produced by discovery may be an attempt to escape, and later to avoid, the subject matter because the problems may threaten rather than challenge the student's intellect and self-concept. As an end, the ability to solve problems is important, but it is not the only important end. One must learn to acquire and comprehend much of his culture as well as to discover new knowledge and to solve problems.

So goes the opposition to learning by discovery, and so goes the dialectic. We shall analyze the fundamentals of this dialectic and discuss the research on these components after a discussion of the widespread interest in learning by discovery. With the variety of subject matter and students encountered in schools, it is surely futile to expect one method of learning to be consistently superior or inferior to other plausible procedures. The dialectic should be replaced by better issues, ones that will allow alternatives to the all-or-none positions common in the literature.

THE INTEREST IN LEARNING BY DISCOVERY

Current Interest

Among writers on human learning and education, there are definite ideas about the sequence and arrangement of stimuli which should be presented to students to produce transfer, savings, ability to discover, intrinsic motivation, and self-confidence. To present some of the excitement and some of the flavor which accompanies the learning by discovery hypothesis, several quotes are presented below. They help to convey accurately some of the enthusiasm and reasons for teaching and learning by discovery.

Suchman (1961) states many of the advantages claimed for teaching and for learning by discovery. About a program to improve inquiry skills, he writes:

> The need for improvement is great. Current educational practice tends to make children less autonomous and less empirical in their search for understanding as they move up the elementary grades. The schools must have a new pedagogy with a new set of goals which subordinate retention to thinking.
>
> It is clear that such a program should offer large amounts of practice in exploring, manipulating and searching. The children should be given a maximum of opportunity to experience autonomous discovery. New goals must be set for the children. Instead of devoting their efforts to storing information and recalling it on demand, they would be developing the cognitive functions needed to seek out and organize information in a way that would be the most productive of new concepts. Both the teacher and the pupil would have to be cast in new roles. The pupil must become more active and aggressive in his learning role. Direction of the concept formation process should be his own, and he should come to re-

gard his environment (including the teacher) as a potential source of information which can be obtained through his own acts of inquiry. The teacher must abandon his traditionally directive mode and structure an environment that is responsive to the child's quest for information. The teacher must see to it that the child's efforts at inquiry are rewarded by success, that the child is able to obtain the information he needs, and that he does discover new concepts on his own. The teacher can help the child by posing problems that are reasonably structured and will lead to exciting new discoveries. The teacher can also coach him in the techniques of data collection and organization that will lend power and control to his searching. The educator should be concerned above all with the child's process of thinking, trusting that the growth of knowledge will follow in the wake of inquiry.

For the past four years, we have been attempting to design and test just such a program to be employed in the elementary school. The following section describes our method, which we call *Inquiry Training* (p. 151).

Interest in the hypothesis is not limited to individual researchers. As early as 1952, the University of Illinois began to prepare materials and teachers to improve the teaching of secondary school mathematics. Max Beberman (1964, pp. 9–34) describes some of the careful organization of materials and some of the objectives of the program. He gives (pp. 11, 23) two operationally defined desiderata for the understanding of mathematics: (1) precision of textbook language and teacher language and (2) student discovery of generalizations. Cause and effect may be somewhat confounded here. These desiderata of the dependent variables of meaning and understanding are also the independent variables—the treatments—which are supposed to produce the understanding of mathematics. For example, by practicing discovery, mathematics is supposed to be made meaningful. How do we know this? Because discovery has been practiced.

But more important than the desiderata is the set of materials developed by the University of Illinois Committee on School Mathematics (UICSM). The Department of Mathematics, the College of Education, and the University High School cooperated in preparing, trying out, and testing the materials. The terminal behavior of students who complete the program seems to indicate that some important improvements in the teaching of mathematics in the secondary school have been introduced.

The UICSM is only one of the groups working on the improvement of the teaching of mathematics. A national effort, rather than a state or local one, is presented by the School Mathematics Study Group

(SMSG), which is financed by the National Science Foundation, and was begun in 1958. A brief history of SMSG is presented by William Wooten (1964, pp. 35–53). The sample textbooks and other materials prepared by this group are characterized by a careful sequencing and structuring of basic mathematical concepts (e.g., numeration, number systems, and intuitive plane geometry in grade 7) and also by involvement of the student in discovery of mathematical concepts. These materials have been enthusiastically received by many teachers, administrators, parents, and students.

The preference among scholars for teaching by discovery is not limited to mathematics. The Chemical Education Material Study (CHEM) by 1963 produced a new course in chemistry (Campbell, 1964, pp. 82–93). With movies, text, and laboratory manual, a series of laboratory experiments was prepared. Through laboratory experiments the student discovered (p. 87) the basic ideas of the course, including such fundamentals as kinetic theory and atomic structure. The discovery precedes the discussion of these concepts in the text. The third major part of the text includes applications of the concepts.

The many dimensions of change these new projects and their courses produce in students are difficult to evaluate. Although these projects are quite new, apparently for many students they present advances in teaching.

However, it is equally clear that the courses themselves involve many complicated dimensions in addition to those of careful sequencing and student discovery. The success of these programs does not, in any serious sense, support or refute the contention that learning by discovery is important for learning the subject matter, for learning a way of solving problems, or, for that matter, important for any other educational objective.

So far as these curricular demonstrations are concerned, learning by discovery is still an hypothesis—an untested one at that. In the sense that learning by discovery involves student selection of the sequence of materials, it is not involved in these projects. They have sequences very carefully designed by scholars and schoolmen. In the sense that learning by discovery implies inductive encounters with problems and raw data and student derivation of concepts or principles, discovery is definitely involved.

One could name other recent curriculum projects, e.g., the American Institute of Biological Sciences (AIBS) project in the teaching of biology. Most of these projects are also sympathetic to a learning by discovery procedure.

Earlier Interest

The current interests described above are rooted in movements in philosophy, education, and psychology. Only a few of the directly relevant leaders of these movements will be mentioned here: J. J. Rousseau, Maria Montessori, and John Dewey. J. J. Rousseau in his book *Emile* insisted that the proper role of the environment is to avoid interference with the internal processes of spontaneous maturation. Teacher direction, goals, and standards were to be replaced by a permissiveness which would allow the innately good child to realize himself best.

Maria Montessori (1912, 1917) pioneered a movement in education. She emphasized the freedom of the child and his choosing for himself the problems or subject matter he would study (1917). The teacher is to give little deliberate verbal direction to the child. She is not often to reinforce the child with words, smiles, or other verbal or social reinforcers.

For example, children are taught discrimination of form and sound by manipulating apparatus. The apparatus is designed to provide feedback to a child without the necessity of intervention of a teacher. In discussing how a child's senses are trained by having him insert objects into a form board, Montessori writes:

> Here instead it is the work of the child, the auto-correction, the auto-education which acts, for the *teacher must not interfere in the slightest* way. No teacher can furnish the child with the agility which he acquires through gymnastic exercises: it is necessary that the *pupil perfect himself* through his own efforts. It is very much the same with the *education of the senses.*
>
> It might be said that the same thing is true of every form of education. A man is not what he is because of the teachers he has had, but because of what he has done (1912, p. 172).

And in another volume, after giving examples of futile attempts of people to control the development of children's legs, noses, ears, heads, and the development of their character and intelligence, she writes:

> It is Nature, "creation," which regulates all these things. If we are convinced of this, we must admit as a principle the necessity of "not introducing obstacles to natural development"; and instead of having to deal with many separate problems—such as, what are the best aids to the development of character, intelligence and feeling?—one single problem will present itself as the basis of all education: How are we to give the child freedom? (1917, p. 5).

Later, she presents an episode important to her in the search for the discovery of a treatment required by the soul of the child which would be analogous to what hygiene prescribes for the body.

I think, therefore, that it is essential to record the fundamental fact which led me to define my method.

I was making my first essays in applying the principles and part of the material I had used for many years previously in the education of deficient children, to the normal children of the San Lorenzo quarter in Rome, when I happened to notice a little girl of about three years old deeply absorbed in a set of solid insets, removing the wooden cylinders from their respective holes and replacing them. The expression on the child's face was one of such concentrated attention that it seemed to me an extraordinary manifestation; up to this time none of the children had ever shown such fixity of interest in an object; and my belief in the characteristic instability of attention in young children, who flit incessantly from one thing to another, made me peculiarly alive to the phenomenon.

I watched the child intently without disturbing her at first, and began to count how many times she repeated the exercise; then, seeing that she was continuing for a long time, I picked up the little arm-chair in which she was seated, and placed chair and child upon the table; the little creature hastily caught up her case of insets, laid it across the arms of her chair, and gathering the cylinders into her lap, set to work again. Then I called upon all the children to sing; they sang, but the little girl continued undisturbed, repeating her exercise even after the short song had come to an end. I counted forty-four repetitions; when at last she ceased, it was quite independently of any surrounding stimuli which might have distracted her, and she looked round with a satisfied air, almost as if awaking from a refreshing nap.

I think my never-to-be-forgotten impression was that experienced by one who has made a discovery (1917, pp. 67–68).

With her willingness to observe children's behavior and to induce classroom innovations from these naturalistic observations, she has produced innovations in educational practice and thought. Unfortunately, she was less interested in the difficult problems of measuring the results of these innovations.

In a quite different way, John Dewey's (1910) preferences for problem solving, laboratory work, and a scientific method produced a decided effect upon education in our own century. He suggested concrete experience, active responses, problem solving projects, and do-it-yourself learning. Although he emphasized social interaction and problem solving as ways to learn, he also recognized three levels of the curriculum. In the third level, subject matter was organized according to the structure of the discipline and not necessarily in terms of the student's own needs or problems. The progressive education movement often seemed to depart from Dewey on this point.

From the above quotes and discussion, it is clear that learning by discovery is used to describe both an end and a means. By discovery a student is supposed to learn regularities and concepts within a discipline. But, more importantly, he is supposed to learn how to solve problems, to go beyond the data, and to behave as a junior scientist. He is supposed to become motivated and enthusiastic about the discipline. He is to know personal satisfaction because he has selected his own sequence of problems and, through active responses of his own, has succeeded at these problems. Attractive as these propositions appear on the surface, they are complicated and do not always survive careful examination.

ISSUES AND PROBLEMS

The literature is fraught with conceptual issues, methodological problems, and semantic inconsistencies in the uses of the word discovery. Some of the problems and different uses of the term should be made explicit before the literature is reviewed.

Conceptual Issues

1. **Discovery as a way to learn subject matter versus as an end in its own right.** Not only is discovery thought to be a way to learn the structure of a subject, but it is a way to teach problem solving. Therefore, regardless of the subject matter a child learns, it is thought to be important for him to discover. These two ends should be kept separate from each other. They can be operationally defined and measured as dependent variables.

2. **What is to be discovered?** Is it a rule, generalization, or a more specific bit of information? Although it is difficult to define the difference between verbal statements of generalizations and more specific information, an attempt should be made to do so. Discovery may differ in its usefulness as a way to learn these ends.

3. **Induction vs. deduction.** Discovery learning is commonly equated with inductive learning where the subject proceeds from the specific to the general. It is just as plausible to assume that the learner begins with a higher order generalization, from which he derives more

specific conclusions and thus discovers answers and even generalizations. That is, there are probably several different processes involved in discovery. Induction has no exclusive identity with discovery learning. Discovery should be viewed as a set of very complex processes.

4. **The depreciation of verbal learning.** Much of the research on discovery learning is highly critical of a teacher's use of words. The argument centers on the necessity for a student to derive his own verbalizations rather than receiving them from teachers.

5. **Control of rate and sequence of stimuli.** For some unknown reasons, the effects of allowing a student to control his own rate and sequence of stimuli are relatively unstudied in the literature. Usually learning by discovery refers to a predetermined sequence beginning with problems and examples rather than with rules or generalizations.

6. **Variety of dependent variables.** From study to study one finds a wide variety of dependent variables: transfer, savings, retention, and especially ability to solve problems. Ability to verbalize rules and conclusions is sometimes an index of discovery. Another important dependent variable is affectivity. If the student discovers, he is supposed to display positive emotions, increased interest in subject matter and in solving problems. Such variety can be healthy, provided the results are carefully related to the particular dependent variables sampled in the study. Obviously, quite different findings cannot be contrasted with one another unless they pertain to the same types of dependent variables.

Methodological Problems

1. **Lack of replicability of the treatments.** In many of the empirical studies, the treatments are not operationally defined. They are complex and lengthy sequences of stimuli which often differ from other treatments in any number of ways. There often are no principles described which could be used by another researcher to generate the same types of treatments to replicate the study. The independent variable is not isolated or carefully varied.

2. **Failure to use random assignment.** Many of the studies called experiments are not experiments. Intact groups are frequently used. Little attempt is made to hold constant the effects of confounding variables.

3. **Inadequate statistical analysis.** Sometimes the statistical analysis of the data is omitted entirely or is given cursory treatment. In few studies is there a complete report of the data and its analysis.

4. **Extrapolation of results**. Although different subject matter and types of students are rarely studied in one report, the results are frequently extrapolated to a wide range of populations unsampled in the research. Discovery may be effective only when the students have already learned the necessary prerequisites and few competing responses. In an arbitrary situation, discovery learning may be highly ineffective and very discouraging.

Semantic Inconsistencies

1. **Labeling treatments in terms of responses they are said to produce.** *Rote* and *Discovery* are two most popular labels. These labels scarcely describe stimuli, but they do indicate responses and mediating processes. The words rote and discovery make it difficult to believe that the rank order of treatment means could be any other than discovery higher and rote lower. Less biased and emotionally loaded names are needed to describe the treatments. In addition, the rote treatment group of one study is sometimes indistinguishable from a discovery treatment of another study. One important function of experimental research on discovery is to determine if the stimuli produce the responses called discovery, not to assume that the issue is closed before the study begins.

2. **Lack of operational definitions and objective indices for the term discovery.** When a variety of specific problems, rather than rules or generalizations, are verbalized by a teacher or researcher, the situation is often labeled a discovery treatment. When concepts are verbalized by the teacher, the situation is usually not named discovery. Sometimes the verbalization of very general or vague cues, rather than specific ones, is also labeled a discovery procedure. Apparently, discovery applies so long as a specific rule or generalization is not mentioned by a teacher. It is usually confined to hierarchically arranged subject matter in which the learner has considerable background. With instructions he has a fairly high probability of deriving by himself correct answers and generalizations. If discovery were accurately indexed in terms of student behavior or knowledge, it would be easier to determine those situations which would preclude his producing that behavior without direction from a teacher.

Discovery is often used to denote a hypothetical, intervening cognitive event. One of the few researchers to try to index it objectively was Hendrix (1947). She used facial and other emotional processes rather than descriptions of teacher behavior or of student answers on a transfer test. If it is useful as an intervening event, we should try to find indices separate from measures of transfer or of treatments.

THE EMPIRICAL RESEARCH

The problems and issues discussed above will become more apparent in this section. In another chapter of this volume, Cronbach discusses some of the methodological mistakes common in the literature. Design and analysis problems will not be considered in detail here. The reader is urged to remember the conceptual and semantic problems described above, especially the comon practice of labeling different treatments with the same name.

Only a representative sample of the studies on learning by discovery can be presented. Any representative sample will include many studies which can scarcely be called research. Many researchers apparently were not aware of the complexity of the problems under study. Their procedures seem grossly inadequate to tease out the cause and effect relationships often boldly reported.

To provide some semblance of organization to the studies below, the independent–intervening–dependent variable framework is used. The studies do not always fall neatly into one of the three major categories, but more is gained than is lost by imposing some structure upon the diversity of studies. Research related to learning by discovery is described at the end of each of the major sections to indicate some of the ways to improve the quality of future research.

The reader is forewarned that the current state of research on discovery is very disappointing and precludes any important conclusions about teaching or learning. The reader is not expected to accept this comment on faith. Many studies are summarized in detail below, to allow one to become familiar with the problems and issues mentioned in the above section.

The literature on learning by discovery does not lend itself to terse summaries. The studies are seldom closely interrelated to one another. The procedures are sometimes naive and crude and evidence only the researcher's preference for a type of treatment. Only by summarizing a few studies in detail can one appreciate the several meanings of the learning by discovery hypothesis, the severe shortcomings of the research, the futility of an attempt to gloss over the particulars of a study, and the meaninglessness of generalizations based on these studies. For other attempts at summarizing these studies, see Ausubel (1963), Kersh and Wittrock (1962), and Wittrock (1963c). What follows below is a review of research only incidentally. Primarily, it is a description and analysis of the fundamental issues and complexities involved in the empirical work on learning by discovery.

The Intervening Variables

The Rote–Meaningful Dilemma. One segment of research began with an interest in deriving and comparing predictions from connectionism and field theory. The recent research on learning by discovery largely grew from this theoretical controversy.

Thorndike's extensive research upon the law of effect, including the relative effects of reward and punishment, stimulated much research upon discovery. A quote from Thorndike often appears in studies on discovery:

> . . . the attainment of active rather than passive learning at the cost of practice in error may often be a bad bargain. . . . The almost universal tolerance of imperfect learning in the early treatment of a topic, leaving it to be improved by the gradual elimination of errors in later treatments, is probably unsound, and certainly risky (1935, p. 147).

These sentences, and others of his, have been interpreted as an attempt to explain complex human learning in terms of simple learning and to de-emphasize the arrangement of stimuli, the meaningfulness of material, and the importance of discovery learning (e.g., Swenson, 1949). In two treatment groups, Swenson operationalized the distinction between meaning-discovery theory and connectionism. She added a third treatment to approximate her conception of the then current practice of the teaching of arithmetic. The subject matter was one hundred addition combinations (e.g., $3 + 4$ and $7 + 3$).

She assigned to the three treatment groups 332 children from 14 different second grade classes. The first group was a Generalization group. The combinations presented to these children were ordered according to an unspecified generalization. By grouping these number combinations, the teachers led the pupils to formulate their own generalizations. The second group, the Drill group, was presented the number combinations in different orders. The children were discouraged from producing answers in any but an automatized procedure. If a pupil hesitated or gave a wrong answer, he was instantly corrected. The third group, the Drill-Plus group, was supposed to approximate common practice in elementary schools. Each number combination was presented by pictures of concrete objects, and each new addition combination was followed by allowing the children to count and manipulate concrete objects. After the counting and manipulating of concrete objects, drill was used. The Drill-Plus method also presented the addition facts in groups organized by the size of the sum. Again, pupils were discouraged from making generalizations of number relations.

For all three groups, instruction lasted for a total of 20 weeks, and was divided into three major sections. An original set of facts (O) an interpolated set of facts (I), and a final set of facts (F) were taught. The 14 second grade classes were assigned by stratified random procedures to the three treatment groups. A test over the 100 addition facts was given on five different occasions: before the original learning (Test I), after the O instruction (Test II), after the interpolated learning (Test III), after two-and-a-half weeks of vacation (Test IV), and after the final instruction (Test V). After the fifth test of learning, three transfer tests were given. One was on 100 untaught subtraction facts. The second was on a test of 100 addition problems in which one of the two numbers to be added was a two-digit number. The third transfer test presented a variety of addition possibilities with one-digit, two-digit, and three-digit numbers.

She reports no means, standard deviations, standard errors, or analysis of variance tables, but states that she tested for homogeneity of variance, and used analyses of variance and covariance. Her analysis of results is complicated and it includes an analysis of gain scores from one of the five tests to the one which immediately followed it. The failure to report numbers and the use of the gain scores make it most difficult to summarize the results. On the learning of the original (O) facts, the Generalization group gained more than either of the other two groups. The Drill group was significantly superior to the Drill-Plus group. On the learning of the interpolated (I) facts, the three groups were not significantly different in gain scores. Neither were there any significant differences in gain scores on the learning of the final (F) facts, although the Generalization group performed better than either of the other two groups at the beginning of the F learning, and also at the end of the F learning.

On the learning of the three sets of facts, the gain scores were significantly different only in the case of the learning of the O facts, where the rank order was Generalization, Drill, and Drill-Plus. Each group was significantly better than the group which immediately followed it. There was no significant gain or loss in retention across the three methods for any of the retention periods.

After adjusting for Mental Age (MA), the transfer within the 100 addition facts favored the Generalization group on most of the tests. Occasionally the Drill-Plus group transferred more than the Drill group. When adjusted for MA and initial learning of addition facts, transfer to subtraction facts ranked, from highest to lowest, Generalization, Drill, Drill-Plus. All differences were statistically significant. On transfer to the upper decade facts, both the Drill and Generalization groups were statistically significantly better than the Drill-Plus group, while neither of the two former groups were statistically significantly different from each other.

Anderson (1949) also tried to compare connectionism and drill with generalization theory and active discovery by the pupils. Against relatively discrete elements and drill, he compared a highly organized system of principles. Practice came after, rather than before, the principles and their rationalization. Connectionism was depicted as a sterile system designed to avoid the practice of errors. He alternately described the two theories as Drill theory and Meaning theory (p. 41).

He also used arithmetic, elementary school children, and two treatments. In the Drill group there were 208 fourth grade students. The experiment lasted for approximately six months. Unlike the Swenson study, in which the teachers were assigned at random to the treatments, he assigned teachers on the basis of interviews and a measure of attitudes. There was no day by day control over the procedure for the teachers of the treatments (p. 44), nor were the teachers held responsible for definite objectives, content, or amount of time spent on instruction and drill.

The teachers of the Drill classes averaged about 11 minutes a day on instruction and 24 minutes a day on drill, while the teachers of the Meaning classes spent about 27 minutes a day on instruction and 18 minutes on drill. Anderson did not specify precisely how the treatments differed from each other. The intent was to implement connectionism in the Drill treatment (discrete elements, responses given to the learner, and repetition or drill on the discrete elements) and field theory in the Meaning treatment (organized patterns, responses not given to the learner, and practice at applying generalizations).

The dependent variables were tests of computational skills, problem solving, understanding of social concepts in arithmetic and vocabulary, and of mathematical thinking. The tests of computational skills included tests of addition, subtraction, multiplication, division, fundamental operations, and an interpolated test of subtraction. The significant differences which did occur indicated that the Drill method was superior for pupils who scored low on the Minneapolis School Ability test but high on the arithmetic pretest. The Meaning method tended to be superior for pupils who were high on the ability test but who were low on the arithmetic pretest. Anderson interprets this to mean that practice is probably most helpful to those who are low on the ability measure but are quite high on the achievement measure.

There were no significant differences among the two groups when social concepts and vocabulary tests were the dependent variables. On the tests of mathematical thinking, the difference between the high groups favored the Meaning group and was significant at the .01 level. The difference between the low groups favored the Drill method and was significant at the .01 level. On a test of long division over the learning exercise, the Drill method was better for both the high groups and the low groups.

In Anderson's study there was little control over the independent variables. It is impossible to draw any conclusions from his data. See Thiele (1938) and Forgus and Schwartz (1957) for further research.

Unverbalized Awareness. Interest in theory about discovery as an intervening variable also appears in Gertrude Hendrix's writings. Her work is interesting for its theoretical approach, not for its serious methodological shortcomings. Her theory departs from the connectionism–field theory dilemma. In several papers (1947, 1950, 1961), she argues that a period of unverbalized awareness is important for obtaining transfer. Here we have transfer as an operational definition of the effect of discovery. She indexed discovery, as described below, by facial and emotional responses. However, she is still using, as the treatment variables, covert responses rather than the stimuli which may or may not produce these covert responses.

In the earliest of the three papers (1947) she presents, in very brief form, her first three attempts at experimentation with discovery learning. With 40 college and high-school subjects, she compared three treatments. In Method I, the generalization was stated first by the teacher, then it was illustrated and applied to new problems. The generalization was, "The sum of the first n odd numbers is n-square."

In Method II, labeled the Unverbalized Awareness Method, a series of problems was presented. First the learners were asked to find the sum of the first two odd numbers, then the sum of the first three, the first four, etc. As soon as the subject noticed (discovered?) the relationship between the totals and the number of odd numbers he was asked to leave the room. The index of his discovering the relationship was, ". . . he started, or gasped a little, or smiled, or grew tense—that is he showed in some way that something had happened to him. Furthermore, he began to give the succeeding answers rapidly. . . ." (1947,

p. 199). In group III, labeled the Conscious Generalization Procedure, the method was the same as for Group II, except that when the indices of discovery occurred, the subjects were asked to state the rule they had discovered. The teacher then shaped the student's verbalization of the rule until it was accurate. Two weeks later, each group was given a transfer test whose items could be quickly solved by the generalization. The results were expressed as a ratio between the number of correct answers obtained by the short cut and the total number of correct answers. The groups ranked, from high to low, II, III, and I. A t-test showed that groups II and I differed at the .12 level, and that groups II and III differed at the .34 level. In other words, no difference was statistically significant at the conventional .05 level. Hendrix, and others subsequently, have cited her study as if the statistical results were significant. However, the n was small, 40 in all three studies combined.

Aside from the serious methodological problems, her results neither support nor refute the discovery hypothesis nor her hypothesis about unverbalized awareness. Hendrix's hypothesis deserves further study, if the treatments can be designed to differ from each other on a single dimension.

Motivation. Kersh (1958, 1962) presents two studies in which he was primarily interested in discovery as an intervening process. Kersh's work indicates a new interest and refinement in conceptualization about the intervening process. He argued that meaning may not be the intervening variable most useful in discovery learning. Instead, motivation may be the construct most useful in explaining the results. In particular, competence motivation may be a useful way to describe the intervening events produced by the discovery treatments.

In his first study (1958), 60 college volunteers were divided at random into six groups. Each subject was taught two rules of addition, the Odd Numbers Rule and the Constant Difference Rule. All the groups were given general instructions which specified the two types, and told that the first type of problem was called the Odd Numbers Problem while the second type of problem was called the Constant Difference Problem. They were then given a sample of the respective types of problems and were told some of the characteristics of the number series which occurred in the problems. Then the three groups, each with two different forms for the presentation of the problems, were given their first problem. The No Help groups were told to try to discover the rule. The two Direct Reference groups were told to discover the rule and were given some hints about the rule. For the two Rule Given groups, the problems and rule were given by the experimenter

(*E*). Each group then continued to work on six problems. Some of the individuals in the No Help groups were unable to discover the intended rules within the time period of 90 minutes. Immediately after the learning period, the first test was given. A retest was given to all subjects four to six weeks after the first test. On the retest, two problems were presented. The first problem asked each subject to sum the first 35 odd numbers. The second question asked them the sum of all the first 35 numbers. However, the dependent variables which interested Kersh were the answers to the following questions:

> Did you add the first 35 (odd) numbers to get your answer? (Yes or no) If your answer is no, explain how you obtained your answer.
> Did you try to recall the rule you learned (or attempted to learn) under our direction several weeks ago? (Yes or no)
> Were you successful in recalling the rule? (Yes or no)
> Describe how you recalled or attempted to recall the rule (1958, p. 287).

His primary interest was the method used in solving the problems, not whether the correct answer was produced. On the test of transfer to new examples of the rules he found that the No Help group produced ($p < .05$) a greater incidence of "acceptable methods" than did either the Direct Reference group or the Rule Given group. On a dependent variable which asked the subject (*S*) to explain the rule, he found that only a small percentage of any group could explain either of the two rules. Initial learning was best for the directed groups. He concludes that motivation and consequent practice, greatest for the discovery group, produced the best performance on the acceptable test given approximately one month after learning.

One clear result of the study is that none of the treatments was very effective at producing transfer to new problems several weeks after learning. The second result is that the self-report data on motivation and practice are difficult to interpret and may not be very reliable. The third result is that a motivational explanation for the performance of the discovery groups is an interesting hypothesis.

Considerable guidance was given to all groups before they were allowed to begin to work on problems. They were all told the names of the types of rules and were given some experience with examples of the rules. It may be that Kersh had introduced into this study the effects of retroactive inhibition.

In his second study (1962) Kersh definitely was studying the effects of retroactive inhibition. He used the same two rules and taught them to 90 high school subjects by a program booklet procedure. After the rules were taught and practiced by each group, one-third of the subjects was given indivdual guidance in discovering an explanation for the rule. This was the Guided Discovery group. The second 30 students were given an explanation of the rules in a programmed booklet. This group was called the Directed Learning group. The last group, the Rote Learning group, was given no further instruction. The tests of retention and transfer, given three days, two weeks, and six weeks later, favored the Rote Learning and Guided Discovery groups. From the questionnaire, it appeared that the Guided Discovery group practiced rules after learning and before testing more than did the subjects in the other groups.

In both studies, he argues that some kind of directed discovery of explanations or relationships motivates the students to continue after the learning exercise is completed. As in the first study, Kersh again used as the primary dependent variable the method used by the students to arrive at answers to transfer items. This is not the same index of transfer often used in other studies on learning by discovery. In his second study, the label of rote learning was used to describe a control condition in which no instruction was given. In earlier studies, rote learning was made synonomous with drill and repetition.

Kersh's work is of interest because it represents recent experimental attempts to index the intervening events. His attention to motivation is described after White's (1959) concepts of competence and effectance. As is characteristic of the research on discovery primarily concerned with intervening processes, one finds less attention given to the independent and dependent variables. One result is that rote and discovery occur as the treatments. Another is that dependent variables, scarcely employed otherwise, become the primary variables of interest because they are likely to index the intervening events. Kersh makes one acutely aware of the problems of measurement of intervening events such as motivation.

Verbal Mediators. Gagné and Brown (1961) taught 33 males, in grades nine and ten, a program on some principles of a number series. All three experimental groups received an introductory program followed by one of three programs. The first treatment was labeled Rule and Example. The second treatment was labeled Discovery, and the third, Guided Discovery.

The Rule and Example program began with the correct formula, which S was asked to copy on his answer sheet; and was followed by several examples for S to work. The Discovery program began by asking S for a rule for the number series. The following frames contained hints to direct S to work at deriving the rule. The questions became more and more explicit; however, they never stated the rules for him. The Guided Discovery program also began with a question, but the question was more specific than the one asked in the Discovery program. The first question was followed by a second to introduce numbers and to make the steps in deriving the rule more apparent than they were in the Discovery treatment. Further items gave examples of the relationships within the number series.

On the second day, each S repeated the first day's program. In this respect, even the Discovery group was given considerable direction. They had seen the items and had been asked to produce the rule the day before. Gagné and Brown state:

> The procedure employed with the three learning programs insured that, although the Ss responded to different sets of learning materials, they all achieved successful answers to questions about the same four number series (p. 316).

The dependent variables were the time to solve the problems, the number of hints required to solve the problems, and the weighted time score combining these. In each case, S had to derive the formula for the sum of n terms in a number series. This type of dependent variable differs from those often used in studies in learning by discovery, where the subject is required to use a previously learned rule to work specific problems. Transfer of a more remote nature—transfer to new rules—is involved in the Gagné and Brown study.

Their results showed the best performance for the Guided Discovery group, the worst for the Rule and Example group, and intermediate performance for the Discovery treatment. All measures were significant by analysis of variance at less than the .01 level. Their results support a Guided Discovery procedure for the teaching of the derivation of new but related rules. However, one must remember that all the groups were given a second day's rehearsal over the material carefully directed the first day.

This study is one of the most carefully controlled ones on the intervening processes in learning by discovery. They described the intervening variable in terms of the subject's history. The concepts newly learned in an experiment were the mediators affecting problem solving and transfer. From this line of argument they state that, provided the concepts are learned, it should not matter how the concepts were learned. The result should be the same. It is not *how* you learn but *what* you learn that is important, according to the argument (p. 320).

Their discussion of the importance of what is learned rather than how it is learned scarcely seems appropriate for this study. This is especially the case since they were careful to mention, as stated above, that all groups learned to approximately the same criterion, and therefore must have differed only in terms of how it was learned. After an analysis of the Gagné and Brown tasks and programs, Della-Piana and Eldredge (1964), question the interpretation that the differences in their study were due to what was practiced rather than how it was practiced.

A study by Bruner (1961) represents an interesting, but not a rigorous, approach to the study of discovery as an intervening event. He used the concept of mediation to predict the results of learning a list of paired-associates. Generic mediation (a superordinate term or idea is the mediator), thematic mediation (a theme or story is the embedding material), and part-whole mediation (e.g., a sentence containing the word 'trees' mediates between chairs and forest) were three types of mediators he intuited and used to measure children's preferences for mediators.

He taught the 30 paired-associates to three groups of twelve year old children. The first group was told to remember the words. In the second group, each child was asked to select some word or mediator which could help to make the association meaningful to him. The third group was supplied with the words selected by the second group and was directed to use these words as their mediators. Since the second group learned in one trial the greatest percentage of the paired-associates (95 per cent), Bruner concluded that discovery was a method superior to prompting or direction.

The mediators for the second group, by virtue of their selection by the learners, were very probably more strongly associated with the stimulus terms by the members of the second group than they were by the members of the third group. It would be interesting to perform this study after controlling for the individual differences in associations. Bruner's dependent variable was initial learning of a list of paired-associates. Percentage learned in one trial is not a type of measure commonly used in studies of learning by discovery.

The study is reported very briefly near the end of his article. No specifics about method or analyses of results are presented. Bruner's study is important because it represents an attempt to apply mediation theory to the study of discovery. As a by-product one can see why self-selection of mediators may be an effective way to increase learning.

For the Future. The recent interest in the intervening variables has changed much from the early studies on connectionism–field theory and rote–meaningful processes. The intervening variables of recent interest include motivation, verbal mediation, and subverbal awareness.

As a description of an intervening process, discovery now competes with verbal mediators, concepts, and the competence motive. Discovery is now seen as an event which should mediate transfer—a theory of transfer. There is also interest in indexing discovery separately from the transfer it may mediate.

One reason why learning by discovery has created such a furor and interest among educators is that it poses an intervening variable, an event called discovery, while at the same time it is a theory of how and under what conditions associations and knowledge are acquired. There are not many theories of verbal learning which predict on theoretical bases, rather than on empirical bases, conditions for forming associations. For example, mediation theory (Osgood, 1953) predicts behavior after associations are formed. That is, if A is associated with B and B in turn with C, then there should be a tendency for C to be produced to the stimulus A. From the theory, one knows little about how to associate A to B and B to C.

One way for discovery to be useful is to lead to productive independent variables. For a useful discussion of functions of theories of instruction see Bruner (1964b).

For the future, one wonders if discovery has any merit as an intervening variable. If it does, the author suggests a behavioral emphasis for discovery as a mediating event. Mandler (1962) presents an important paper on association and structure. He discusses the distinction between cognitive and association theories in the use of the term response. From empirical evidence on the effect of overlearning on transfer and from the concept of learning set, he indicates that events which have been given structural and cognitive explanations are amenable, at least in part, to associative explanations. In research on discovery learning, the term response has little usefulness because the type or mode of response is often unimportant. If one chooses to use an associational theory to predict the results of learning by discovery, he must remember that the term response is deceptive and is narrow in its implication. A term such as answer might be more useful (Gagné, 1962).

The measurement of the behavioral results of mediating events is covered in a well known volume on the measurement of meaning (Osgood, Suci, & Tannenbaum, 1957). However, in this volume, the future researcher on discovery will find most attention given to the affective and connotative dimensions of mediating events. Little attention is given to denotative meaning and its transfer.

The second important part of this course for the future would be to relate discovery to its behavioral antecedents. Gagné (1964, pp. 310–317) discusses the nature of problem solving and presents paradigms to describe the hypothetical intervening events which occur in human learning and problem solving. He differentiates among the types of learning according to their complexity.

> Increasing complexity is seen to reside not so much in what is learned, as in the nature of what has to be *preavailable* . . . in order for various types of learning to occur. Thus, verbal paired-associate learning in its pure form occurs when the responses (or response-connections) are already available (cf. Underwood and Schultz, 1960), originally made so presumably, by previous learning . . . And so on until the most complex form, problem solving is reached, which depends upon the preavailability of capabilities acquired in all the other forms of learning (pp. 311–312).

Although it may be too much to expect that a behavioristic approach will improve the usefulness of discovery, the attempt should be made. Unless the concept of discovery can be objectively indexed, it has little usefulness in behavioral research on learning and instruction.

The Independent Variables

The second major segment of research on learning by discovery is grouped under the heading of independent variables. These studies are focused on the functional relations between independent variables and dependent variables. Compared with the studies described under the Intervening Variables section above, there is relatively less attention given to indexing or theorizing about the hypothetical covert behavior of the subject. Instead, the researchers are primarily interested in discovery treatments and in comparing them with other treatments. In some of the latest studies, there are attempts to define operationally the independent variables separately from the dependent variables. The old rote–discovery labels are replaced gradually by names for treatments which imply little about the subjects' behavior, but describe the stimuli in more objective ways, e.g., answers given. The dependent variables are given less attention in these studies than are the independent variables.

The studies summarized below differ from one another in many ways: subject matter, age of learners, variety of treatments, and measures of the dependent variables. The reader is especially cautioned about the labels for the treatments and even for the tests. Quite different treatments are sometimes given the same name, and sometimes one research-er's rote treatment is highly similar to another's discovery treatment.

Principles and Answers. One of the earliest and best known of empirical studies on rules and principles, a precursor of studies on learn-ing by discovery, is by Judd (1908). He used transfer as a criterion and studied the teaching of a relationship between the depth of water and the refraction which results when one looks from a less dense medium (air) into a more dense medium (water) with an angle of incidence ap-propriate to produce a refraction. One group was taught, in verbal form, the principle of refraction. They then practiced throwing darts at a sub-merged target. Another group was given the same total instructional time, but the time was used to practice throwing darts without the teacher's verbalization or explanation of the principle. On a transfer test with a change in the depth of the water, the group given the prelimi-nary verbal training performed better.

Thorndike's admonition to avoid the practice of errors which may occur in discovery learning prompted a chain of studies on rules and principles. A type of task used by Thorndike was adopted in these studies. It involves eliminating the one word which does not belong among five. Craig (1953 and 1956), Kittell (1957), and Stacey (1949) used this task. Stacey studied information given before the learner made a response and also reinforcement and knowledge of results.

He divided 100 sixth grade pupils into five groups. Group A was told nothing about why a particular choice was correct. Group B was told only that there was a reason why one of the words did not belong with the other four. This group was also given three examples to work before they began the learning task. With the examples appeared the correct principles and the correct answers. Stacey called the above two groups his discovery groups. For the remaining three groups, correct answers were specified in advance for each item. Group C was given only the item and the correct answer. Group D was given the items, the correct answers, and the information and examples given to Group B, described above. Group E was given the same as Group D plus the correct reason for the answer to each item. Each subject was also given imme-diate feedback. The experimenter announced "right" and "wrong" as appropriate. A correction procedure was used, and S was allowed to continue until he selected the correct word.

Stacey found no interaction between amount of information given to the subjects and ability level. When gains from pretest to posttest were measured, there were no significant differences either among abil-ity levels or among the five treatments.

57

When the dependent variable was ability to give the proper reasons for the responses, the results indicated that those given the minimum amount of information (method A) or just about the minimum (method B) and just below the maximum (method D) gave the correct reasons in a higher proportion of cases than the subjects given the median (method C) amount of information. There were not any significant differences among methods A, B, and D. In other words, the two methods which Stacey thought involved discovery, methods A and B, produced greater ability to state reasons for correct responses. However, method D, which emphasized identification rather than self-discovery, produced similar mean scores.

Stacey's results indicate one danger of naming the stimuli in terms of behavior one hopes the stimuli will produce. Groups C and D might also be considered discovery groups if it is discovery of a generalization or principle rather than specific answers which is most important. Neither C nor D was given the correct principles. Stacey's results must be related to the dependent variables he sampled. The studies which follow often use other dependent variables.

Stacey's study influenced a series of later studies. Craig (1953, 1956) and Kittell (1957) used the same type of task. Craig (1953) reacted to the line of argument developed by Stacey. Craig felt that guidance could produce a positive effect on discovery. He described his independent variables as different types of stimuli. This description of variables represents an important step towards defining more precisely the learning by discovery issue and a step away from the rote-understanding issue and from the definition of treatments in terms of responses made by the learners.

He investigated the effects of cues about principles. There were four groups of 50 male college graduates. The task was the same as that used in the study by Stacey above: i.e., to determined the one word among the five of each item that did not belong. The first group was a minimum guidance group and was given no cues. For the second group, the items were arranged according to common principles. The third group received a blank space between the sets of items grouped by a common principle. This group was told that all items in a group were organized into a common principle. The fourth and final group, a maximum guidance group, was given the information described for the third group and also was given a short statement of each principle.

On initial learning, the amount of guidance was directly related to the number of correct responses. When transfer was a criterion, the same relationship held, that is, the more the cues, the greater the ability to discover.

In his second experiment, Craig (1956) divided 106 college sophomores into two groups, a No Help group and a Directed group. The No Help group was told only that one principle was used to answer all five items which were grouped together as a unit. The Directed group was given the same information as the No Help group, except that the principle was stated above each group of four items. Each item consisted of five words. The subject was to sort out the incorrect one of the five. He gave an immediate test, and retention tests 3, 17, and 31 days later. On the immediate test, the Directed group did better than the No Help group. Although there were no significant differences between the two groups on the 3- and 17-day retention tests, there was a significant difference between the two groups on the 31-day test. The Directed group did better than the No Help group. These tests all contained new examples of the rules previously learned. Another retention test, which consisted of new rules and examples of these new rules produced no differences between the groups. He interprets his study to indicate that external direction can help learners to make future discovery by providing them with an adequate background of information. Craig summarizes his experiment as follows:

> Many have advocated relatively independent problem-solving in the belief that learning situations should be similar to anticipated transfer situations. This point of view rests on the assumption that future discovery of principles will be through independent problem-solving, hence, more like pupil self-discovery than directed discovery. A different view is that problem-solving and discovery are never independent except in the sense that no one is physically present to prompt the learner. Principles previously learned in an area serve to direct discovery. Out-of-school discovery is not independent but directed by the knowledge gained under the direction of previous teachers. The more direction of this kind available to the learner, the more effective his discovery of new relations. The cumulative effect of greater learning through directed discovery over months or years may offset the effect of any lack of similarity between learning and transfer situations and prove to be the best preparation for new discoveries (Craig, 1956, p. 233).

Of course, it should be remembered that he found no effect upon transfer to new principles, a finding which has been often repeated by other researchers. He also found no differences on two of his three retention tests.

To study the effects of guidance upon problem solving, Corman (1957) used forms of Katona's match tasks which were presented to

255 twelfth grade students. He varied the information about the principle and about the method of solving problems. All possible combinations of these three factored variables (no information, some information, and much information) gave nine different treatments ranging from no information about either the principle or the method, to information about both the principle and the method. The dependent variables were initial learning, transfer to simple and complex problems, and ability to verbalize the principles.

His results are complicated. For the simple transfer problems, specific information about the rule, with explicit information about the method, was the best for the more capable students. On the test of complex transfer, the indirect clues (either to method or to the rule) produced for the more capable students performance worse than other combinations of information. But for students of less than average ability, performance on complex tasks was best when guidance, either specific or less explicit, was given about the method. When acquisition of the rule was a criterion, performance increased as the amount of information about the rule also increased. That is, explicit information about the rule was superior to no information about the rule.

When writing the rule was the criterion, the students who were given the most explicit information about the rule performed best, although their performance was better only than that of the No Information group. No statistically significant effect on this criterion was found for information about method. Corman concluded that appropriate guidance was beneficial for learning and transfer and that failure to provide it would delay rather than prevent solution; and that the effectiveness of the guidance may interact with student ability as described above.

One interesting part of this study was the attempt to define the independent variables in terms of two types of information (information about a principle and information about methods of solving problems) and three quantities of information (no, some, and much). His attempts to define the treatments in terms other than those which also describe the type of responses (rote or discovery) represent a step toward objectivity. However, the terms 'some' and 'much' leave much to be desired. At best they are on an ordinal scale. They still are defined in terms of assumptions about the learner's background, when these assumptions may not be valid. Another interesting part of the study was a dependent variable, ability to verbalize the principles, which he added to the usual dependent variables of initial learning and transfer to new problems. His study is of interest primarily because he elaborates the number and type of variables and studies all possible combinations of them.

The primary interest in dependent and independent variables rather than in intervening processes, characteristic of Corman's study and of the two Craig studies mentioned above, occurs again in a study by Kittell. He hypothesized that giving the underlying principles, in verbal form, was better for transfer and retention than not giving these principles. He used the same type of items as did Craig. He divided 132 sixth grade children into three groups. The Minimum Direction group was told that each group of three items had a principle in common and was told to look for the principle. The Intermediate Direction group was given the same direction as that given to the Minimum group plus a verbal statement of the principle. The principle was printed above the appropriate items and was also read twice, aloud, by the E. The Maximum Direction group was given not only the same information as the Intermediate group but was told the three correct responses to the three items in each group.

On a difficult test of transfer to new examples of previously learned principles, the Intermediate group did the best, the Maximum group next best, and the Minimum group did least well. The Intermediate group also retained more of the previously learned principles. On initial learning, the Intermediate and Maximum groups did not differ from each other significantly and each was better than the Minimum Direction group. His tests were difficult. The mean scores were less than five out of a possible 15.

Compared with Craig's two studies, Kittell increased the amount of direction by adding a group which was given both the relevant rules and the correct answers. Kittell's Intermediate group was probably more highly directed than was Craig's Directed group.

His results offer an interesting hypothesis about the relationship of direction to transfer. The hypothesis would be that when the material is most difficult the direction should match the population of items to which transfer is desired. For example, direction with specific rules produces transfer of these rules, even to situations where the rules do not apply.

That the most highly directed group would do as well as or better than any other group on initial learning of several specific responses agrees with much earlier research and is a surprise to no one. It is interesting that the group given the rules but not the correct answers produced the greatest transfer to new examples of the same rules. Perhaps the learner discovers how to apply the rules and receives extinction for incorrect attempts to apply these rules. The direction toward certain rules may make it likely that he will use these rules again in the future. One wonders what Kittell's results might have been had he used one transfer test which contained quite new and different items.

Craig and Kittell's studies also show that labels such as maximum and minimum are largely meaningless. Kittell's Intermediate Direction group was probably more highly directed than was Craig's (1956) Maximum group.

It was inevitable that the Craig and Kittell studies (which found that by giving rules transfer could be increased) would excite at least one rebuttal. Haslerud and Meyers (1958) used 100 college students as subjects, and 20 enciphering problems as the learning task. The two treatments consisted of either no directions or specific directions (including the rule) for deciphering the code printed above the problem. They used a treatment by subjects design; that is, each subject was given both treatments. There were 10 items for each treatment. On initial learning the specific directions produced the greatest mean performance on the test of transfer to new sentences, which involved the same 20 rules used during training. They found no statistically significant difference.

However, they give a dubious interpretation of the results and conclude that the No Directions Given treatment was the better of the two because the percentage of loss from the immediate to the test given one week later was less for this group than for the other group. Since each subject was given practice on each of the two experimental conditions, one might expect that the practice at discovering would generalize from one set of items to the other and that the treatments would then be contaminated. Again, the directed procedure was better on the original learning, even when there was no significant difference on a later transfer test.

Wittrock (1963) divided 292 college students into four experimental groups. The task was to decipher transpositional codes. To one group the rule as well as the answer to the specific item were given simultaneously with the encoded item. To a second group the rule was given but the answer was not given. To a third group the rule was not given but the answer was given. And to the fourth group, neither the rule nor the answer was given. It was hypothesized that with difficult materials (low association value also) direction toward the rules or specification of the rules enhances transfer to new examples of these same rules. It was also hypothesized that learning both rules and answers produces the greatest initial learning of a few correct answers, but would interfere with transfer, because S would not be practicing applying a rule or extinguishing his associated and incorrect answers. The results supported ($p < .01$) the hypotheses. An intermediate amount of direction produced the greatest retention and transfer but maximum direction produced the greatest initial learning. The minimum direction treatment was least effective on initial learning, retention, and transfer. This study exemplifies how the studies primarily interested in relationships between independent-dependent variables have recently tended to use materials which are simple, of low-association value, and somewhat foreign to the type commonly used in elementary and secondary schools. The use of coding or selection of one word from among five as tasks for experimentation is justified when one needs control over stimuli which he cannot get with sequenced materials. However, for the use of these materials one pays a price in ability to generalize.

These studies on rules and answers differ from one another in so many ways that no definite conclusions can be stated. However, some of them are better controlled than most of the studies described under the section on intervening variables. The learning by discovery hypothesis is being operationally defined better than before. Some of the complexities and oversimplifications of the earlier studies are being exposed. (See Grote, 1960; Moss, 1960; Ray, 1961; Rowlett, 1960; and Tomlinson, 1962 for further discussion of the effects of discovery treatments upon learning, retention, and transfer.)

Verbal Cues. One reaction against the complexity and diffuseness of the treatments common in learning by discovery is to design treatments that differ from one another by only one word or one sentence per problem and, in preliminary training, to teach a hierarchy of associations to these words or sentences.

In a series of experiments by Wittrock, Keislar, and Stern it was hypothesized if one knew the subjects' associations to these words, he could predict verbally mediated transfer, learning, and retention. One way to know many of the associations is to take unknown stimuli and associate a hierarchy to them. In the first study in the series (Wittrock, Keislar, and Stern, 1964), 52 kindergarten children were, over a period of three months, taught associations to the verbal cues used later in the experiment. By looking at pictures of 12 common objects and animals, and by hearing their French names pronounced aloud, each child was taught to say the French names whenever the appropriate picture was presented. Half of the 12 French names were masculine nouns and half were feminine nouns. After each child had learned to label the pictures, the next level of the hierarchy was taught. The children learned that each French name had an initial *la* or *le* sound. They were taught to say *la* or *le* and to discriminate *la* or *le* when a French name was spoken. Finally, they were taught to associate the words *la* and *le* with the word 'article.' During the experimental training all treatment groups were given a sequence of slides each of which showed three pictures—a model at the top and two alternatives below. The children were asked to select one of the two bottom pictures which matched the top picture in a certain way. The basis for matching was always the gender of the French name for the top picture. One of the alternatives at the bottom always had a masculine name and the other always had a feminine name. While they looked at each slide the verbal cues were presented. The children in Group I were told to press a button. In Group II the children were told the word 'article.' In Group III the children were told *la* or *le*, depending upon the correct basis for matching. In the fourth group the children were told the correct alternative.

The dependent variables were measured by learning and transfer tests given immediately and also three weeks later. The learning test consisted of items constructed from the six objects used during the experimental training. The transfer test used only the other six objects which had been named by the students during the preliminary training but had never been used during the experimental training. By analysis of variance and by a specific comparisons test, the mean of the group told *la* or *le* was statistically significantly greater ($p < .01$) than any of the other three groups on the transfer test.

Apparently, after the preliminary associations were learned, transfer to new instances of the same concept was facilitated by explicit verbalization by E of the name for the correct concept, followed by practice and reinforcement for applying this label. The study indicated that kindergarten children may not learn and transfer if they are given only general or very specific cues or if they are left to discover answers on their own—at least when the stimuli are of common objects. It should be emphasized that all tests presented problems with no verbal cues. The child had to discover the correct basis for answering any set of ten or fifteen items. The study also indicated that whether or not discovery is effective may depend on the learner's history of associations to the items and the cues. A history of working with similar problems and similar materials may make discovery learning or reception learning a more effective way than the other to solve problems.

The second study in the series (Wittrock and Keislar, 1965) was performed with 160 second and third grade children and used the concepts color, size, shape, and number familiar to the children. The dependent variables were the same as those mentioned above, except that one which sampled transfer to new concepts was added.

By analysis of variance and covariance, both the group given the specific cue and the group given the concept cue did significantly better than the group given the most general cue. This was true on the tests of learning, transfer to new instances, retention, and the delayed test of transfer to new instances. None of the groups was any better than any other on the transfer to new concepts test. It seems that when the subject has a history of associations to cues, they help him eliminate many possible answers and mediate discovery on his own. At least he appears to be able to do this more readily with familiar materials of few dimensions than with comparable materials learned over a few days or months during an experiment. In both studies the group given the name for the concept did as well as, or better than, any of the groups.

In both studies, the most general cue was not effective on initial learning, retention, and transfer, including transfer to new concepts. This may simply mean that in order for the general members of a hierarchy to become effective cues in problem solving, some procedure other than what was used in this study must be attempted. With proper training, it may be possible to make these most general cues effective for transfer to quite different concepts than those learned in the experimental training.

From these two studies, it would appear that the subject's history and his associations to the terms E gives him are important variables. Certainly these associations plus those associations S has to the entire problem stimulus are variables which must be considered in future research.

Instructions. The studies grouped under the heading of Instructions differ from those under the Principles and Answers heading in two ways. First, they include among the independent variables vague or general cues. Second, they are taken from the literature on concept learning; but they are directly relevant to the learning by discovery hypothesis.

Maier (1930) studied the role of direction on reasoning and problem solving. His double pendulum problem was solved by eight of the 22 subjects in the Direction group. Only one of the 62 subjects solved the problem without the added cue ("Observe how easy the solution would be if you could only hang the pendulums from two nails on the ceiling"). Providing additional information here resulted in improving the problem solving process. Saugstad (1955) showed that performance on these problems can be improved if availability or prerequisite associations is induced.

Luchins (1942), in another well-known study, showed that a general cue, "Don't be blind," increased the problem-solving of the adult subjects, but not of school children. Here a very general cue changed negative transfer, which was produced by working six problems of one type, into positive transfer for problems seven and eight. However, the sentence was not effective with children.

Ewert and Lambert (1932) gave their subjects three cardboard disks, one in each of three circles drawn on a board. The three circles formed a triangular pattern. The cardboard disks were graduated in size and the object was to maintain the order of size within the stack and yet to transfer the disks one at a time, from one circle to another circle. One of the groups was given minimal instructions about the general rules of the game. A second group was told to try to find a general principle. A third group was given the principle in verbal form, while a fourth group was given the principle and a demonstration of how to solve a problem. The groups given the verbally stated principle did significantly better than the groups which were not given the principle.

Reed (1946a) investigated the effect of instructions on learning and retention of concepts. He found that instructions to learn the meaning of, as well as the name of, a stimulus produced a much higher rate of learning and degree of retention than did a set to learn only the names. The condition which produced the best learning did not involve giving the subjects detailed information about the meaning of the cards. However, the direction which he introduced did increase learning and retention. It seems that a minimal amount of direction improves performance over a situation which does not contain this type of verbal direction. Wittrock, in several experiments, found that with adolescents and with adults, a general cue which contains no information about the subject matter can still increase the learning of principles. This was true whether the subject matter was principles of economics (Wittrock, 1963b), Buddhism (Wittrock, 1963a), or history, American government, and English (Wittrock, 1962).

Underwood and Richardson (1956) studied concept learning as a function of instructions and of dominance level of concepts. Unrestricted instructions (UR) gave the subjects nothing about the nature of the concepts to be learned. They were told only that it would be a good idea to vary their responses from trial to trial. Partially restricted

(PR) instructions gave the subjects a class of responses needed to form the concepts. The experimenter probed the subjects about simple ways to describe common objects. Completely restricted (CR) instructions gave the subjects the six correct responses which they were allowed to keep before them and to study during the experiment. The results showed that the greater the amount of information given the subjects concerning the content or the nature of the concepts to be learned, the more rapid was the acquisition of concepts.

The above studies on instructions indicate that problem solving and concept learning can be facilitated by guidance upon discovery. In many instances, quite direct and specific guidance, which specifies the correct concepts, can also facilitate problem solving and concept learning. This is not to say that learning cannot occur incidentally or that it cannot occur without awareness or without instructions (Adams, 1957; Bugelski and Scharlock, 1952; Postman, 1964; Postman and Sassenrath, 1961; Sassenrath, 1962).

Verbalization by S. After reviewing Katona (1940) and Haslerud and Meyers (1958), Gagné and Smith (1962) studied the effects upon problem solving of two independent variables: Ss' verbalizations during practice, and instructions to find and to state a general principle. There were 28 ninth and tenth grade boys in the study. They were divided randomly into four groups which were composed from all possible combinations of the two, two factored independent variables (i.e., verbalizing versus nonverbalizing, solution set versus no solution set). The task was the three circle task used by Ewert and Lambert (1932). On transfer to new problems, the groups required to verbalize did significantly better than those who were not required to verbalize. This was true both in terms of number of moves and in terms of time. All other differences between pairs of groups were not statistically significant. They also found that the groups who were required to verbalize performed better than the nonverbalizing groups on a test of ability to state verbal principles. They summarize their results as follows: "The results appear to indicate that requiring Ss to verbalize during practice has the effect of making them think of new reasons for their moves, and thus facilitates both the discovery of general principles and their employment in solving successive problems" (Gagné and Smith, 1962, p. 18).

For the Future. The great variety of complex treatments, subject matter, students, and dependent variables used in the above studies on the independent variables makes it most difficult to compare results across studies. Any conclusions about learning by discovery are highly tenuous. However, several things can be learned from these studies and there are several possibilities for the future.

First, the results of a study should be generalized only to students, subject matter, and situations directly comparable to those sampled in the experiment. Although the future may show that broad general principles do encompass a variety of people and subject matter, the present state of the science warrants no such conclusion. Obviously, interactions among types of students, subject matter, and methods of instruction will not be found unless designs are used which will evidence them. With complex human behavior, we should expect these interactions to occur and measure them when they do occur.

The second thing to be learned from these studies is that future studies should give greater attention to individual differences and to the history of the learners. The effects of the treatments must be related to the learners' proactive influences. In a culture where children are customarily taught by reception rather than discovery, we should not be surprised if their histories are more influential than our brief treatments. Neither should we be surprised if a new discovery procedure is interesting and motivating, at least until the novelty wears thin.

The third thing to be learned is that considerable research on concept learning and problem solving is often relevant to the problems encountered in research on learning by discovery. For the future, researchers on discovery learning would do well to build on these results and procedures.

For example, Gagné (1962) has developed a model and a procedure that considers the history of the subjects, individual differences, knowledge and instructions, all important variables in learning by discovery. He reasoned that for the learner to perform on a dependent variable, certain knowledge is prerequisite and certain instructions from the experimenter are necessary. His term *knowledge* refers to information, ideas, etc., that are particular to a certain subject matter. His term *instructions* pertains to sentences which include information not peculiar to a certain subject matter. Instructions perform at least four functions. First, they help the learner to identify the required terminal performance. Second, they identify elements of the stimulus situation which are important. Third, they enhance recallability of learning sets. Fourth, they guide thinking. He introduces the history of the subject with the term *learning set*. Learning sets apply to subordinate classes of tasks necessary for the learner to be successful on the dependent variable, provided he is given instructions. These learning sets are hierarchically arranged. The lowest members of the hierarchy must all be present before more advanced members of the hierarchy can be performed. The lowest members mediate positive transfer to the higher levels. If one of the lower members cannot be recalled, transfer from one learning set to another would be zero. If the lower members can be recalled, transfer will range up to 100 per cent. Although one can question what Gagné means by one learning set being prerequisite to another, or being simpler than another, the results he obtains with this model are impressive.

For example, in the study by Gagné and Paradise (1961), they asked the question, "What would the individual have to be able to know how to do, in order to be able to perform this (new) task, being given only instructions?" (pp. 16–17). They studied the effects of mental ability factors and learning sets upon the solving of linear algebraic equations. Among the important findings were those which indicated that subordinate learnings sets mediate positive transfer to other members in the hierarchy. The proportion of transfer ranged from .91 to 1.00. They also predicted and found that while the correlation between relevant basic abilities and rates of attainment of learning sets progressively decreased at higher levels of the hierarchy, the correlation of basic abilities with achievement of learning sets increased at these higher levels. The correlation between rate of attainment and relevant basic abilities should decrease, according to Gagné and Paradise, because as one proceeds up the hierarchy, transfer depends increasingly upon the immediately subordinate learning sets or upon specific knowledge. The correlation between basic abilities and achievement of relevant learning sets should increase because, since the learning program is not perfect, high and low ability students will become more differentiated. This increase in the correlation indicates the ineffectiveness of the learning program.

Although again one could give other interpretations to these data and predictions, Gagné and his associates present an excellent model for much of the future research on learning by discovery. By analyzing complicated and hierarchically organized subject matter into its prerequisites and components, he has been able to produce impressive results on learning and transfer tests.

Stolurow and Bergum (1957) present a model which may also have usefulness in discovery learning. They tested the effects of different methods of training upon trouble shooting. They analyzed the symptom-cause and the cause-symptom relationships into their stimulus and response components. They described response sharing, that is, where one stimulus is associated with more than one response, and stimulus sharing, where several stimuli are associated with one response. Last, they described stimulus-response sharing, or many stimuli to many responses, where several stimuli are each associated with each of several responses. They argued that before one can learn new associations, such as symptom-cause relationships, he might have to engage in stimulus learning or response learning. Stimulus learning involves differentiating the occasion for one rather than another response. Response learning involves the acquisition of the response repertoire. By analyzing the complex problem of trouble shooting into its stimulus and response learning components, and by hypothesizing that learning would be more or less difficult in relation to the associations in the learner's repertoire, they predicted and found an interaction between the learner's experience with learning style and the direction of association, and the conditions under which he would acquire generalized habits of learning. This type of careful analysis of stimulus and response factors, as well as the analysis of the learner's history, is greatly needed in studies of learning by discovery. However, as discussed earlier, in discovery learning one probably should not think of particular responses. Instead, classes of responses or answers is probably a more useful term because the particular form of the overt response may not be crucial to learning.

Although many more lessons can be learned from the studies on the independent variables, only two more will be mentioned here. Treatments should be designed to vary one element at a time. If an experiment is performed, its treatments should differ from one another in a meaningful way. It does no good to know that a discovery treatment is more effective than a rote treatment if the two treatments are not systematically related to each other. This is more than a problem of labeling treatments. Perhaps standardized treatments, as suggested by Della-Piana and Eldredge (1964), are needed.

The last lesson to be mentioned here is that the rote versus discovery issue is a meaningless one and should be replaced by several, more useful issues. One way to rephrase part of the issue would be to look at the effects of the teacher's use of language. Discovery could be viewed as a condition to contrast with uses of different verbal stimuli. Another part of the issue is the use of language by the subject. Each of these fundamental issues could be studied as to the effects of the rate, variety, sequence, etc., of presenting stimuli in interaction with the subject's history. When supplemented with an analysis of the dependent variables discussed below, the result should be a substantial improvement in research, and should bring the study of the independent variables of learning by discovery into the areas of research on concept learning and problem solving.

However, the problems of studying the independent variables of discovery learning will not be solved simply by joining the ranks of researchers on problem solving. When Duncan (1959) reviewed the recent research on problem solving, and Schulz (1960), the research on transfer of training, they indicated a need for studies to relate stimulus events as antecedents to behavior as consequents. Duncan writes, "Problem solving particularly needs research to determine the simple laws between dimensionalized independent variables and performance" (1959, p. 426). Schulz writes:

> Until we know what the variables are that cause problem solving behavior to vary in predictable ways, our teaching is less likely to be as effective as it might be. Therefore, it is prerequisite to our success as educators that we discover the laws which describe the functional relations between various kinds of antecedent variables and later problem solving performance (1960, p. 62).

The problems of doing research on the independent variables of learning by discovery are not yet solved by researchers in problem solving.

The Dependent Variables

The lack of empirical research. Needless to say, the learning by discovery researchers have done almost no empirical work on the analysis or measurement of dependent variables per se. They have been interested in a few variables, described vaguely as transfer, motivation, and ability to solve problems. These variables tend to differ widely across studies. For example, Kersh (1958) was interested in the methods the students used to solve problems, not the number of correct answers. Some researchers are interested in the child's ability to solve examples of previously learned concepts. Others are interested in the child's ability to solve problems much different from those he encountered during the experiment. Gagné and Brown (1961) were interested in the child's ability to derive formulae, rather than in his ability to solve numerical problems. The identification and measurement of the results of discovery learning is a necessary prerequisite to improving research on the independent variables. There is no greater problem in the area today.

For the Future. A multi-dimensional analysis of the outcomes of learning is sorely needed. See Cronbach's chapter in this volume for his

71

identification of important dependent variables. In addition to the common and overlapping dependent variables of transfer, motivation, and ability to solve problems, at least the dependent variables of savings and time should be included whenever possible. Savings can be quantified. It is important that a student be able to use the subject matter to further his learning in the same area and to avoid problems in that area.

The measurement of the dependent variables is also important. Della-Piana and Eldredge (1964) argue for standard types of treatments which could be used to compare one mode of presentation with another. One can argue for the development of standardized measures of dependent variables used in learning by discovery. At present there are very few of these types of measures of achievement available to researchers in learning by discovery.

Gagné, Foster, and Crowley (1948) reviewed the area of the measurement of transfer of training and summarized the methods which have been used to quantify transfer of training. Not much of a creative thrust has been made in the measurement and evaluation of the differences among groups of learners after they have been exposed to complex instructional treatments. Glaser (1963) has written about this problem. Criterion referenced tests and measures designed to discriminate among treatments should be developed. These would be useful in experiments on learning by discovery.

DISCUSSION

At the beginning of this chapter it was stated that the independent–intervening–dependent variable framework helps one to explicate some of the complexities and inconsistencies in research on learning by discovery, and it helps one to develop suggestions for the future. Throughout the chapter, the framework has been applied and has been used to suggest improvements for the future. There is no reason to repeat all those suggestions here. Instead, an evaluation of the learning by discovery hypothesis will now be made.

The early simple conception of the hypothesis carried much surplus meaning. The early field theory-versus-connectionism controversy involved far more than discovery. In fact, one could argue that Thorndike's treatments which specified correct answers but not explanations left much room for student discovery. Field theory, which sometimes injected explanations and verbalizations of generalizations, left reduced opportunity to discover these verbalizations. The early conception of the hypothesis is no longer useful. It injected serious oversimplifications and ignored distinctions made later.

Since the early conception of the problem, confusion has existed among researchers about the complex nature of the issues in the hypothesis. The framework for this chapter has helped to expose some of those issues. Induction-deduction is a variable commonly confused with the discovery hypothesis. The learner can discover from either very general or very specific cues, one presented before the other. When applied to independent variables, induction-deduction pertains to the order in which general and specific cues are presented. When applied to hypothetical, logical processes, the learner can still discover a principle or generalization by either procedure. It depends upon where he starts and what he is asked to discover.

Whether he succeeds or fails in the process is not only a function of the treatment he is given, but it is also a function of his individual history. Proaction and individual differences have complicated the simple, early hypothesis.

Discovery as a Way to Learn

Perhaps the most useful distinction which the framework helps one to make is that learning by discovery denotes both a way to learn and an objective of learning. As a way to learn or to teach, discovery may not be an effective treatment when measured by the criteria of learning, retention, transfer, affectivity, and time. It depends upon what is meant by learning by discovery as a treatment. The treatment may refer to the way a teacher uses verbal stimuli—their sequence, nature, and variety. It may also refer to the learner's use of verbal stimuli. The result also depends upon the dependent variable sample, e.g., learning or transfer.

For example, as a way to learn a few specific associations, discovery may be inferior to more highly directed procedures. When the criterion is the learning of concepts and hierarchically ordered subject matter, discovery may fare better. If the criteria are transfer to new concepts, originality, and learning by discovery, learning by discovery as a treatment may fare well. There are no carefully gathered experimental data on this last issue. As Bruner stated the hypothesis quoted above, it has not been given a fair test. In no experiment has anyone carefully studied learning by discovery both as a treatment and as a dependent variable. Both conditions are necessary to test the practice hypothesis.

As a way to learn, discovery may also produce definite, positive or negative affectivity, and may not produce an affective loading near zero. Along with the other above mentioned tenuous hypotheses, this last one depends upon the individual learners and upon the subject matter.

From the above analysis of discovery as a way to learn (a treatment), there emerge several learning by discovery hypotheses, not just one. Research is needed upon each of them and upon the fundamental psycholinguistic variables relevant to discovery learning. Many of the discovery enthusiasts have quickly rejected or disparaged E's use of verbal statements of rules and principles. These variables should be studied. The literature on concept learning and problem solving indicates they are important for many outcomes.

Discovery as an Objective of Learning

As an objective, ability to discover is important in its own right; this is a value judgment. As an agreed-upon objective for teaching and learning, we can still ask whether learning by discovery as a treatment is as effective at producing learning by discovery as are other treatments. In other words, is practice an important independent variable? Many researchers feel that it is. Many others, including the author, feel that alternatives to practicing the terminal behavior deserve study. Perhaps a sequence of verbal materials, given with some practice at discovering would be better than an equal amount of time devoted exclusively to practice at discovering. Again it probably depends on many subject and subject matter factors. One can scarcely do better than to agree with Bruner that the practice hypothesis is an important one, and it should be tested—in the schools.

Summary

The aging but still elusive learning by discovery hypothesis has outlived its usefulness to researchers. It has not been one hypothesis but a set of several hypotheses. The practice hypothesis, discussed in detail above, is only one of this set of hypotheses. Embedded within the discovery hypothesis were other issues, such as: (1) rote versus discovery learning; (2) student control versus teacher control of the rate and order of presenting stimuli; (3) inductive versus deductive learning; (4) interaction of methods of learning with individual differences among students; (5) the order of presenting to students rules, principles and more specific information and problems; (6) the teacher's classroom use of verbal abstractions; (7) the separation of independent and dependent variables; (8) the operational definition of terms, especially of the dependent variables such as transfer and savings; and (9) the teaching of rules and generalizations.

We have progressed beyond the rote versus discovery issue. We should be directing our energies to operationally defined issues and hypotheses, such as number 9 above. Let's take one important objective now commonly cited in research on discovery but amenable to research on the teaching of rules. It is the ability to go beyond the data or to go beyond the specifics.

In more mundane terms, this is usually called positive transfer. One issue immediately follows: How can a student be taught rules, principles, and problem solving strategies which will transfer positively to new problems or show a savings in further learning? Now theories of transfer and of teaching can be applied to this operationally definable problem. We might investigate the savings and transfer obtained from hierarchically organized verbal stimuli and sequences taught to students. Instead of disparaging the teacher's use of verbal abstractions, we could now analyze them and study their effects upon learning as these effects interact with individual differences among students and among ways to learn. For example, one interesting conjecture is that there is an interaction between the specificity of the information taught to students and the amount of transfer obtained. A method which produces sizable results upon the learning of a few specific associations may produce only a limited amount of transfer. Methods which produce transfer may be slow at producing learning of a large number of specific associations.

The problems involved in the teaching of rules and principles are basic to the study of education. The area of rule and principle learning is open and ready for creative, theoretical and empirical research.

It remains to be seen whether the above conceptualization of discovery learning as one issue in the teaching of rules and principles will be more productive for research than was the discovery hypothesis. But we should have learned not to repeat two mistakes of the researchers on learning by discovery. When we state an hypothesis we should make explicit its independent, intervening, and dependent variables. When we begin our research, it would be better to start with the problem, the teaching of rules and generalizations, rather than to begin with a ready made solution to the problem, learning by discovery.

Chapter V

The Logic of Experiments on Discovery

LEE J. CRONBACH

IN SPITE OF THE CONFIDENT ENDORSEMENTS OF TEACHING THROUGH discovery that we read in semi-popular discourses on improving education, there is precious little substantiated knowledge about what advantages it offers, and under what conditions these advantages accrue. We badly need research in which the right questions are asked and trustworthy answers obtained. When the research is in it will tell us, I suspect, that inductive teaching has value in nearly every area of the curriculum, and also that its function is specialized and limited (Cronbach, 1963, pp. 378–382). The task of research is to define that proper place and function.

Honest research is hard to do, when learning by discovery is the battlecry of one side in the ardent combat between educational philosophies. We have, on the one hand, the view of education as cultural transmission, which hints strongly that it is the teacher's job to know the answers and to put them before the pupil. On the other, we have the view of education as growth, arguing that the only real and valuable knowledge is that formulated by the pupil out of his own experience. The second position, which appeals to liberal, humanitarian, and instrumentalist biases, has a long history. In the last thirty-odd years the bias favoring do-it-yourself learning has been very strong, as educators and psychologists have united in attacks on teacher dominance and pupil conformity. Consequently, we have had almost none of the cut-and-thrust debate needed to define issues and to expose implications or fallacies of the evidence.

It is time to put aside the polemic question, Is teaching through discovery better than didactic teaching? (*Didactic* is perhaps not the ideal brief label for the pedagogy in which the teacher sets forth knowledge, but among the words that come to mind it has the advantage of being least value-loaded.) We shall have to ask subtle questions and exhibit both patience and ingenuity in unravelling them. How to frame research studies to get the right information is not at all clear; sometimes we can meet one of the supposed requirements of research design only at the expense of another, and if all my recommendations were to be followed, research would become impossibly elaborate. One of the hopes is that discussion among investigators and educational innovators can generate some agreement as to which subquestions and which improvements in research design should have priority in the next stages of investigation.

I propose that we search for limited generalizations of the following form:

> With subject matter of this nature,
> inductive experience of this type,
> in this amount,
> produces this pattern of responses,
> in pupils at this level of development.

Since this sentence constitutes an outline of the remainder of my paper, let me clarify each segment of it before I proceed.

First, the subject matter. Surely we cannot generalize over all educational content indiscriminately, yet the literature on discovery reads as if a general conclusion is sought. Moreover, unless learning tasks are comparable to those of the classroom, they are unserviceable as a basis for educational recommendations.

Second, the type of training. I can amplify this sufficiently for the moment by referring to type and amount of guidance as a significant aspect of the training.

Third, the amount of inductive experience. I have no faith in any generalization upholding one teaching technique against another, whether that preferred method be audiovisual aids, programmed instruction, learning by doing, inductive teaching, or whatever. A particular educational tactic is part of an instrumental system; a proper educational design calls upon that tactic at a certain point in the sequence, for a certain period of time, following and preceding certain other tactics. No conclusion can be drawn about the tactic considered by itself.

Fourth, the pattern of outcomes. Education has many purposes, and any learning experience must be judged in terms of all those goals. To take a simple example, there must exist some method of teaching arithmetic that produces graduates who compute brilliantly—and who hate all work involving numbers. It would be improper to advocate this method on the basis of research that considers only its effect on computational skill. It is no defense for the advocate to say that computation is the only objective that concerns *him*. If he recommends an educational change, it is his responsibility to consider how that change will affect all the outcomes that reasonable men consider important.

Fifth, the pupils. I suspect that inductive teaching is more valuable for some learners than others, and that we should not generalize over all pupils.

As I go on to illustrate wise and unwise research decisions, I am restricted by the content of past, studies. In these studies the learner is nearly always to discover some simple connection or, at best, a formula or inductive generalization. When a writer argues that discovery is a thrilling personal experience he seems to have in mind the sort of startling reorganization of interpretation illustrated on the grand scale by Kepler, and on a lesser scale by Kekulé. These "retroductions" (Hanson, 1958) are Discoveries that appear to be quite different psychologically from discoveries of simple regularities. Big-D discoveries are infrequent even in the life of the scientist. I doubt that the pupils in today's innovative classroom are having many big-D experiences, and I doubt that the psychologist will be able to arrange conditions so that Discovery will occur while the subject is under his eyes. Hence my account is limited to research on little-d discovery. We should not, however, allow ourselves to think that in these studies we are learning about the effect of retroductive discovery. (E. R. Hilgard draws my attention to the fact that we are equally without research on a "really fine kind of discovery: discovering problems rather than discovering solutions" [Mackworth, 1965]).

SELECTION OF LEARNING TASKS

Since the question before us is educational, experimental tasks ought to have psychological properties closely similar to those of educational subject matter. Discovery surely becomes more valuable as the linkage between the stimulus and the correct response becomes more rational. Rationality is at a maximum in tasks where the correct response can be deduced from the givens of the problem or from a network of established ideas. For example: finding the number of diagonals from any vertex in a polygon of n sides. Once a child understands the question, he can confirm or infirm any rule he proposes, with no help from an instructor. While the younger child confirms empirically, the older child can see that the rule is a logical necessity. There is a natural (but not necessarily a logical) linkage in tasks where the response has a readily discerned consequence. Do apples taste good? The answer might in principle be deduced from the chemistry of plants and the physiology of taste, but in practice the discovery is made through a provisional try followed by natural reinforcement. At the opposite extreme from rationality are those tasks where the S-R linkage is arbitrary, so that the person can know what is correct only because the experimenter tells him so. An example is Duncan's experiment (1964), where a digit is presented along with three adjectives and the learner has to guess which adjective has been selected randomly as correct. Discovery at this point has been reduced to sheer trial and error.

Learning by discovery is said to teach a sort of intellectual self-reliance. The child who understands the structure of the number system believes that he can work out subtraction combinations for himself, believes that he can check his own answers, believes that the answer to an arithmetic problem is always the same, believes (more broadly) that any new quantitative problem has a discoverable solution. Piaget and Smedslund (Ripple and Rockcastle, 1964) consider intellectual self-regulation—checking the consistency among one's beliefs before converting a belief into action—to be the chief ingredient in operational thought. Where inductive teaching is to promote intellectual self-reliance, is it not obvious that it must use tasks whose answers are rationally determined? Where we want to teach an experimental attitude, must we not use tasks whose solutions are empirically confirmable? Arbitrary tasks cannot possibly generate the important attitudes sought in serious inductive teaching of educational content.

Many experimental tasks that have value for other problems seem too lacking in rationality for the proper study of discovery. The task of Wittrock et al. (1964) where the child selects a picture representing a *la* or *le* French noun is arbitrary; the child's task is primarily to discover what the experimenter has in mind. The rules and codes used by Stacey (1949), Haslerud and Meyers (1958), and others are likewise arbitrary. The subject has to detect a pattern or regularity, but the patterns change from example to example. The patterns are not 'principles' (even though mistakenly given that name), and they do not fit into any system of mutually supporting propositions.

If we are concerned with the implications of discovery for understanding a discipline, the task should be part of a whole system of subject matter. The summation-of-series task of Gagné and Brown (1961) is well chosen. A solution called correct is correct in the eyes of God as well as of the experimenters. The training tasks are representative of series problems and, insofar as one task can be representative, of all mathematics. But we should not generalize from mathematics to other school subjects. If it is proposed, for example, to apply inductive methods in history by requiring pupils to draw conclusions from source documents, then there had better be experiments with such lessons. We might learn, for example, that the pupil who forms his own historical generalizations becomes much too confident of the dependability of his inferences, since social data cannot be counted on to contradict an error unequivocally.

TYPE OF TEACHING

With regard to experimental treatment, the first requirement is that each treatment be given a fair chance to show what it can do; by and large, educational innovators have violated this rule. What usually happens is something like this: John Doe contends that programmed presentation of college geology is better than conventional lectures. He assembles a writing team and spends two years drafting material, editing every sentence, trying it on pilot classes, and revising. Then Doe runs a grand experiment in which 10 classes are taught with his material, while 10 classes take the regular lecture course. Unless his writers were painfully inept the test scores favor the new method, and unless Doe is a very saint of an experimenter, he concludes that programmed instruction is more effective than the lecture method. Doe *has* shown that his programs give better results than the lectures in their casual, unedited, tired old form, but the outcome would very likely to have been reversed if he had put the same two-year effort into tuning up the lectures. Nothing of explanatory value has been learned from his study.

Studies of discovery have rarely given didactic instruction a fair shake. The control group suffers from one or another of the following impediments in nearly every study:

1. **Shorter training time.** In the Hilgard-Irvine-Whipple (1953) study with Katona's card tricks, the students who developed the rule for themselves worked with the material two to four times as long as those given the rule; they had to, to reach the criterion. In such a case, differences in transfer scores are interpretable only if the discovery group, with its greater opportunity to learn, *fails* to surpass the contrast group.

2. **Limited goals.** The nondiscovery group is often led to think that manipulation of a formula is the only goal of instruction. Any insight into the nature of the formula is incidental rather than inten-

tional learning for them, whereas the discovery group is oriented toward the meaning of the formula. Consider the Gagné-Brown experiment. The rule-and-example group practiced substituting numbers in the formulas for summation of various series, and was trained to criterion on that limited decoding skill. The guided-discovery group was taught to look for a pattern relating the terms of a particular series and the corresponding sums, to use a symbolic code for term number, term value, and sum, to translate the pattern into a symbolic formula, and then to substitute numbers into the formula. These students met a four-fold criterion. Gagné and Brown are right in asserting that instructional effectiveness depends more on what is learned than on method of instruction, but their study is interpreted by them and others as supporting the *method* of guided discovery. For a fair test of the value of discovery, their rule-and-example program should have explicated the structural relationships that the discovery group was led to find for itself, and these relationships should have entered the end-of-training criterion for the rule-and-example group. (Note that my comments on this aspect of the Gagné-Brown study do not agree with those in Wittrock's paper (pp. 52–54).)

Mental set is an important variable in the training, as we see in the Hilgard experiment. One of his treatment groups was shown how to find the rule in one card-trick problem after another, but often the student who found a rule set about at once to memorize it. Because no one had conveyed to him that he was supposed to learn the rationale and the rule-finding technique, he put them out of his mind. Rarely is the experimental subject told, even in general terms, what transfer tasks constitute the objectives of instruction. Keeping the objectives of instruction secret from the learner is pedagogically unsound, and an experiment where this is done is an improper base for educational generalizations.

3. **Rote instruction.** The McConnell (1934) studies of arithmetic and others like it allegedly compare discovery with didactic teaching— but note these excerpts from McConnell's description of the second method: "The [number fact] is identified by the teacher dogmatically and autocratically. There is a studious effort to keep the child from verifying the answers. He will not know why $8 + 5$ is 13. [The method] does not tolerate concrete teaching, discovery, or insightful manipulation." Thiele (1938) shows a similar exaggeration; his nondiscovery group was given "isolated facts as though each fact had no relation to any other fact taught." Such experiments with nonrational drill may once have been justified by the challenge of Gestalt theory to that of

Thorndike (as it stood before he introduced "belongingness" as a principle in 1932), but they are not pertinent today.

Didactic teaching can and should develop meaning out of concrete experience and lay bare the mathematical structure behind an algorithm. Only comparing that kind of didactic teaching with discovery methods tells us anything of value today. We may note that Forgus and Schwartz (1957) found no difference at all between discovery and meaningful didactic teaching.

4. **Prejudicial data analysis.** As Olson (1965) points out, one of the studies most often cited as supporting discovery attains this result by illogical analysis of the data. Haslerud and Meyers (1958) had the student work with codes, each sentence requiring a different encoding rule. For any one person ten sentences were in this G form:

> Write each word backwards.
> (A) THEY NEED MORE TIME
> YEHT DEEN EROM EMIT
> (B) GIVE THEM FIVE MORE

On the G rules the subject merely practiced encoding. The D form for the other ten sentences was the same except that the rule was omitted and had to be inferred from the A example. The G and D sentences were presented alternately in a single list. The G_1 score was the number of sentences correctly encoded from the G list; the D_1 score was the number of D sentences for which the code was found and applied. The transfer measure presented multiple-choice items like this:

> THEY CAME AND WENT a. MNEN ECTE
> ATA HWYD
> b. DOBM RGHO
> CKF DEIN
> c. YEHT EMAC
> DNA TNEW
> d. HPZC OHAT
> RRS FSHZ

One of the four alternatives is a transformation of the given sentence by a rule that was in either the G or D list during training. The G_2 score was the number of items based on G rules where the subject chose the correct alternative, and the D_2 score was similarly based on the ten items involving D rules. The score means were as follows:

G_1	8.6	G_2	7.8	Difference	−0.9
D_1	5.4	D_2	8.0	Difference	2.7

The Haslerud-Meyers report gives these facts, but puts all the emphasis on the difference scores. The authors first run a significance test to show that the mean difference for the discovery group departs from zero. This is wrong for many reasons, not the least of which is that with a free-response first test and a multiple-choice second test, one would expect a gain of 2.5 points among persons performing entirely at random. But the more fundamental error is to use difference scores at all. Test 2 is the only measure that is operationally the same for both groups and therefore the only fair basis for comparison. The difference of 0.2 points is trivial and nonsignificant. The much-cited conclusion, based on the difference in difference scores, arises simply because the D_1 task was much harder than the G_1 task, and so there was lots of room for an increase from D_1 to D_2.

I turn now to a pervasive dilemma in experimental design and analysis. Shall we train every subject to criterion under both D and G methods, in which case the D training ordinarily gets more time to produce its effect? Or shall we equate time, and if so, how shall we treat the nondiscoverers? In the latter design an average over the whole D group, while assessing the net utility of the treatment, has no explanatory value. Using a principle one has discovered is one thing; performing on a problem whose principle was not discovered during training is another. We might discard those who fail to discover, but that biases the experiment by throwing out the weaker members of the experimental group. To pair experimental and control subjects and to discard every nondiscoverer along with his opposite number in the control group is better, but places too much faith in our imperfect matching. I am inclined to think that transfer data for all subjects have to be analyzed in a way that takes initial scores into account. One possibility is to treat separately the discoverers in the D group and the nondiscoverers, since their transfer scores have different meanings. I am not content with this resolution of the difficulty, however, since there are probably degrees of discovery and nondiscovery (cf. Travers, 1964, p. 498).

One further complication. Surely it is good pedagogy to apply a further treatment to the child who fails to discover. In most studies prior to 1960, the subject who could not discover the answer simply left the problem unsolved. We may contrast this with Baddeley's little study (1963), where, after a minute of effort to unscramble an anagram, the unsuccessful subject was given the answer and went on to another anagram. Interestingly, his subjects later recalled more of the answers given to them than of the answers they had worked out for themselves. The finding, like Kersh's (1958), begins to make a case for learning by trying to discover and failing! Or, at the very least, suggests an aspect of the discovery treatment that has been given very little attention.

The fact that experiments are often loaded against the nondiscovery group leads naturally to a recommendation to make the discovery and didactic treatments alike in every respect but one, but this is too facile a recommendation, as can be seen if we think further about duration of training. Suppose we agree that the discovery instruction is to continue until nearly all the pupils pass a criterion test. Then there is no way to make the treatment uniform even for members of that treatment group. A certain child reaches the criterion early: if we terminate his training we allow him less training time than others; if we have him work on additional relevant problems, he encounters content others in his group do not. It is even less possible to hold constant the experience of different groups. The didactic group can be expected on the average to master the solution earlier. Do we shorten their instruction? Give them more problems on the same rule at the risk of boring them? Take them on to additional rules? Whatever we do, it is clearly impossible to give desirable instruction for each group while keeping all variables constant save one.

I doubt that any recommendation will fit all studies, but my inclination is to fall back on optimization within a fixed time. In education, a certain amount of time is allocated to a particular course, and experimentation should tell us how to use that time (cf. Lawrence, 1954). I would fix a certain period of instruction, say, 400 minutes, and compare two styles of instruction by arranging the two best instructional plans we can within that time limit. For style A, then, we have to select subject matter suited to that style, arrange whatever length and spacing of instruction fits that style, and similarly adjust explanations, reinforcements, etc. Likewise for style B. In the Gagné-Brown summation task, for example, I can imagine that the series problems used to develop insight by a rule-and-example style would differ from the set of problems best suited to the discovery style. If so, not even the content studied would be held constant.

Have I now completely contradicted my criticism of experimenters who confound other variables with discovery? I think not. An educational procedure is a system in which the materials chosen and the rules governing what the teacher does should be in harmony with each other and with the pupil's qualities. If we want to compare the camel with the horse, we compare a good horse and a good camel; we don't take two camels and saw the hump off one of them. My objection is to didactic treatments that do not use sound didactic pedagogy. Wherever we can reasonably predict that giving a concrete experience or explaining clearly or stating the aims of instruction will make the didactic teaching more potent, we should adopt that good procedure. We should likewise optimize the discovery treatment in *its* own terms, though it is impossible to adjust all the parameters experimentally. When the study is finished, and style A produces the better result, a colleague can always argue that a change in one another parameter would have reversed the result. That trouble we can never escape. Even after the most highly controlled experiment, our colleague can contend that style B would have been superior if one of the controlled parameters had been held constant at a different level.

On the whole, I would favor more attention to comparisons of different inductive procedures than to further studies with a didactic contrast group. Experiments have shown a good deal about how to optimize didactic procedures, but there has been little analytic work on discovery methods. The study of Hilgard, Edgren, and Irvine (1954) where different groups were led to the solution in different ways is, I think, unique. We have seen useful studies on degree of guidance, but there has been less attention to the character of the guidance. We have some studies where the instructor gives hints about solution of the problem at hand (e.g., Gagné and Brown), others where the instructor gives hints about information-processing technique for solutions (Corman, 1957; Wickelgren, 1964), and, in the Hilgard studies, didactic teaching of an algorithm for generating (discovering?) a solution to a certain type of problem.

An important aspect of the treatment is the extent to which the pupil puts what he discovers into words. The instructor may or may not urge the learner to formulate his generalization in words and may or may not monitor the formulation for correctness. Closely related is the choice of criterion for deciding that a pupil has reached the solution and can go on to new work. A discovery emerges through several stages, and one can solve quite a few similar problems before he consolidates the intellectual basis for the solution. It is hard to say which decision on these points would make for the best inductive teaching; right now the need is to make an explicit decision in the experimental plan and to report it clearly. The Gagné-Smith (1962) study is a model in this respect. It puts considerable substance behind George Stoddard's famous remark that we learn not by doing but by thinking about what we are doing.

I shall draw attention to just one more of the variations in teaching procedure that must be studied. The experimental psychologist has invariably studied discovery by the isolated learner. He arranges conditions so that the learner cannot profit—or be handicapped—by what other members of the class do and say. Educators, however, are concerned with group instruction in which many pupils face a problem together and all of them throw their partial insights into the discussion. The teacher may lead out one pupil Socratically; if so, are the others discovering vicariously or are they learning a solution given to them? Studies of isolated learners tell us nothing about the effect on bystanders or those who share a discussion. There have been some controlled studies of group problem-solving (Lorge et al., 1958) and team-learning (Glaser, Klaus, and Egerman, 1962), but they are rather remote from our present topic. I have seen no studies of inductive teaching that analyze the group process and its effects on pupils who play different roles.

EXTENT OF INDUCTIVE TEACHING

Educational recommendations seek to optimize the student's development over a long time span. The educator is not nearly so concerned with the mastery of a single principle as with the student's cumulative development of insight and skill. Studies of inductive teaching have generally employed very brief instruction, yet the recommendations apply to whole courses or whole curricula. I am dubious about such extrapolation, and join Carroll (1963) in urging studies of instruction continued over a substantial time span.

Even as small experiments, the discovery studies have been too miniature. Typically, there is an hour of training and one delayed transfer test. But consider the moral of Duncan's study (1964) with five consecutive days of work and a new learning task each day. He found negative transfer from Day 1 to Day 2, and positive transfer thereafter. A study confined to two days would have given a false conclusion. Something like a minimum length for an educational experiment is seen in Kersh's 1964 study with 16 hours of instruction and McConnell's with 35–40 hours (1934).

I am impressed by the possibility that *some* experience in discovering principles in a field of knowledge will radically alter the relation the learner perceives between himself and the knowledge, and his way of behaving when he forgets a solution or encounters an unprecedented problem. I offer the hypothesis, however, that this can be accomplished by devoting only a small fraction of the instructional time to inductive procedures.

To illustrate, let me offer a hypothetical plan for teaching cooking; if nothing else, this will provide relief from too much talk of mathematics and physics. Although recipes can be discovered or invented, I would start by giving experience in following recipes, along with reasons for measuring exactly and following directions. This is didactic teaching. The pudding scorches if not stirred according to directions, and the girl discovers that authority was right in its warnings—but that surely is not what we mean by a discovery approach. Around, perhaps, age 12, my class would experiment. The most elementary experiment might be to vary the amount of water added to one cup of pancake flour and observe the product under standard baking conditions. Trivial as this is, it can float profound enough notions in its wake: optimization, control of experimental conditions, interaction of variables, variation in criterion with the purpose or artistic taste of the judge, etc. While these simple experiments would initiate new thinking about recipes and cooking, I'd guess that six such parametric inquiries could teach nearly as much as six dozen. We might well shift back to prescription and demonstration when we teach the girl to make pie crust. Once she has some experimental background, she should have no difficulty in accepting the teacher's statement about what chilling the crust before rolling does to the texture, particularly if the teacher supports the statement with photographs and samples. We had her make discoveries to establish an attitude. This attitude, once established, can be sustained in subsequent didactic teaching. Later exposition can and should continually hold in view the experimental base of recipes, the legitimacy of adapting them to fit personal criteria, and other such concepts. From time to time there will need to be further experimentation, in inventing recipes, for example. When I propose that some small fraction of the course use discovery methods, I am not saying 'and let the rest of the course remain as it was.' On the contrary, I want didactic teaching modified to capitalize on the meanings and attitudes that were established through discovery.

Now there may be those who argue that a girl simply cannot fully understand the technique for making piecrust if she is told how to do it. Then what is the right experiment to determine how much discovery is needed? No short-term treatment can provide any evidence. Instead, we need experiments lasting at least a semester, and ultimately extending into studies of long-term growth.

Some of the advantages claimed for discovery in past experiments may arise from its novelty, and would vanish in a long-term treatment. Kersh (1958) had students learn or discover rules for summation of series and found a sleeper effect. Many in the discovery group had not mastered the rules at the end of the training hour, but a month later they outperformed an instructed group. Their side comments at the time of retest convinced Kersh that the discovery method had aroused such interest that they puzzled over the problem on their own time or looked up the answer in the library. Something similar was found in Kersh's 1962 experiment. I have long felt that this result can be attributed to novelty. I doubt that a discovery approach causes typical pupils to work on math for their own satisfaction when further problems are put before them day after day. I was therefore somewhat gratified by Kersh's 1964 experiment. After sixteen training sessions there was no difference between didactic and inductive groups in tendency to use the information outside of class. This supports my argument for reasonably extended studies.

OUTCOME VARIABLES

Although in general writings we preach that education has many outcomes, this view is not much honored in planning research on educational learning. Only gradually are we moving away from the experimental paradigm in which amount or rate of learning is the sole dependent variable, and into a timid attempt to appraise educational development multidimensionally. Recent studies on discovery usually include both retention and transfer tasks, but even so the dependent variables are few compared to the outcomes that spokesmen claim for discovery methods. If we put together these various claims, we have a list somewhat like the following. To facilitate discussion I have offered a neat label for each class of outcomes, but I do not take the labels as constituting a taxonomy. I make no attempt to list all available illustrations of studies that assess a given outcome.

1. **Time to criterion.** Ordinarily, a criterion of performance on the tasks on which the subject is trained. May require ability to verbalize principle. (E.g., Gagné and Brown, 1961; Corman, 1957).

2. **Application.** Ability to solve problems where the discovered rule is relevant, for example, applying the formula for the sum of an arithmetic series to a set of numbers not encountered in training (e.g., Kersh, 1958).

3. **Retention.** Ability to recall a rule or to rediscover or reconstruct the rule (e.g., Ray, 1961). While delayed tests calling for verbal statement or application are common, the experimenter rarely finds out which mode of retention the subject is using.

4. **Conviction.** Adherence to a principle in a confusing stimulus situation where perceptual cues support an answer contrary to the principle. This type of resistance to extinction is best represented in Smedslund's study (1961) of the Piaget plasticine problem, where the tester palms a bit of material and so it seems that the conservation principle has been violated. Evaluation of conviction is also illustrated by the social psychologists' studies of propaganda and counterpropaganda.

5. **Rationale.** Understanding of the consistency between this principle and other concepts in the discipline. This might be exemplified by the child's explaining the equal-angle reflection of a billiard ball in terms of vectors. Interviews used by McConnell to obtain data on how pupils account for number facts are also pertinent.

6. **Epistemology.** Concept of the logic of the field of study, of the criteria of truth in the field; knowing, for example, the relative weight in judicial decisions of *stare decisis*, the election returns, and the judge's digestion.

The foregoing all represent different levels of knowledge of the subject matter.

7. **Specific rule-finding technique.** Ability to find rules for closely similar problems. Gagné and Brown develop this, for sum-of-series problems, by teaching the subject to line up in a table the term number, the term, and the sum to that point, and then to look for patterns. (See also Hilgard et al., 1953.)

8. **Heuristics.** Ability to solve diverse problems in the discipline by having acquired general search and information-processing behaviors. E.g., Kersh's (1964) observations of attack on new problems.

9. **Aptitude.** Ability to learn subject matter in the field, whether by improved motivation or tendency to look for meaning or to criticize preliminary solutions. The changes that increase aptitude for learning from one type of instruction may not be helpful under other instruction. McConnell (1934) had taught number facts; as one measure of effect he presented a silent-reading lesson on two-digit subtraction and tested how well pupils could perform after that instruction. Since the operation took just twenty minutes, it is not a very adequate measure of learning ability. (Cf. Carroll, 1963, and Cronbach, 1965).

10. **Interest.** Concentration or voluntary effort at the time of training. Represented in Kersh's studies and in an attitude questionnaire of McConnell.

11. **Valuation.** Enduring interest, desire to study in the field, appreciation of the value of knowledge in the field.

12. **Creative urge.** Finding gratification in coping with problems, making efforts to construct knowledge for oneself, being less dependent on authority.

If, in referring to one of these objectives, I have cited no illustrative measurement of that objective, it is because no example in the literature on discovery is known to me. Hence our first conclusion is that many possible consequences of discovery have not been investigated. It seems to me that our interest should concentrate on those wide-ranging objectives that have to do with the pupil's broad educational development, rather than on his mastery of the particular lesson. I believe that inductive teaching is rarely superior to other meaningful teaching for putting across single generalizations, but I share the hope that it has special power to make a practicing intellectual out of the student. I want to see a heightened effort to collect data on theoretical understanding, heuristics, aptitude, valuation, creative urge, and epistemology. These are the variables least considered in the past research, and not surprisingly, since it is scarcely credible that a 50-minute experimental treatment will confer any of these benefits on the learner. Educational development comes through continued instruction with intellectually significant subject matter and that is what we should investigate.

INDIVIDUAL DIFFERENCES

Discovery surely has more value for some pupils than for others. We should expect an interaction between the discovery variable and pupil characteristics, such that among pupils classified at the same level some respond better to inductive teaching and some better to didactic teaching. Perhaps the simplest question to begin with is the matching of instructional technique to age, or to some subtler measure of general development such as mental age, along the lines suggested by Osler's studies (Osler and Fivel, 1961: Osler and Trautman, 1961).

The interacting variables may have more to do with personality than with ability; I am tempted by the notion that pupils who are negativistic may blossom under discovery training, whereas pupils who are anxiously dependent may be paralyzed by demands for self-reliance. If that were to be found, however, it might imply that those of the latter group especially need training in intellectual independence rather than that they should be allowed to learn passively.

Ultimately, enough knowledge should permit us to say that a

fourth-grader with one profile of attainment needs discovery experience, whereas another will move ahead more rapidly on all fronts if teaching is didactic. A pupil who already accepts the meaningfulness of the number system and who has the confidence to look for generalizations on his own will only be delayed, I suspect, by having to figure out his own rules for multiplying decimals. Conversely, for the pupil who has plenty of arithmetic skill and very little understanding of the origin of the rules, nothing could be more important than some experience in discovering such rules.

CONCLUSIONS

The educational psychologist is torn between two responsibilities. His responsibility as educational specialist is to give schools advice on matters where the evidence is pitifully limited. His responsibility as scientist is to insist on careful substantiation of claims for each educational innovation. In education, unfortunately, there is great furore about whatever is announced as the latest trend, and the schools seem to career erratically after each Pied Piper in turn. This giddy chase keeps them almost beyond earshot of the researcher standing on his tiny, laboriously tamped patch of solid ground, crying in a pathetic voice, "Wait for me! Wait for me!"

Knowing that panacea-mongers always have the last word (even though the word changes from year to year), knowing that it will take decades at best for research to catch up with the claims, what stance are we to take? I suggest a judicious blend of these not-incompatible attitudes:

Hospitality to new ideas.

Skepticism about slogans and ill-defined terms, and about doctrines that promise to cure dozens of educational ills out of the same bottle.

Resolution to make research incisive rather than polemic, to clarify what about the new proposal is valid and why, rather than to score points for or against the innovation.

Willingness to advise educators along whatever path we can extrapolate from what we know, but to make clear that this advice is extrapolation and nothing more.

I have indicated a number of reasons why the existing research on inductive teaching has not begun to give the answers needed for firm recommendations to the schools. I have suggested that there will need to be more complex experiments, planned along quite different lines from those of the past literature. We have to explore a five-fold interaction—subject matter, with type of instruction, with timing of instruction, with type of pupil, with outcome. Understanding will be advanced by each experiment, so long as the investigator is open-mindedly curious, and keeps the whole problem in mind while interpreting his exploration of one small corner of it.

Chapter VI

Educational Objectives

THE SECOND SESSION OF THE CONFERENCE WAS CLEARLY THE ONE IN which the questions concerning dependent variables became paramount, sparked primarily by Cronbach's list of suggested outcomes. The discussion began with the suggestion that, in Piaget's terms, our profession is at the stage of concrete operations, while our educational criteria, our discussions, and our research are at the stage of formal operations. This is an enormous gap which we must bridge; and it is difficult enough to describe in some meaningful sense what we are doing in any particular teaching effort, much less try to contrast two different approaches to educating children. Furthermore, what we are teaching is an important variable in these discussions. The organization of one subject matter is different from that of others. We are in great need of some system of classification.

Following a lengthy and heated discussion about the role of the psychologist in the determination of educational goals, the extent to which consensus might be obtained on the desirability of each of Cronbach's outcome variables, and the relationship between individual differences and educational objectives, the group turned to consider the nature of goal-setting in teaching.

A distinction was made between seeing a 'shaping' process as the instructional approach most adequate for attaining the objectives of education, and seeing an 'opening-up' process as the appropriate technique for achieving those objectives. A shaping process is an attempt to elicit progressively from a child a complex of behaviors that sequentially approximate more and more closely a desired set of terminal behaviors. This is quite different from an opening-up process. The latter is an attempt to teach the child to match his own cognitive structures with what is 'out there' in the environment in order to provide greater meaning for him in what is around him. The instructional strategy is

93

one of making it possible for the child to have experience in this match-making process. Part of the secret here is letting the child take a natural course: Let the child try whatever he has. Let the child go, see how what he has operates and where he must run up against a wall. Let him collect data and accommodate. The role of the teacher here is to suggest alternative models for the child to try out and to elicit from the learner his own hypotheses. A plea was made for opening up the learning process instead of focussing on the method and the objectives, whether discovery-like or not; we should simply watch the process.

The position just described was characterized by another discussant as the mind-unfolding approach, which leads to the dangerous notion that one is teaching for nothing. In reality, it would be quite possible to formulate in behavioral or operational terms the educational goals implicit in the opening-up process.

The first participant responded that the important concept here is that of openness. The child must negotiate this match-making between his internal structure and the external world for himself. It is not the same if someone else decides the sequence. If our goal is to get him to make this match, we will get more cues from the learner himself than we can from our theories. He knows what is bothering him. Just open up the situation and in effect let the learner be free to write his own program. Put him in what we might call a responsive environment. Let the teacher be sensitive to the ideas that are shaping up in the child's mind and reflect them back to the pupil, as it were, Socratically. Have him reexamine his position and then let him move on. The notion of education as engineering is severely limited; it ultimately leaves the child dependent on someone else. This participant wanted the child to know two things: (1) knowledge is a transient thing, and (2) he can participate in the process of creating knowledge and testing its validity for himself.

A second participant agreed. He too would leave substantive goals open. He preferred more abstract or stylistic kinds of goals. For example, the real pay-off for the student is the ability to evolve his goals as he goes along. In this sense, the goals are stated in terms of operating styles of students.

In rebuttal to this position it was suggested that there are different meanings to the term 'opening up.' One can open up the classroom situation in order better to observe what is going on. A very different meaning, however, refers to the process itself, that process called match-making by one participant. Such an inference about the kind of process that is going on may in turn be adopted as an indication of what ought to go on. Here, we dangerously leave the level of observation and enter the realm of the polemic. If our goal is, in fact, to study the process, we must close it up someway by means of some controls. Too much respect for style gets one into the position of the Chinese where style becomes everything. We must identify, however broadly, the changes in behavior desired and then train teachers to change behavior in this direction. The alternative is a romantic position of simply watching the kids and believing they will show us where they ought to go. It was pointed out that research on clinical versus actuarial judgments had pretty much shown that the more you put human judgment into the system, the more noise you get. We cannot attempt to adapt to every child from moment to moment without getting wild oscillations in the system—and poor education. The romantics have to recognize the kinds of teachers we actually have today, not the kind they would like to create. We have no alternative but to standardize.

Another participant denied that this position was romantic. It was the very antithesis of an undisciplined approach to education. This discovery approach to teaching requires preparatory work that is so detailed and so complex that neither most teachers nor most children can do it themselves. We must make provisions ('we' in the sense of those who developed curricula) for them in the form of the indexing of materials and the like. If this constitutes romanticism, then let it be considered a good word.

It was then suggested that we need not place all our trust on the ability of the teacher to diagnose what is happening inside the student. We must provide for both the teachers and the students a range of exemplars of what is to be learned, so that if the student falls off one track he can climb back on another. The point is not to avoid the stating of objectives, but to state them in a sufficiently broad sense and in a sufficiently general manner that different styles of learning are anticipated and hence planned for. One major advantage of the new curricula is that they do not provide one route, e.g., discovery, but rather are replete with multiple alternatives for different kinds of students, and, for that matter, teachers.

There are certain terminal behaviors which all agree must be mastered. It is important to distinguish between these kinds of goals, which Schwab calls *axiomatic*, and those goals which are not axiomatic. Critical evaluation of one's own thought processes is not generally seen by society as one of the axiomatic skills. If we see this as a goal, we then must make attempts to produce cultural change in order to make such objectives axiomatic. If teachers uncritically reinforce the dominant values of the present culture, they may unwittingly undermine the innovative features of new educational programs.

Since Glaser's definition of discovery implied the inevitability of mistakes, the group now turned to a consideration of the use of the term 'error.' The discussion began with an examination of the differences between correct and incorrect responses. One participant maintained that the desirable response to be elicited by the educational process is not necessarily the specific behavior of writing or speaking a given response, but rather internal changes of the concept or of the total linguistic structure of the child. He thus raised the issue of whether, in the programmed learning approach, what is being changed is a specific response, a particular conception, or the full linguistic structure of the child.

It was countered that we never teach a specific response, but rather a response class. That is, we intend to teach a general conception of which any specific response is but an instance, even though the shaping process in programmed instruction in fact forces one response. Unless the experimenter uses a transfer design, which is not in the typical program, he never knows whether it is the specific response or a response class which has been learned. Yet, the response is always seen by the experimenter as an instance of a response class. The idea of teaching a single response is a sterile one. This position was buttressed by a quote from Bradley that "associations marry only universals."

Error is also a function of the subject matter with which one is dealing. In some subject matter you can define quite easily and dichotomously the difference between right and wrong. In other subject areas, error points out simply the necessity for revision and emendation of a concept to be acquired. When there is no clear-cut correct response, error becomes a process of constant correction.

In the context of correction, the relationship between language and discovery becomes somewhat clearer. Because animals do not have language, there is in most experiments a finite set of contingencies, such as withholding reinforcement, when an incorrect response is made. Hence, in the language-free animal learning situation, you get either positive or negative instances, reinforcement or extinction. In contrast, with language comes correction, for the experimenter (teacher) can now say, not only Don't do that, but also Do this, instead!

There are circumstances in which the concept of error may become quite meaningless. These occur when the consequences of different courses of action are rendered equivalent, as in a setting where all behaviors are equally rewarded or unrewarded. For example, in Tolman's latent learning experiments, the rats have no sharp criterion of error when they are in their Platonic (unrewarded) state. Hence, they do not regard a blind alley as a wrong place to be. Error is the wrong word, until the individual is given or develops a specific sense of where he *ought* to be going. Thus, by loosening up the objectives, we lower the probability of nonreinforcing error, while increasing the likelihood of profitable, nonthreatening exploratory behavior. The error concept is irrelevant when the goal is exploration. There are 'goodies' at every turn. Here was another way of contrasting the implications of the shaping and opening-up positions.

PART THREE

THE CURRICULUM

Chapter VII

Some Elements of Discovery

JEROME S. BRUNER

I FIND THE TOPIC OF THE CONFERENCE A LITTLE BIT PUZZLING. I AM NOT quite sure I understand anymore what discovery is and I don't think it matters very much. But a few things can be said about how people can be helped to discover things for themselves.

A word of caution first. You cannot consider education without taking into account how a culture gets passed on. It seems to me highly unlikely that given the centrality of culture in man's adaptation to his environment—the fact that culture serves him in the same way as changes in morphology served earlier in the evolutionary scale—that, biologically speaking, one would expect each organism to rediscover the totality of its culture—this would seem most unlikely. Moreover, it seems equally unlikely, given the nature of man's dependency as a creature, that this long period of dependency characteristic of our species was designed entirely for the most inefficient technique possible for regaining what has been gathered over a long period of time, i.e., discovery.

Assume, for example, that man continues to adjust when he learns a language and certain ways of using tools. At that particular point, evolution becomes Lamarckian in the sense of involving the passing on of acquired characteristics, not through the genes, but through the medium of culture. On the other hand, it becomes reversible in that one can lose parts of culture in the way that Easter Islanders or the Incas of Peru seem to have lost some of their techniques. Culture, thus, is not discovered; it is passed on or forgotten. All this suggests to me that we had better be cautious in talking about the method of discovery, or discovery as the principal vehicle of education. Simply from a biological point of view, it does not seem to be the case at all. We ought to be extremely careful, therefore, to think about the range of possible techniques used for guaranteeing that we produce competent adults within a society that the educational process supports. Thus, in order to train these adults, education must program their development of skills, and provide them with models, if you will, of the environment. All of these things must be taken into account, rather than just taking it for granted that discovery is a principal way in which the individual finds out about his environment.

You make no mistake if you take the phenomenon of language-learning as a paradigm. Language-learning is very close to invention and has very little in common with what we normally speak of as discovery. There are several things about language-learning that strike me as being of particular interest. For example, in language-learning, the child finds himself in a linguistic environment in which he comes forth with utterances. Take the first syntactic utterances. They usually have the form of a pivotal class and an open class, like 'All gone, Mommy,' 'All gone, Daddy,' and 'All gone this; all done that.' The child, exposed linguistically to an adult world, comes forth not with a discovery but with an invention that makes you believe somewhat in innate ideas, in a linguistic form that simply is not present in the adult repertoire. Such language learning consists of invention or coming forth with grammar, possibly innately, that then becomes modified in contact with the world. The parent takes the child's utterances which do not conform to adult grammar. He then idealizes and expands them, not permitting the child to discover haphazardly but rather providing a model which is there all the time. It is the very earliest forms of language learning.

Thus, within the culture the earliest form of learning essential to the person becoming human is not so much discovery as it is having a model. The constant provision of a model, the constant response to the individual's response after response, back and forth between two people, constitute discovery learning guided by an accessible model.

If you want to talk about invention, perhaps the most primitive form of uniquely human learning is the invention of certain patterns that probably come out of deep-grooved characteristics of the human nervous system, with a lot of shaping taking place on the part of an adult. Consequently, wherever you look, you cannot really come away with a strong general consensus that discovery is a principal means of educating the young. Yet, the one thing that is apparent is that there seems to be a necessary component in human learning that is like discovery, namely, the opportunity to go about exploring a situation.

It seems to be imperative for the child to develop an approach to further learning that is more effective in nature—an approach to learning that allows the child not only to learn the material that is presented in a school setting, but to learn it in such a way that he can use the information in problem-solving. To me, this is the critical thing: How do you teach something to a child? I am going to say teach even though I know that the word teaching is not very fashionable anymore. We talk about the child learning, or about programming the environment so that he can learn, but I want to raise the following question: How do you teach something to a child, arrange a child's environment, if you will, in such a way that he can learn something with some assurance that he will use the material that he has learned appropriately in a variety of situations. This problem of learning by discovery is the kind that guarantees a child will use what he has learned effectively.

We know perfectly well that there are the good rote techniques whereby you can get the child to come back with a long list of information. This list is no good, however, because the child will use it in a single situation and possibly not even effectively then. There must be some other way of teaching so that the child will have a high likelihood of transfer. This problem of how to teach a child in such a way that he will use the material appropriately breaks down, for me, into six subproblems.

First, is the attitude problem. How do you arrange learning in such a way that the child recognizes that when he has information he can go beyond it, that there is connectedness between the facts he has learned with other data and situations. He must have the attitude that he can use his head effectively to solve a problem, that when he has a little bit of information he can extrapolate information; and that he can interpolate when he has unconnected material. Basically, this is an attitudinal problem—something that will counteract inertness in that he will recognize the material that he has learned as an occasion for moving beyond it.

Second is the compatibility problem. How do you get the child to approach new material that he is learning in such a fashion that he fits it into his own system of associations, subdivisions, categories, and frames of reference, in order that he can make it his own and thus be able to use the information in a fashion compatible with what he already knows.

Third involves getting the child activated so that he can experience his own capacity to solve problems and have enough success so that he can feel rewarded for the exercise of thinking.

Fourth is giving the child practice in the skills related to the use of information and problem solving. This is a highly technical problem that has to do not only with psychology but with learning those valu-

able short cuts within any field that we speak of as heuristics. I do not think that psychology stops at the level of psychological terminology, by any means, when we talk about learning in this particular context. But it is a feature of the thought process when a child learns some basic principles in mathematics he can use. Essentially, the tools of the mind are not only certain kinds of response patterns, but also organized, powerful tool concepts that come out of the field he is studying. There is no such thing, to be sure, as the psychology of arithmetic, but the great concepts of arithmetic are parts of the tool kit for thinking. They contain heuristics and skills that the child has to master and the great problem here is how do you give the child practice in the utilization of these skills, because it turns out that however often you may set forth general ideas, unless the student has an opportunity to use them, he is not going to be very effective in their use.

Fifth is a special kind of problem that I want to speak of as 'the self-loop problem.' The child, in learning in school settings, will very frequently do kinds of things which he is not able to describe to himself. We see this all the time in our new studies—namely, children who are able to do many kinds of things, for example, to handle a balance beam quite adequately by putting rings on nails on both sides of a fulcrum and getting quite interesting balances, but are not able to say it to themselves and convert this fact into a compact notation which they could hold in mind and push around. They can't, to use some barbarous computer language for a moment, develop adequate subroutines until they can get the responses right and describe them to themselves. Phil Rizzuto, playing baseball, does not field a grounder in a certain way because he understands the differential equation of how the ball will move. Rather he is combining one act with another; using a sensorimotor skill fitted to the situation. But there is also self-loop, a turning around on your own behavior, a chance for reflection. One goes from this skill at action to a deeper cognitive understanding. Various people have talked about this idea in different ways. I see it as a separate and special problem in discovery—discovering what it is that you've been doing and discovering it in a way that has productive power to it.

The sixth factor involves the nature of our capacity for handling information flow manageably so that it can be used in problem solving.

Let me spell out these six problems in more detail, giving examples from a curriculum on which we are now working.

First is the matter of attitude. We have talked about being corrupted by the vanity of teaching something oneself. I am going to illustrate some of that corruption not only because I am full of my own ideas but also because I have been teaching children, and one's little successes corrupt in a most intoxicating way. Discovery teaching generally involves not so much the process of leading students to discover what is 'out there,' but, rather, their discovering what is in their own heads. It involves encouraging them to say, Let me stop and think about that; Let me use my head; Let me have some vicarious trial-and-error. There is a vast amount more in most heads (children's heads included) than we are usually aware of, or that we are willing to try to use. You have got to convince students (or exemplify for them, which is a much better way of putting it) of the fact that there are implicit models in their heads which are useful.

Let me give you some cases, though you will have to forgive me while I tell you a little bit about the course that we are putting together. We are a group of anthropologists, psychologists, linguists, and so forth. This elementary-school course is one which we are at the moment trying out with children in the fifth grade, children who are 10 years old, taught in small groups of 10 children at a time. The course is on the emergence of man as a species. It deals with the kinds of things that lead to the humanization of the species *Homo*. It is based on a great quantity of powerful work that has been done in the last decade and a half, by linguists, by archaeologists, by physical anthropologists, and so on. It centers on four humanizing factors in man's history: tool-using, language, social organization, and the uniquely human child-rearing practices. We are operating on the assumption that in order for the children to understand what role these factors played in man's evolution, they have got to understand the nature of each one of the functions. We are, therefore, teaching them a good deal of anthropological linguistics, structural linguistics, with a main emphasis on the design features of the languages as you get it from Hockett, as well as on linguistic productivity. They get some idea of what a flexible tool system language is, and what it has done in the way of opening up the range for man coping with his environment. With respect to tool-using, what we are trying to do is to give them some sense of what a tool is, how a tool fits into a program of skill. I will tell you something about this particular thing later on. Social organization is the hardest part to teach. We are using a variety of techniques. We have some very high-brow game-makers who work mostly with generals in the Pentagon when they are not working with us. They have devised some games, one of them called Hunters. It is based on the way in which Bushmen operate in the Kalihari Basin in Southwest Africa. Their social organization has to do with hunting; therefore the game deals with social organization. The child-rearing section starts off with our making a census of the kids' skills, and analyzing when they learn certain kinds of things. It is centrally concerned with the idea of the human life cycle.

The course is based on a fair amount of contrasted material; we try to give them the sense of comparison of human languages with other forms of communication. We use also the social organization of modern Western man as compared to the traditional Eskimo to give them some sense of recognition of their own culture. We have a store of material on Bushmen as well. We also look at free-ranging baboons in East Africa. That is enough about the course for a moment.

Let me just say one thing about the attitude problem, to give you an example of how we try to have the children recognize that they can use their own heads in their own education. We wanted the children to learn that, generally speaking, one can reduce a language into what is called *type* and *order*. I, therefore, used a trick that I got from an experiment by my colleague, George Miller, which consists of the following. First write a sentence on the board. Then get the children to form similar sentences as follows:

The	man	ate	his	lunch.
A	boy	stole	a	bike.
The	dog	chased	my	cat.
My	father	skidded	the	car.
A	wind	blew	his	hat.

At this particular point, we have the children provide other sentences *ad libitum*. And they provide them. Sometimes they are wrong. Usually not. We then shift them to the following puzzle: How is it that one can go from left to right across the sentences in practically any row and still come out with a sentence: The boy chased the cat; A father chased a lunch; The man stole my bike; A father stole his hat. Some of the sentences are rather silly, but clearly sentences. Soon they will say things like, There are five places and you can put lots of things in each place. But which kinds of words will fit into each column? Type and token begin to emerge as ideas. Now we reach a very critical point. Ask, for example, whether they can make up some more columns. One child proposed the following, something that put the class on a new level of attitude toward the use of mind. He said that there is a 'zero' column that could contain the word 'did.' I asked what other particular words this column could contain. The children said, 'did,' 'can,' 'has.' This was the zero column. Then one of the pupils said that this did not quite fit and that you would have to change the word in the third column too but it would not be very much of a change. They were ready and willing now to get into the syntax of the language, to invent it afresh. They talked about the family of words that would fit and that two columns affected the families each could carry. Only then did we introduce some terminology. We talked about *type* and *order*, and that in sentences there were words that were types and they appeared in a certain permissible order. One of the children said of types, "They're called parts of speech. A noun, for example, is a 'person, place or thing.'" To produce a pause, we asked about 'dying' and 'courage.' They were quick to grasp the syntactic distinction of 'privilege of occurrence' in a certain position, in contrast to the semantic criterion of 'person, place or thing' and found the idea interesting. They soon began on the alternative ways a sentence could be said and have the same meaning. We were soon building up the idea of productivity.

We were struck by the fact that once the children break into an idea in language, once they get a sense of a distinction, they quickly 'turn around' on their own usage and make remarkable strides toward linguistic understanding. The only point I would make is that you must wait until *they* are willing reflectively to turn around before you begin operating with the abstractions. Otherwise they will become obedient and noncomprehending. In time, the habit of or attitude toward reflecting on what you habitually do or say becomes well established. I put this matter first for I feel that it is the one thing that children most rarely encounter in school—that it is a good practice to use their heads to solve a problem by reflecting on what they already know or have already learned. Are college students so different from fifth graders?

Consider activation now. I do not want to say much about this. I think that the reward that comes from using materials, discovering regularities, extrapolating, etc. is intrinsic to the activity. It probably goes beyond the satisfaction of curiosity. It has more to do with the form of motivation that Robert White speaks of as effectance or competence. Extrinsic rewards may mask this pleasure. When children expect a payoff from somebody, they tend to be drawn away from or distracted from the behavior that provides intrinsic rewards. You can corrupt them all too easily into seeking your favor, your rewards, your grades. But enough of this subject.

The compatibility problem is next in our list and it is interesting. Let me describe it in terms of the behavior of some of our pupils. We were treating tool-using as a problem. I would remind you that our children were suburban. They had not used many tools, nor thought much about what a tool is. A tool was something to get at the hard-ware store. Could we relate tools to something that they themselves knew about? Our aim was to present tools as amplifiers of human sensory, motor, and reflective powers—which includes mathematics in the range of tools.

To get the children away from their parochial notions about tools, we prepared a set of drawings of all kinds of tools and devised an exercise whose object was to restore some manner of awareness about tools. We would present a hammer. What is its use? One child said it is used for beating in nails. What do you want to drive in nails for? You drive nails in because you want to have the nail in the board. Why do you want to have the nail in the board? To hold two boards together. Why would you want two boards together? Well, to make a building steady or to support something like a table. Any other way to do it aside from hammer and nails? Yes, you could use string. String and nails do the same thing? Etc., etc., etc. Along the way, it was quite apparent that when you got the pupils to rephrase uses in their own terms and kept pushing them as to how something could be used, eventually they would find some place where it connected with a structured body of knowledge they already had. This is what I mean by the 'compatibility problem'— finding the connection with something they do know.

Frequently, you came upon some very striking surprises. Let me give you a couple of examples of this. One of the pictures was of a compass—the kind that is used for drawing circles. One child, a particularly interesting one, was asked about it. What is that for? It's a steadying tool. What do you mean, a steadying tool? She went to the board and took a piece of chalk. You see, if you try to draw a circle, you're not steady enough to make a real circle, so a compass steadies you. The other children thought the idea was great and came forth with a stream of suggestions for other steadying tools. One suggested a tripod for a camera. Another said a stick could be a steadying tool. He had seen a sign painter the other day, resting his arm on a stick.

I was struck by the fact that they were doing something very much like Wittgenstein's description of concept formation. Recall his description of a game. What is a game? There is no obvious hierarchical concept that joins tennis and tag. What these children were doing with steadying tools was forming a concept in which neighboring elements were joined by "family resemblance," to use Wittgenstein's phrase. The concept that emerges is like a rope in which no single fiber runs all the way through. The children are getting connections that allow them to travel from one part of the system to the other and when something new comes in, they find compatible connections. You can, at your peril, call it association. By calling it that you forget the systematic or syntactic nature of their behavior, as when they dealt with the idea of type and order in language. They were dealing with tools as governed by a rule of filling certain requirements—the different ways of getting steady or of holding things together. But the rules are not as simple as formal concepts. It is this kind of binding, this kind of exercise, that helps solve the compatibility problem, the problem of how to get a new piece of knowledge connected with an established domain so that the new knowledge can help retrieve what is likely to be appropriate to it as needed.

The compatibility problem turns out to have some surprising features. Let me illustrate by reference to a junior high school course which I will not tell you about except for one particular unit. In this unit we deal with an episode in which Julius Caesar must decide whether to cross the Rubicon, leave Cisalpine Gaul to penetrate Italy and try for Rome. The children have the commentaries of Caesar, nothing from Pompey who was Caesar's opponent, and letters from Cicero to various characters around Italy. The data are insufficient. The pupils must pull all the shreds together. Amusingly enough, the class divided into Caesarians and Pompeyans, comparing their heroes to people they knew about. The discussion was dramatic; they reasoned like politicians! Caesar must have had friends along there. He'd never have taken his army through a narrow valley like that if he hadn't some friends in there to count on! As a result, one group of pupils set off looking through Cicero's gossipy letters to find out whether Caesar might possibly have friends who had been passing information to him about the people along his narrow valley. The connections they were making were with their knowledge of the human condition and how people got on with each other. We did not care whether they made connections through the imagery of unsavory Boston politicians (with whom they at once equated Roman politicians). The interesting thing is that they connected. We tried out the Caesar unit in a 'problem' class in Melbourne, Florida—a group of leather-jacket motorcycle kids. They went completely for Caesar! They were exquisite analysts of the corrupt Roman system. Pompey just could not hold them. He was a fink without guts. The transcripts of these lessons are marvelous! It was only when they found the connection between Caesar and their strong-arm fantasies (and not always fantasies) that Rome and Melbourne came together. Forgive me for going on about something so obvious. It is just that it was not so obvious to us when we started.

Consider next the skill problem. It has had fewer surprises to it, but let me say a few things about it anyway. One of the skills is pushing an idea to its limit. Let me give you an example. A question came up in one of our classes of how to get information from one generation to another. One fifth-grader said that you did it by "tradition" and this empty formula satisfied most of the pupils. They were ready to go on to the next thing. I said that I did not quite understand what they meant by tradition. One child said that a tradition is that dogs chase cats. The others laughed. Well, the laughed-at boy responded, some people say it is an instinct, but he had a dog who did not chase cats until he saw another dog do it. There was a long silence. The children picked the issue up from there, reinvented the idea of culture, destroyed the idea of instinct (even what is good about it), ended up with most of their presuppositions rakishly out in the open. Had I stopped the discussion earlier, we would have been contributing to the creation of passive minds. What the children needed were opportunities to test the limits of their concepts. It often requires a hurly-burly that fits poorly the decorum of a schoolroom. It is for this reason that I single it out.

Training in the skill of hypothesis making has a comparable problem. Let me give you an example of what I mean. We got into a discussion in one of our classes of what language might have been for the first speaking humans. We had already had a similar session with one other class so I knew what was likely to happen. Sure enough, one child said that we should go out and find some "ape men" who were first learning how to speak and then you would know. It is direct confrontation of a problem, and children of 10 like this directness. I was teaching the class. I told the children that there were various people in the 19th century who had travelled all over Africa on just such a quest, and to no avail. Wherever people spoke, the language seemed about the same in sophistication. They were crestfallen. How could one find out if such ape men existed no longer? I thought I should take drastic measures and present them with two alternative hypotheses, both indirect. It is usually a fine way of losing a 10-year-old audience! They had the week before been working on Von Frisch's bee-dance 'language' so they knew a little about other than human forms of communication. I proposed, as a first hypothesis, that to study the origin of *human* language they look at some animal language like bees and then at present human language, and perhaps *original* human language would be somewhere in between. That was one hypothesis. I saw some frowns. They were not happy about the idea. The other way, I proposed, was to take what was simplest and most common about human language and guess that those things made up the language man first started speaking.

This discussion, weighing the worth of the two hypotheses took the whole period. What struck me was that in the course of the discussion the children were learning more how to *frame* hypotheses than how to test them, which is a great step forward. One child asked whether what would be simple in one language would necessarily be simple about another. They were trying to invent a hypothesis about language universals. Or another pupil suggested that the way babies speak is probably the way in which man first spoke. They enjoyed discussing not only whether the hypotheses were 'true' but also whether they were testable. I told them finally that the Cercle Linguistique de Paris in the 1880s had voted that nobody should be permitted to give a paper on the origin of human language, and that they were not doing badly, all things considered. They took a dim view of Paris as a result! I was struck by the avidity of the children for the opportunity to make hypotheses. I believe children need more such practice and rarely get it.

Training in being concise is, like limits testing and hypotheses making, a neglected though crucial area of skill-training. I heard one fifth-grader answer another who asked about a movie by starting off to recount it from the beginning. He was prepared to give a blow-by-blow account. They have little training in condensing information. I feel reasonably convinced that we could take a lesson from a game that Ford Maddox Ford and Joseph Conrad are alleged to have played on Sunday outings. Who could describe a landscape before them in the smallest number of words? I do not have much experience with this kind of training. All I do have is a sense of the overwhelming prolixity that gets in the way of the children I have observed.

Consider now the fifth or 'self-loop' problem. Edward Sapir once made the remark that language is a dynamo that we use principally for lighting little name plates, for labelling and categorizing things. When human beings some day learn how to use language effectively, we will probably spend much more time grasping the logical implications of how we say things. Let me start the discussion of the self-loop with that thought. When the child becomes aware of what he is saying, when he turns around on himself, he will gain a special advantage from his language.

Let me give you some examples. One child said to the class that all they were doing that day was saying the same thing over and over in different ways. Another child responded that the things in question being talked about did not say the same thing. Still another argued that they were the same thing. Now, the distinction between the syntactic and the semantic mode is an extremely difficult one. The children sensed, though, that the word 'same' needed to be decomposed into different kinds of sameness—a sameness of words and of things. This is an example of turning around on your own language, the self-loop that permits you to recognize what you are up to.

Another instance happened quite by accident. A child, smitten by the intersubstitutable sentences, put down a list of two-word expletives:

jeepers	creepers
leaping	lizards
aw	gee
good	grief
my	goodness

I asked how they were alike. The children suggested you could substitute in each column as with the sentences: 'gee creepers,' and 'oh lizards,' etc. It is an interesting kind of substitutivity. But the more interesting thing is that some children said that these phrases are the same though they do not stand for a thing that is the same. If you speak of this as discovery, I would agree. But it is discovery via self-consciousness, and these I esteem as of particular importance.

Let me move on to the last point: How one engineer's discovery so that it takes place in a context of problem solving—so that one can retrieve and combine information in an appropriate setting rather than under the spell of 'inspiration.'

One of the most powerful tools we have for searching is contrast. Contrast can be engineered or self-engineered. Indeed, it can become an acquired taste. We have gone out of our way to present material to children in contrastive form—film of baboon juveniles playing followed by human children playing in an identical 'habitat.' The children discover quite readily that little baboons play mostly with little baboons and do not play with things, that human children play with things and with each other. This is engineering a situation. It provides a start for a discussion of tool use, free hands, and so on. Later, give them kittens (who play with things) and then have them deal anew with the problem. They will very quickly understand that cats play with things, but not by holding them.

We believe that by getting the child to explore contrasts, he is more likely to organize his knowledge in a fashion that helps discovery in particular situations where discovery is needed. I need not go into an elaborate justification of the method of contrast here, and will only note that its efficacy stems from the fact that a concept requires for its definition a choice of a negative case. Man is a different concept contrasted to standing bears, to angels, to devil. Readiness to explore contrasts provides a choice among the alternatives that might be relevant.

In conclusion, let me take a very pragmatic position. Develop the best pedagogy you can. See how well you can do. Then analyze the nature of what you did that worked. We do not yet have enough good principles at this point to design an adequate experiment in which this group gets this 'treatment' and that group another 'treatment.' The experiments of this type have been grossly disappointing. The best things that you can do at any given point, I would urge, is to design a pedagogical 'treatment' that works extremely well, and then work your way back. Later on, design hypotheses to determine what you did. But for the moment, can we not declare a moratorium on little experiments that produce miniscule effects? Instead, use contrast, use different kinds of representations, use such formalisms as you can, develop self-consciousness. With a mixture of psychology, common sense, and luck you may produce an effect on learning that is worth studying. Then purify and experiment. But first invent and observe. That seems to me to be the pragmatic strategy. It is not in the grand experimental tradition of physics. But is experimental pedagogy in the grand tradition of physics at this point in history? It may very well be that it is more like economics, a mixture of models and pragmatics. It is in this spirit that I have suggested six ways of possibly aiding a child to discover something for himself. The formal experiments can wait until we have shown that some 'treatment' is worth the trouble.

Chapter VIII

Discovery in the Teaching of Mathematics

ROBERT B. DAVIS

WHETHER ONE THINKS OF THE AERONAUTICAL ENGINEER VERSUS THE pilot, or of the pure mathematician versus the engineer, or of the economist versus the businessman, virtually every major field of human endeavor is split between a group of theorists and a group of practitioners. It seems to me that it is a sign of health when the two groups are able to communicate, and when they attempt to work closely together. Speaking as one of the clinical people or practitioners, I want to thank the theorists for their efforts at bridging the gap which sometimes seems to separate us.

My remarks are made from the practitioner's point of view, which is the only one I can legitimately claim. Based on the Madison Project work of the past eight years, I want to cite a few examples and a few ideas related to them.

Specifically, I have three goals: first, I want to give examples of what we have regarded as discovery experience for children, in the hope that some of you will be able to suggest a few of the ways in which these experiences differ from exposition, and even differ from one another. This last remark deserves emphasizing, for it is my present notion that there are many different kinds of discovery experience, and we confuse the issue badly when we treat discovery as a single well-defined kind of experience.

My second goal is to offer a few remarks attempting to interpret or describe some of the things we mean by discovery, and to explain why some of us believe in its importance.

Finally, I shall list a few things that might be called objectives of Madison Project teaching, for this, too, may clarify why we think we believe in 'discovery.'

SOME EXAMPLES AND SOME INTERPRETATIONS

The students in my first example were some low-IQ culturally-deprived children in the seventh grade, some of whom were older than normal for grade seven. The topic was the matter of finding pairs of whole numbers that would satisfy linear equations of the form

$$(\Box \times 3) + 2 = \triangle$$

Although we found that $\Box$, $\triangle$ notation useful, and consequently did use it with these children, what I have written above could be translated into traditional x, y notation as

$$y = 3x + 2$$

We passed out graph paper and suggested that suitable pairs of whole numbers be recorded according to the usual Cartesian use of coordinates.

Very nearly all of the students made the obvious discovery that there is a simple linear pattern to the resulting dots. A considerable number of them actually applied this discovery, by extrapolating according to the pattern, then checking to see if their new points gave numbers that satisfied the equation.

It is these students who used the discovery this way whom I wish to discuss. Some of them spent several days working with various linear equations, using the patterns to find points, then checking by substituting into the equation. This was one of the earliest things the project ever did that seemed to fascinate children far beyond their normal degree of involvement with school.

My conjecture is that the important aspect of this was perhaps a combination of achievement in making their own discovery, competitive gratification vis-a-vis those classmates who did not make the discovery, autonomy of having set the task for themselves, some intrinsic esthetic or closure reward, and the existence of a verification that did not depend upon the teacher.

These were culturally deprived children, with a middle-class teacher and a middle-class curriculum. Previous observation had already convinced us that these children were at best *tolerant* of a schoolish learning that was *wrong* in every important respect. The children were always checking up, between school and social realities outside of school, and invariably found the school to be wanting.

The school taught you to speak the language incorrectly—for example, the school taught, 'It is I' in a world where the social reality was, 'It's me'—the school taught personal economics incorrectly, the school taught civics incorrectly, and so on. Nothing ever checked when you tried it out against actual reality. (For example, if a majority of people in the county don't like the sheriff, he won't be reelected—according to what they teach in school. But in reality, perhaps a majority of the people are not even allowed to vote—to use an example that is in our newspapers at the present moment.)

Here, in their *own* discovery, they had found something that *really worked!* If you tried it out, it checked out perfectly!

In any event, some of the children were captivated, and spent several days on the matter, asking to take graph paper home and so on.

(Incidentally, in the long run—i.e., over the year that we worked with this class—truancy decreased markedly, and parents reported their children taking an unprecedented interest in school—for example, by discussing it at mealtime.)

My second example is perhaps somewhat similar. We wanted to give children in grades 3–9 some experience with *variables* and with *the arithmetic of signed numbers*. It is one of our principles that such experience should always be provided *in a sensible mathematical context*, and (if at all possible) in a form which would permit a student to make one or more interesting discoveries. We believe that this procedure helps get the children in a frame of mind where they are always poking around looking for interesting patterns that may be lurking just beneath the surface.

I should emphasize that the discoveries in question will usually not be part of the basic purpose of the lesson, and it is not essential for a child to discover them. They are primarily a bonus for those who do discover them.

In the present instance, remember, we wanted the children to get some experience using *variables*, and working with the *arithmetic of signed numbers*. We consequently gave them quadratic equations to solve, beginning with

$$(\square \times \square) - (5 \times \square) + 6 = 0$$

and gradually progressing to harder problems, such as

$$(\square \times \square) - (20 \times \square) + 96 = 0$$

Now, at first the only method available to the student was, of course, trial and error. If he makes no discoveries, the student continues with this method, and gets full benefit from the basic part of the lesson; that is, he gets a great deal of experience using variables and signed numbers, and in a situation where he does *not* regard this as drill.

But—if the student discovers the so-called coefficient rules for quadratic equations, his use of trial-and-error can be guided to maximum efficiency. He has discovered a secret—and one which many of his classmates don't know. They may *never* know!

Torpedoing

In both of the previous examples, we make use of a technique which we call 'torpedoing.' After a student has discovered what he believes is the pattern for linear equations from working with

$$(\square \times 1) + 3 = \triangle$$
$$(\square \times 1) + 5 = \triangle$$
$$(\square \times 1) + 2 = \triangle$$

and so forth—*after* he is confident of his mastery, we unobtrusively slip in a problem like

$$(\square \times 2) + 3 = \triangle$$

He uses his pattern, he checks—and the numbers don't work!
What shall he do?

With a little thought, he discovers there is a pattern here, also—indeed, there is a more general pattern of which he had discovered only a special case.

In a similar way, with the quadratic equations, we begin by using only unequal prime roots, so that one of the two coefficient rules (the product rule) is extremely obvious. Using it alone leads to easy solution of the equations, such as

$$(\square \times \square) - (5 \times \square) + 6 = 0$$
$$(\square \times \square) - (12 \times \square) + 35 = 0$$
$$(\square \times \square) - (13 \times \square) + 22 = 0$$
$$(\square \times \square) - (7 \times \square) + 10 = 0$$

and so on.

Here also, once the student is really pleased with his discovery, and with the new power it has given him, we confront him—unobtrusively and unexpectedly—with a variant problem which will tend to confound his theory.

In this instance, we slip in a problem having composite roots, instead of the prime roots the student had previously dealt with.

The product rule now seems to indicate more than two roots: for example, with

$$(\square \times \square) - (9 \times \square) + 20 = 0$$

many students will say the roots are

$$\{2, \quad 10, \quad 4, \quad 3,\}$$

Trial by substitution shows that this is wrong. Again, by persevering, the student finds that there is a broader theory, of which he had found only a narrower part.

Why do we like Torpedoing?

It may seem that what I have described is simple sadism, or How to Be One Up on Your Students Without Really Teaching. We *feel* that it is not so (although, unfortunately, it *can* be in the hands of a teacher who really *is* a sadist.)

Why do we use this technique of torpedoing some of our students' best theories?

It is important to realize that, at the outset, we don't know. We use the technique because, intuitively, it feels right.

But, in the years while we have been using this technique, we have, of course, discussed it often, and even made some analytic attempts at constructing an abstract rationalization for it.

Perhaps we like the technique because:

i) It gives the brightest students something to work on while the others catch up on more basic work;

ii) It is a friendly challenge from teacher to student, and students rise to such bait better than fresh-water fish do to flies;

iii) Perhaps Piaget's processes of 'assimilation' and 'accommodation' need to be practiced, and this is where you practice them;

iv) Or, to put point iii in less technical language, perhaps the security of a friendly classroom is the best place to gain experience in fixing up theories that used to work, but somehow don't seem to work any more—the classroom is a better place to learn this than, say, the political meetings of anti-integrationists or the radical right;

v) Then, too, it is worth learning that science does not deal in absolute truth. Sufficient unto each day are the theories thereof—and an irreconcilable contradiction may be discovered tomorrow! (Or, for that matter, a better theory!) If your theories work, make the most of them —but keep a wary eye out, just the same.

vi) Finally, this is one of the ways that we go about bringing *history* into the classroom. If one wishes to *understand* history, one must have some background of relevant experience. Since the history of mathematics is an unending story of trials, failures, break-throughs, temporary successes, new points of view, and so on, it is unintelligible to the person who has no background experience in trials, failures, break-throughs, temporary successes, revised points of view, and so on. Torpedoing theories in the classroom provided background experience that parallels important historical phenomena. Can you *realize* what the discovery of irrationals meant to the Greeks if you, yourself, start out with the sophisticated viewpoint of the 20th century?

The 'Crisis' dilemma: seeking the unit matrix

This next example involves a different kind of discovery situation. In the previous examples, the discoveries were merely optional bonuses added to the meat of the lesson; moreover, students discovering any secret patterns kept the secret to themselves, revealing their knowledge only indirectly, by using the secrets to solve difficult problems easily and quickly.

In the present example, all eyes are focussed upon a central problem which we wish to solve, if possible—or to recognize as unsolvable, if a logical argument shows that no solution can exist. If anyone finds an answer, he will announce his discovery at once.

Specifically, we look at the system of 2-by-2 matrices and ask how this new mathematical system compares with the familiar old system of rational numbers. One question is this: is there a 2-by-2 matrix which plays a role analogous to that of the rational number zero? The answer turns out to be that there is, and it is the matrix

$$\begin{pmatrix} 0 & 0 \\ 0 & 0 \end{pmatrix}$$

So far so good. Now—is there a matrix that plays a role analogous to the rational number *one*? Students invariably—and wisely, on the available evidence—guess

$$\begin{pmatrix} 1 & 1 \\ 1 & 1 \end{pmatrix}$$

but a quick computation shows that this is *not* satisfactory.

Here we have the dilemma: *IS* there any matrix that behaves like the integer one? Has our failure to find one been a symptom of the impossibility of the task, or have we merely failed due to personal reasons, not reasons of fundamental impossibility. Is it worth-while trying any longer? If so, how shall we proceed?

This has proved to be a consistently exciting lesson for fifth-graders, or anyone older who doesn't already know the answer.

Going Beyond the Data or the Task

In the filmed lesson entitled, "Graphing an Ellipse," at the end of a lesson on graphing

$$x^2 + ky^2 = 25, \qquad 0 \leq k,$$

a seventh-grade student (Debbie H., according to her nametag) asks: "Why couldn't you use matrices, and make a graph for k less than zero?"

Since these students have previously used matrices to introduce complex numbers, this is an ingenious and appropriate suggestion. The teacher does not immediately respond, but another student (whose nametag reads Lex) answers: "No, you can't, because you won't be able to graph matrices." This answer is essentially correct—but both of these remarks go beyond anything the teacher had planned or anticipated.

The teacher's contribution to this is mainly a genuine appreciation of the students' contributions—but we believe this is important. Children somehow act far cleverer when their cleverness is welcome and appreciated.

Do It Your Own Way: Kye's Arithmetic

Somewhat similar is this example. A third-grade teacher was introducing subtraction, with borrowing and carrying:

$$\begin{array}{r} 64 \\ -28 \\ \hline \end{array}$$

She said: "You can't subtract 8 from 4, so you take 10 from the 60 . . ."

A third-grade boy named Kye interrupted: "Oh, yes you can!

$$4 - 8 = -4$$

$$\begin{array}{r} 64 \\ -28 \\ \hline -4 \end{array}$$

and $60 - 20 = 40$

$$\begin{array}{r} 64 \\ -28 \\ \hline -4 \\ 40 \end{array}$$

and $40 - 4 = 36$

$$\begin{array}{r} 64 \\ -28 \\ \hline -4 \\ \hline 40 \\ \hline 36 \end{array} \text{."}$$

The teacher did nothing here to *solicit* originality, but when she was confronted with it, she *listened* to the student, tried to understand, and *welcomed* and appreciated his contribution.

This was an unusual, but actual, occurrence. The more common, 'traditional' response would have been to say: "No, Kye, that's not the way you do it. Now watch carefully and I'll show you . . ."

Where does this traditional rejection of his contribution leave Kye? He is given the feeling that mathematics is a stupid subject that never works out the way you'd expect it would . . . Given enough experiences of this sort—and in a traditional situation he will be—Kye will probably transfer his interest and his energy to some other field of endeavor.

This example has always seemed to me to suggest the essence of good 'modern' teaching in mathematics, as opposed to 'traditional' teaching. In a phrase: *listen* to the student, and be prepared for him to suggest a better answer than any you know. The 'modern' teacher *actually learns from his students!*

Kye's algorithm for subtracting was an original contribution of a third grade boy. It is in many ways the nicest algorithm for subtracting that I have ever seen—and it was invented by a boy in the third grade.

The traditional teacher assumes from the outset that such a thing is impossible. Is it any wonder that the traditional teacher somehow never encounters such clever behavior from students? Like the spirits that move Oui-ja boards, such clever student behavior rarely appears before the eyes of those who don't believe in its existence.

Autonomy and Proliferation

In introducing graphical integration and differentiation to an eighth-grade class, we proceeded as follows: We obtained a print of the PSSC film "Straight Line Kinematics" which is an *expositional* treatment of these topics in relation to velocity and acceleration. The students could view this film whenever they wished—and as often as they wished. They were then given a shoebox full of simple equipment—the PSSC ticker-tape equipment—to take home if they wished, and were asked to devise their own experiments and work up their own data. They later performed their experiments in school, at a session which has been recorded on film.

The effort and ingenuity that some students put into this went far beyond their normal effort for 'schoolwork.'

What Questions

In one instance, we give physical apparatus to students and ask them *what questions* might be worth studying about this apparatus. The point here is for the student to identify appropriate *questions*. An eminent mathematician, Professor McShane of the University of Virginia, has said that his favorite mathematics problem is stated in a textbook as follows:

A pile of coal catches on fire.

These seven words are the *entire* statement of the problem—in a *mathematics* book!

Now—what *mathematics* questions does this pose?

Leaving Things Open-Ended

Many mathematics problems occur at a stage in the child's life when he is not yet prepared to answer them. An honest use of logic seems to compel us to leave these questions open for the time being. The alternative would be to 'answer' them on the basis of authority—but we believe this would tend to make the child think that mathematics is based upon the pronouncements of authorities. We prefer to leave the question open—after all, aren't most scientific questions open at the present time? Or, perhaps, *always* open?

Example: Is

$$\square \times 0 = 0$$

an *axiom* or a *theorem?* Ultimately the child will learn that it is a theorem:

$$\square + 0 = \square$$
$$0 + 0 = 0$$
$$\square \times (0 + 0) = \square \times 0$$
$$(\square \times 0) + (\square \times 0) = \square \times 0$$
$$\therefore \square \times 0 = 0$$

This proof, however, involves some subtle and awkward points, so that the child cannot settle the question when it first occurs to him, and we leave the question open. The child knows that if he is ever able to *prove* the result, he will be able to classify it as a theorem. In the mean-time . . . Who knows which it is?

Where Does It Come From?

The Madison Project approach to *logic* is, so far as we know, completely unique and unprecedented. Virtually every existing book on logic *tells* you what *modus ponens* is, *tells* you what the truth-table is for 'and,' 'or,' 'if . . . then,' and so on.

But why? Where does all of this come from, anyhow?

Given the transitory nature of scientific knowledge, we can hardly settle for facts which are static pieces torn out of the fabric of time past, time present, and time future.

Where does all of this logic come from? How would we go about making up our own logic if we wished to do so?

In order to answer these questions—at least, according to our own view of the answer—the Madison Project proceeds like this:

First, we ask children (grades 7, 8, 9, or older) to analyze statements of their friends, and to classify them as true or false. They realize that this is a vast oversimplification, for most ordinary statements in the ordinary world are neither true nor false; there's some truth in them, but one still has some possible doubts or reservations.

We then ask the children to focus on actual usages of 'and' and 'or', and to record *as many different uses of 'and' and 'or' as they can find* by means of truth tables.

Ordinary language has a great many different uses of both words. One of my favorites—we might label it 'and₁', in order to distinguish it from *other* uses, which can be labelled 'and₂', 'and₃' and so forth—is this one:

Keep driving like that and you'll kill somebody.

A somewhat similar use of 'and' occurred prior to the 1964 election, in the radio admonition: Vote, and the choice is yours, Don't vote, and the choice is theirs. If you fail to register, you have no choice. Consider, also, the poem: "Laugh, and the world laughs with you, Weep, and you weep alone." The result of this activity is an extensive truth table with many different columns, headed 'and₁', 'and₂', 'and₃', etc, and 'or₁', 'or₂', 'or₃', and so on. Usually some students insist on moving into a more-than-two-valued logic, in order better to reflect nuances of meaning which seem to them to be present. Once we have collected together this large truth table, we have completed stage one, which might be labelled Observing the Behavior of the Natives.

We move next to the Legislative stage: In order to gain clarity, we agree on one single meaning for the word 'and,' we pick one column in the truth table to define this meaning, and we legislate that 'and' shall henceforth be used in that single sense only.

The study of logic proceeds further: after the Sociological stage, and the Legislative stage, we move on to the Abstract stage, and so forth—but the point is that these children have made up their own systems of logic. As a result, they know where logic comes from. In the same way, you understand Beethoven differently after you, yourself, have written some music of your own composition.

An Active Role, and Focussing Attention. Discovery of another sort is perhaps involved in teaching students (second-graders, say) to plot points on Cartesian coordinates. The teacher plots a few points, but the students learn more by imitation than by following a careful exposition. Learning by imitation of course involves a kind of discovery, since you must figure out how the teacher is doing it.

As David Page has pointed out, the best mathematics students have always learned by discovery—even when listening to a lecture, they are *actively thinking*: asking Why? Why not? How about doing it this way? Now what do you suppose he meant by that? Why can't you do it *this* way? and so on.

Games Using Clues. One of our most successful lessons goes like this:

Three students, working together, make up a rule. For example, Whatever number we tell them, they'll double it and add twenty. They do *not* tell us their rule; instead, we tell them numbers. They apply their rule to each number we tell them, and tell us each answer. It's our job to guess their rule.

There is a great deal of mathematics involved in this lesson—for example, the distinction between formula and function, and such properties of functions as linearity, oddness, evenness, rate of growth, and so on. But perhaps the main *discovery* aspect resembles closely Suchman's (1964) work on inquiry: By choosing wisely the numbers we tell them, we can get *clues* as to the nature of the function they are using. No single clue will usually be decisive, but a suitable combination will be.

A somewhat similar format has been used by David Page in his lessons on Hidden Numbers. A few numbers are written on a piece of paper, and the students are to guess the numbers from a set of clues. To make matters harder, *some of the clues are false*, so that the students must recognize *and make use of the contradictions* which are contained in the set of clues (grades 4, 5, 6, 7, 8, or 9).

Two Theoretical Interpretations

An extremely valuable approach to analyzing communications in class has been developed by Professor J. Richard Suchman. The data inside a student's mind at an instant in time can be classified (as an oversimplification, of course) into three categories: facts, unifying mental constructs (roughly, 'theories'), and applications. The possible communications can be diagrammed as follows:

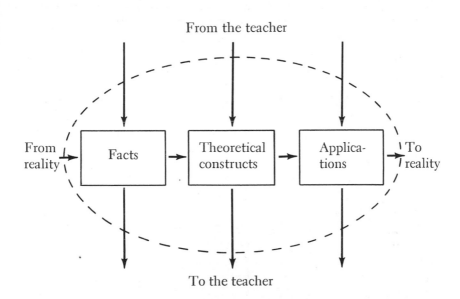

Using this analytical approach in interpreting classroom lessons can be very exciting and gratifying—which, as J. Robert Oppenheimer has remarked, is perhaps the most valid test of a theoretical approach.

Because of limitations of time and space, I shall not attempt to illustrate the use of Suchman's diagrams, beyond remarking that on a Suchman diagram, discovery communications seem to appear as conspicuously horizontal channels, whereas expositional and rote communications appear as conspicuously vertical channels. Particularly in connection with the work of Piaget, Tolman, Lewin, Kohler, White, and Bruner, Suchman diagrams are a powerful analytical tool for the practitioner seeking a rationale for understanding what goes on in the classroom.

Another aspect of discovery experiences is being emphasized in the motivation studies by Richard de Charms (in press) in relation to the analytical dichotomy of the learner's perception of his role, which de Charms polarizes as 'origin' versus 'pawn.'

THE GOALS OF EDUCATION

It is worth remembering that the life of a human being, or the inter-related lives of many human beings, are in reality unified wholes, not separated into pieces in any way whatsoever. When, in order to analyze life abstractly, we break off pieces by invoking *categories*, we do a violence to the reality whole that can impede comprehension as easily as it may, hopefully, facilitate it.

In particular, motivation is not separate *in reality* from perception, personality, learning, social interactions, or communication. Still more specifically, *reality* does not begin with a statement of *explicit goals*. If a teacher begins with an attempted statement of explicit goals, he does so by choice, and may easily do so in error, for his subsequent behavior may not reveal the same goals as his initial words did.

In our own Madison Project teaching, our original conscious goals were general and nonspecific: we wanted to find some of the best experiences with mathematics that children could have. To choose among alternatives we relied upon our intuitive assessments.

From this highly general purpose we spun out a sequence of specific activities in the classroom. In order to *discuss* these experiences, *after they were created*, we have attempted to work out some suitable analytical categories. In particular, we have identified what appear to be some of our probable goals. Here is a tentative list, surely somewhat incomplete:

i. We want to give students experience in *discovering patterns in abstract situations;*

ii. We want students to have experience in *recognizing potentially open-ended situations,* and in *extending open-ended situations by original creative work;*

iii. We want the students to be familiar with the basic concepts of mathematics, such as *variable, open sentence, truth set, function, Cartesian coordinates, mapping, isomorphism, linearity, matrices, implication, contradiction, axiom,* etc.

iv. We want the students to build up, in their own minds, suitable *mental* imagery (in the sense of Lewin, Tolman, Piaget, Leibnitz,

Polya, et al) to permit them to perform mental manipulations involving the basic ideas of mathematics (such as *function, linearity, isomorphism, mapping*, etc., as mentioned above);

v. We want the students to acquire a modest mastery of the *basic techniques* of mathematics;

vi. We want the students to know the basic facts of mathematics, such as $7 + 3 = 10$, $-1 \times -1 = +1$, and so on;

vii. We want the students to possess considerable facility *in relating the various parts of mathematics one to another*—for example, using algebra as a tool in studying geometry, or recognizing the structure of the algebra of linear transformations of the plane into itself, and so on;

viii. We want the students to possess an easy skill in *relating mathematics to the applications of mathematics* in physics and elsewhere;

ix. We want the students *to have a real feeling for the history of mathematics*, derived partly from having been eye-witness observers (or participants) on the occasion of mathematical discoveries.

We regard the preceding nine points as intellectual matters; but they must be accompanied by some emotional or value goals, namely:

x. We want the student to know that mathematics *really and truly is discoverable* (something few people believe);

xi. We want each student, as part of the task of knowing himself, to get *a realistic assessment of his own personal ability* in discovering mathematics;

xii. We want the students to come *to value 'educated intuition'* in its proper place;

xiii. We want the students *to value abstract rational analysis* in its proper place;

xiv. We want the students—as much as possible—*to know when to persevere, and when to be flexible*;

xv. We want the students to have a feeling that *mathematics is fun or exciting, or worthwhile.*

The preceding goals do not sound like the goals of a traditional arithmetic or algebra program. They are not.

Space and time do not permit us to pursue the matter, but implicit beneath all Madison Project work is the notion that *education* and *training* are different, that education is for people, and training is for electronic machinery (which usually doesn't need it anyhow)— indeed, all repetitious routine tasks are basically nonhuman.

One example of the distinction—a tragic and highly suggestive example—will have to serve where many might be cited:

A few years ago in a hospital nursery in Binghamton, N.Y., the formula for new-born babies was made with salt instead of sugar. By the time the error was discovered, a dozen or so babies had either died or suffered severe and irreparable brain damage.

Now,—who or what was at fault? Many babies—indeed, virtually all of them—*simultaneously* developed feeding problems. Some of the *mothers*—but none of the nurses!—tasted the formula and complained that it was unusually salty.

No nurse heeded either clue. The nurses had been trained to soothe a new mother's anxieties, lest they be passed on to the infant and create feeding problems.

Those of us who have children of our own know how much this episode meant to the parents of the babies involved.

New York State has responded by passing a new law, which, I believe, makes it illegal for a hospital to store salt in a room in which nursery formulas are prepared.

This is a significant step in the wrong direction.

Every time we attempt to by-pass human resourcefulness—by laws, rote training, or otherwise—we move toward, and not away from, the unintelligent behavior of the nurses who were trained but not educated. The response of the *mothers* was more appropriate than that of the nurses, but the nonadaptive blind weight of authority decided the outcome in favor of the 'trained' nurses.

I think it important for every teacher always to remember that *he, the teacher, does not know the right answer or the right response*— he can only hope that, when the time comes, his former students will respond appropriately.

Those theorists who study education are on shaky ground indeed if their analysis assumes that they can separate right answers from wrong answers. If the matter in question is trivial, perhaps they can; but if it is important, they surely cannot.

The present emphasis on creativity and divergent thinking would never have occurred—and should never have occurred—but for the fact that we had gone all too far down the road labelled training, and had, surprisingly, lost sight of education.

Chapter IX

Teaching and Discovery

DISCUSSION

WHAT ARE THE RELATIONSHIPS AMONG THE ACT OF TEACHING, THE content of the curriculum, and the concept of discovery? The conference group turned to this set of questions in their third meeting. The starting point for discussion in this third session of the conference was a film of Dr. Robert Davis teaching a junior high school mathematics class a unit on the multiplication of matrices. This was the first concrete example of a teaching sequence which purported to be learning by discovery that the members of the conference had had the opportunity jointly to observe. In the film, Davis repeatedly provided a series of cues for the students and then led them to appropriate generalizations by using a sequence of leading questions or prompts. As in most recitation or discussion situations, not all the children participated equally. A small number of students seemed to dominate the discussion. After the showing of the film was completed, Davis turned to the participants and asked, "All right, gentlemen. You saw the film. What did I do?"

One participant suggested that the term which best characterized Davis' instructional tactics was "commando teaching," genuinely eliciting responses from the students, rather than telling them the answers. You may lecture, but you leave 'empty boxes' for the students themselves to fill in, which is quite different from a straight, didactic presentation of materials. It differs from a pure discovery approach in that the students are not at all just "messing around," in Hawkins' terms. It is like a discovery approach in that they are called upon to discover or invent material to fill in gaps.

There appeared to be two independent axes operating in this definition of teaching by discovery. One was the extent to which 'messing around' was characteristic of the behavior of the students. The second was the extent to which students were called upon to

129

invent or discover facts or generalizations in the subject matter, in contrast to being told the given statements directly. In messing around, the students may generate a wide variety of possible gap-fillers, all of which may be equally acceptable to the teacher. In Davis' approach, the students, though inventing or discovering constantly, were essentially seeking those responses which filled the gaps in the same way Davis wanted them filled. Thus, in contrast to messing around, the object of discovery was to come up with one right answer.

Another relevant distinction is whether it is the teacher or the student who selects the order in which questions or materials are examined. When the children themselves are selecting the order in which the materials are handled, the consequences for learning might be quite different than when the teacher is making these decisions.

One participant now protested that the argument over whether a piece of teaching behavior was discovery or not, was quite unnecessary. Why must there be such hard and fast distinctions? Why can there not be a continuum for looking at discovery, just as there is for looking at many other variables such as *intelligence* or *rigidity*? There was no question that the film was full of kids making discoveries.

Another participant agreed with this position. He went so far as to maintain that not only was a 'pure discovery' approach absent in the film, but that no educator would ever suggest using one. The *pure discovery* notion is *pure nonsense*, he asserted.

In further analyzing teacher and pupil behavior in the film, and the relative purity of the discoveries, it became clear that the teacher was not the sole guide to the student's exploration. Several kinds of things guide individuals in this kind of instructional situation. First, in mathematics, a student checks his discovery against reality. That is, the student has alternative means of checking the response he has generated and of determining whether or not it is accurate. The students are constantly called upon to check their findings against an incontrovertible reality.

Second, the other students in the group can guide the individual. In the case of the film which the group had observed, the students were constantly monitoring each other and correcting each other's responses. Finally, there is the kind of guidance with which we are most familiar, in which it is the teacher who is the primary corrector of the behavior of the student. A major criticism of the individual exploratory 'messing-around' approach to teaching is that, under these conditions, children are deprived of all except the first kind of guidance. They work individually and can thus only check their results against reality.

With this in mind, the group now shifted the focus of discussion to the differences inherent in teaching individuals and teaching in a group. One participant raised the possibility that, in the film shown by Davis, it was unnecessary for the teacher to state whether a response was right or wrong because the children themselves played this role for each other. Thus, the students acted as teacher-surrogates. What happens if you try to work with only one child utilizing this same method?

There was a good deal of consensus here that working with one child using this form of discovery technique was not at all as successful as using it with a group. The reasons for this were now examined. One suggestion was that in a group situation, you simply have more teachers. Another suggestion was that the group situation is superior because it supplies either competition or simply an appreciative audience. A third suggestion was that in an individual teaching situation there is too much of a work or information overload for the individual child. In a class situation he can sit back and relax for a moment, while others carry the ball. Conversely, a classroom atmosphere can sometimes be so tense or competitive that no one can relax, because each student feels called upon to come up with a new and brighter idea than his classmate. When the overall atmosphere is this tense, the level at which the class operates is often rather 'surfacy' and banal.

Most research in human learning, however, takes place under conditions where individual subjects cannot communicate with others. If the discovery techniques are so much more effective in a group situation, much more research is needed in investigating the process of learning in a group. For example, is the learning of the individual who offers an insight during a discussion qualitatively different from that of other individuals who are just listening to it? One way we could test the discovery principle is by checking the differential abilities to transfer their training of those who actively provide insights during a discussion and those who more passively sit back and listen.

A participant now observed that the group had been focusing almost exclusively on problems of understanding, and subsequently manipulating, the child and his environment in such a way as to elicit the learning desired. Equally important is the question of how to prepare the teacher so that she in turn may affect the child in a given way. Unlike the former problem, this is a topic which has not been explored very fully. It is quite apparent, though, that for purposes of dealing with problems of instruction, an understanding of the processes of learning alone is not sufficient.

Is it possible to enumerate a range of instructional strategies which reflect the concept of discovery? It became apparent that even in the heuristic sense of generating descriptions of teaching tactics, discovery was not a sufficiently precise term. We must be able to outline specific discovery-type strategies which are distinctive and amenable to systematic examination. In this way, we can discuss with teachers the kinds of things they now do, and more effectively categorize and evaluate instructional procedures.

For this kind of task, we need a meta-language of education which will allow psychologists to communicate with educators in the same language. We need a theory of instruction stated in these same terms. That is, we need ways to bring our knowledge of perception, storage and retrieval, mediating processes, motivation and the like within the framework of the classroom in some meaningful sense. To fulfill this function the teaching of psychology may need to be improved.

College students of psychology perceive this discipline at a pre-operational level, in Piaget's terms, while the instruction proceeds at a formal level. Then, when these students become teachers, we find, to our surprise, that their perceptions are not very refined. They seem only to recognize the primitive extremes of differences and cannot even associate these with the terms we have taught them to use. One strategy may be to infiltrate the training of these youngsters at an earlier age and begin teaching them to think about their own mental processes and those of others when they are much younger. This kind of learning can possibly grow out of courses like that which Bruner, for example, describes in this volume. Thus, the long-range key to preparing teachers adequately to function in the 'discovery-oriented' classroom, may lie in the introduction of behavioral science concepts to potential teachers in their own elementary school experiences.

PART FOUR

PSYCHOLOGICAL INSIGHTS

Chapter X

Varieties of Learning and the Concept of Discovery

ROBERT M. GAGNÉ

IN VIEW OF WHAT HAS BEEN SAID IN THE OTHER PAPERS, IT IS UN-
necessary to point out that *discovery* is a word tending to call forth
distinctly positive reactions in the world of education. Discovery is a
'good' word for describing one aspect of the educational process and,
on the whole, this state of affairs is probably a good thing in itself.
One effect is that the consideration of the nature of *instruction* as a
central part of the educative process increasingly emphasizes student
behavior, as opposed to teacher behavior, classroom conditions, and so
on. Discovery is something that the student does, beyond merely
sitting in his seat and paying attention. What the student does, or to
say it another way, the events that transpire within the student, are
bound to be of crucial importance for learning.

These processes that take place within the student are traditionally
of interest to the psychologist. He wishes to study them, not primarily
because they are good or bad, but in order to determine how they can
be employed to account for instances of actual learning. He is interested in constructing a useful model, or theory of learning, which will
incorporate such constructs as 'discovery,' if this is possible. Some theories
of learning have not made use of a construct like discovery, to be sure.
The reason may be either (1) that the theory actually rejects such a
construct as unnecessary, or (2) that the varieties of learning situation
to which the theory of learning is applicable are restricted to those
which do not, in fact, involve such a process as discovery.

In any case, if the psychologist is to use a construct like discovery,
he must seek to define it in terms of observable events. This is what I
shall try to do in this paper. At the very outset, it seems highly likely
that discovery will turn out to have more than a single meaning. When
Gibson (1941) examined the concept of mental set, a number of years
ago, he found it to have a bewildering variety of meanings. I hope this

will not be true of discovery. But if discovery is to be useful as a scientific term, the search for its meaning or meanings must be made, whatever the outcome may be.

LEARNING: EXTERNAL AND INTERNAL EVENTS

It is obvious that the change in performance potential that is called learning involves phenomena that are directly observable, located outside the organism, as well as other phenomena that are inferred as taking place inside the learner, that is, in his nervous system. One would not expect the learner to discover the external events, since these are the 'givens' in bringing about the act of learning. In contrast, certain internal events or states are said to be 'discovered' because they are not supplied by the learning experimenter as a part of the situation which he controls. The implication is that discovery of these internal events must involve (1) a process of *search*, and (2) a process of *selection*, each of which takes place within the learner's nervous system, and each of which may be idiosyncratic to the individual learner.

What is it that must be searched for and selected in this activity called discovery? In attempting to answer this question, we are soon led to realize that the object of the search is not always the same kind of thing. And if this is a possibility, we then can ask, What kinds of entities can be searched for and selected within an act of learning? Since what is sought must be internal events or states, we must presumably look for them inside the learner. The tools to be used are inference and reasoning from external observations; and these, of course, are fairly good tools. Using them, I shall attempt to answer the question, What is discovery? for several types of learning situations.

Simple Associative Learning

As nearly everyone will agree, there is a type of learning which may be called simple associative learning, or connection learning. In a dog, an example is learning to raise his paw when his master says, Shake hands. In a human child, it is learning to imitate saying a previously unfamiliar word. In a human adult, it may be such a thing as learning to pronounce *ch* in German. As each of these examples illustrates, there is often a motor component in connection learning. In fact, it is doubtful whether the prototype of connection learning can be considered truly typical unless this motor component is present. This, however, is a subject too complex to consider here, and I must leave it with a reference to Mowrer (1960).

Can it be that there is discovery in connection learning? Many investigators have said there is. For example, consider some of Thorndike's results (1898) concerning the behavior of cats in getting out of "problem boxes." I need not show you a slide to illustrate the difference exhibited by Cat No. 10 in getting out of Box D, and the same cat in getting out of Box C. The first of these problems required him to pull a short string, and showed a decrease in time from seven minutes to 25 seconds following the first trial, with a small reduction thereafter. The second required the cat to rotate a button, and showed variable times of release from seven minutes to two minutes to four minutes to 40 seconds to three minutes, and so on and on, for 30 trials. Thorndike interpreted the gradual reduction in time as a gradual strengthening of the connection. This, however, will not begin to explain why there should be such a difference between the two boxes. Apparently, one connection was strengthened right away, whereas the other showed great variability over many trials.

It seems simpler and more reasonable to interpret the cat's variable fumbling around as indicative of a process of search and selection. At least, nothing in the cat's behavior contradicts such an interpretation. Why was the string-pulling performance established rapidly? It was because the motor-feedback aspect of the stimulus (that is, the kinesthetic part of the stimulation) was quickly discovered. Why did it take so long to establish the button-turning performance? It was because the kinesthetic parts of the stimulus were not quickly discovered. The difference no doubt has something to do with the native constitution of cats, as the Brelands (1961) point out. This analysis suggests, therefore, that connection learning does indeed involve discovery, and that what is being discovered is the internal (kinesthetic) part of the stimulus. It also suggests that much, if not all, of the 'gradualness' of learning motor acts is an indication of the process of discovery, of internal search and selection. It will be evident that such an interpretation is most consistent with modern learning theories that emphasize stimulus selection (e. g., Estes, 1959).

This interpretation is also quite compatible with what is known about human motor learning. Learning a motor act does seem to be a process in which there is discovery of the proper kinesthetic stimuli. As the lady golfer said when she holed a ball from the edge of the green, I wish I knew what I did right. Practical methods of establishing human motor acts are almost entirely concerned with facilitating the process of discovery. Sometimes they do it by getting the learner to take the proper stance, sometimes by means of verbal or pictorial instructions. But always there appears to be the necessity for repeating the action over and over again in the attempt to discover the proper response-generated stimuli.

It is worth pointing out, perhaps, that this is not a novel view of the process of simple associative learning; the occurrence of discovery in such learning has been recognized for many years by those investigators whose thinking is not hindered by rigid theory. Melton (1950, p. 671) has written:

> Problem situations may also be described in terms of the extent to which they require the discovery and/or fixation of responses which are *available* in the repertoire of the individual . . . [Thus] in motor learning, learning to wiggle one's ears is different, in terms of this dimension, from learning to push the proper switch (an already available response) on a certain signal.

The function of practice in this kind of learning may be conceived to be that of providing repeated occasions on which the discovery process can take place. If the German word *ich* does not come out quite right the first time, the individual practices some more. Over several trials, it may be supposed that the kinesthetic stimuli become more and more precisely selected so that the performance meets some established criterion. In this meaning of the term, it is fair to say that if we want discovery to occur, we must provide practice, or repetition of the learning situation.

Discovery in Verbal Associate Learning

Learning psychologists have been fond of studying the learning of associations between pairs of verbal terms, like GUZ-FIV, or 22-Green, and the like. While one may reasonably deprecate the idea that such learning forms a large part of what is learned in school, it nevertheless seems true that verbal associations do have to be learned, on occasion. There are many kinds of codes or translations that must be acquired in the course of learning academic subject-matter. Perhaps the clearest example is learning the translations of foreign words into English, and vice versa.

Does discovery play a part in this paired-associate kind of learning? Is there a process of search and selection which can be identified in connection with such learning? There certainly seems to be mounting evidence that paired-associate learning is a far more complex thing than the connection of a stimulus with a response. Let me mention here some of the evidence that supports this view, and attempt to point out what this shows about the occurrence of a discovery process.

The evidence marshalled by Underwood and Shulz (1960) adds up to a pretty clear indication that much of the gradualness of the typical paired-associate learning task must be attributed to the process of becoming familiar with the response members (nonsense syllables or words). There is also evidence that the paired-associate task diminishes in difficulty when the learner is more highly familiar with the stimulus terms (Noble, 1963). While the question of the nature of the process underlying familiarity has not yet been answered fully, it seems clear that the process is not one that involves discovery. Familiarity seems to be graded in amount, but not to involve search and selection.

Undoubtedly, the major event which dominates the learning of sets of paired associates is *interference*, as Underwood (1964), Postman (1961), and others have emphasized in summarizing the experimental findings in this area. Interference may be an extinction-like phenomenon, as the study of Barnes and Underwood (1959) suggests. But again, one can find little evidence of a discovery process here.

It is when one asks the question, How does a *single* pair of verbal associates get connected? that the possibilities of discovery reveal themselves. The occurrence of mediation in such learning is by this time a well-established fact. For example, Jenkins (1963, p. 213) reports a study by Sacks and Russell which had the following procedure: First, learn verbal associations of the sort ZUG-Table, BOP-King; then, learn a second set of associations of the sort ZUG-Chair, BOP-Queen. The subjects learned the second set in virtually one trial.

Taken as a whole, the evidence on mediated verbal learning makes it fairly clear that verbal associates are increasingly more easily learned to the degree that there already exists in the learner a readily available mediating link (cf. Jenkins, 1963; Russell, 1963; Staats & Staats, 1963). Some writers (e.g. Gagné, 1965) consider verbal association to be typically a process of mediation, while others (e.g. Underwood, 1964) caution that a mediation process need not necessarily be involved. It is noteworthy, though, that when subjects are asked how they form associations, in a very high proportion of instances they report what Underwood (1963) has called a "functional" stimulus, which is usually not the same as the "nominal" stimulus. The events of association, as distinguished from those of word-familiarity and interference, do appear to provide the conditions for a search-and-selection process—in other words, for a process of discovery.

If the possibility of discovery exists in verbal association, how does it come about? It is a reasonable hypothesis, perhaps not yet fully established, that the words or syllables to be associated generate a process of recall in which the learner discovers a link between them. In the Sacks and Russell experiment, the discovery is easy, because the links between *table* and *chair*, and between *king* and *queen* are highly available. In contrast, links between such words as *cheese* and *river* may be less readily available, while the discovery of a link between GUZ and RYK may be a relatively difficult task. Is there an advantage to reducing the need for discovery by actually supplying a link (as is typically done in experiments on mediation), or is it better for learning and retention if the learner discovers his own link? According to Bruner (1961), the latter procedure has the advantage: in one study, 95 per cent of the associations were recalled when the learner had to supply his own mediator, whereas less than 50 per cent were recalled when the mediator was supplied for him.

In learning verbal associates, then, there is evidence that a process of discovery enters into the learning activity in an important way, as *discovery of mediating links*. There is an important difference to note between this kind of learning and the simple connection learning previously described. In the former case, it was notable that practice provided the opportunity for discovery. But practice does not appear to have this function in verbal learning. It does not take repetition of the verbal associates to bring about discovery of the mediator. Rather, what it takes is a rich store of mediators, established by *previous* learning. Learning facility will be increased to the extent that mediators are readily available, and this in turn will be determined by the previous learning of word associations. The individual who has earlier acquired a great store of verbal associations will presumably have the advantage in learning new verbal associates. This is also the reason for the advantage to meaningfulness (in one of its meanings) in verbal learning: discovery is easier when many associates are available (cf. Deese, 1961).

Concept Learning

Another typical variety of learning, bearing some relation to verbal associates, is called concept learning. As a result of this kind of learning, the individual becomes able to perform identically toward stimuli which may differ markedly in their physical appearance, but which are responded to as a class. A fairly clear and simple example of a concept is provided by Harlow's (1949) "oddity problem." The individual, whether animal or human being, presented with stimuli which may be varied in their physical appearance, responds by choosing the odd one: if there are two triangles and a circle, he chooses the circle; if there are two books and a pencil, he chooses the pencil. In related studies of an earlier period, Hunter (1913), in studies of delayed reaction, showed that raccoons and children could learn to choose the middle one, or the left one, or the right one of three stimuli. The point of these techniques used to study concept learning is to set up a situation in which it can be shown that the learner's behavior is not controlled by specific external stimuli. Instead, the learner himself must supply an internal "symbolic" stimulus (as Hunter called it) that represents the class of stimuli being presented to him. He must somehow represent to himself 'odd,' or 'middle,' or 'left,' or whatever, and be able to transfer this capability to new situations of the same class.

Experimental controversies generated by these basic studies of concept learning have centered around the question of how logically tight is the demonstration that a self-generated mediating process *must* be inferred, as opposed to the idea that behavior is controlled by some sort of external cue. Techniques to insure the soundness of this inference are still being invented. Besides those previously mentioned methods of Harlow and Hunter, there are the transposition experiments of Spence (1937) and Kuenne (1946), and the reversal technique of the Kendlers (1961). However thorny the arguments against them, it is really quite difficult to believe that all these instances can somehow be 'reduced' to simple associative learning; and, accordingly, it is not difficult to believe that both human beings and many animals can learn concepts.

Is there evidence of a mediational process in concept learning? Yes, indeed there is; in fact, this is what most of the evidence is all about. If it can be demonstrated that consistent responses can be made in the face of widely varying external stimulation, then one is forced to infer that there must be a consistent *internal* process supplied by the individual's own nervous system. Hunter's raccoons generated an internal symbolic cue. Harlow's monkeys acquired learning sets. When an individual is able to respond to 'stimulus relationships' in some transposition problems, this is taken as evidence that some mediational process must have guided the behavior. Seven-year-old children are able to switch rapidly from choosing the black card to choosing the opposite (or white) card, because they are able to represent 'opposite' to themselves, whereas four-year-olds cannot.

Mediation, then, is characteristic of concept learning. Some internal process must be searched for and selected which makes it possible for a great variety of specific stimuli to be represented as a class. It is an interesting question, though, as to how such a discovery process might be affected by a greater or lesser amount of guidance, particularly verbal guidance.

Guidance in Concept Discovery. One can certainly set up a learning situation to require that concepts be learned by discovery with a minimum of external guidance. In fact, this is the procedure that Harlow did use, in having his monkeys learn to choose 'the odd one,' or to acquire the other concepts he required of them. They solved one particular problem, went on to the next, and the next, and so on, until they reached a point at which the new problem (involving the same concept) was solved almost immediately. The animals *had to discover* the concept; Harlow gave them no help, only practice.

It is of some importance to note that a learning situation can readily be set up to require human beings to discover concepts with almost no guidance. Goldstein and Weber (1965) arranged a learning situation in which learners of high school age were asked to make a choice on successive exposures of two nonsense figures. Confirmation of correct responses was provided in such a way that in one group of learners 'position' was the correct choice (i.e., the one on the right), and in another group, a particular appearance was correct. The subjects were asked simply to indicate choices, and minimal verbal directions were provided. The positional concept turned out to be much more difficult for these human subjects to discover than was the appearance concept. But in either case, it took a relatively large number of trials before the discovery was actually made.

If one examines these kinds of situations dispassionately, they lead naturally to the following conclusion: Discovery without guidance makes the learning of concepts a terribly slow process. It is quite evident that adult human beings do not typically learn concepts by this method. If one wants an adult to learn to choose the one on the right, he says, 'on the right,' and the concept is attained in a single trial. If one wants efficient behavior in a reversal problem by seven-year-olds, he says 'opposite,' and the concept is available for use at once. Examples from school learning situations are not different in principle. The student does not start to learn what a *cell* is by discovering that this is its name; he is *told* what it is. The child does not begin the process of discovering what a circle is by searching for a drawn circle; he is told what it is. That is to say, when the mediators have been previously learned, as verbal responses or some other kind, it is considerably easier to arouse their recall by means of some verbal instruction than it is to expect them to be discovered. If the monkey or ape could respond to verbal instructions as a human being can, he too would probably be able to acquire concepts in a small number of trials. To expect a human being to engage in a trial-and-error procedure in discovering a concept appears to be a matter of asking him to behave like an ape. It is of psychological interest to do this, of course, but possibly not of much educational interest.

It is true that there must be a difference between the use of a previously learned concept by an adult in a new situation, on the one hand, and the absolutely brand-new learning of a concept by a young child, on the other. Perhaps the latter is not and cannot be done simply by transferring a previously learned verbal label, acting as a mediator, to a novel situation. The young child must have to respond to a certain number of instances of a given class before he is able to respond conceptually to any member of the class; and in addition, he must have differentiated negative from positive instances. Unfortunately, we seem to have too little evidence on this point. We know that the four-year-old learners in the Kendlers' study could learn to reverse by means of a period of trial-and-error learning. But could they have learned the concept 'opposite'? And how might they have learned such a concept most efficiently? These are the questions which seem to me to be unanswered at present.

As a hypothesis concerning how a child might learn a concept, the following is offered (cf. Gagné, 1965):

(a) Show the child one instance of the concept (e.g., edge, as the edge of a piece of paper), and say, This is an edge.

(b) Show him another instance, such as the edge of a swimming pool, and say, This is an edge.

(c) Show him a negative instance, such as the side or top of a cylinder, and say, This is not an edge.

(d) Show him still another object, such as a cup, and pointing appropriately, say, This is an edge, and, This is not an edge.

(e) As a test, give the child a box and say, Show me the edge.

I think this method might work, although I have not tried it. More examples, both negative and positive, might be needed for some children than for others. A teacher might prefer to use a questioning form of statement in most cases, rather than the declarative form. But it is most important to note that this is a highly guided procedure, which requires communication through language for its success. There may be an internal process of discovery in the attainment of the concept, but the external learning situation is one which uses extensive guidance.

Discovery in the Learning of Principles

A still more complex kind of learning pertains to the learning of principles or rules. This sort of learning constitutes a very large part of what is accomplished in school situations. Principles, in their ideal form, are combinations of concepts. They range from such a relatively simple set of ideas as Birds fly, to considerably more sophisticated combinations such as that represented by $F = ma$.

It should be clear that when I speak of principles I do not refer to the simple expression of the principle as a verbal sequence, such as Birds fly. Learning this as a verbal sequence is quite a different matter, already described in terms of learning verbal associates. If one wants to determine whether the individual has acquired the principle, he must ask him to *apply* it, or *supply* an instance of it. Often the person can also say it, but this is not directly relevant. Brown and Fraser (1963) make this point vividly in their discussion of the learning of syntactic rules by children.

A different and equally important point about the learning of principles is that what is learned is the *combination*, and not the concepts of which it is composed. If a learner is to acquire the principle, $F = ma$, in an efficient manner, he must previously have learned the concepts of *force* (as push or pull), of *mass*, of *acceleration*, of *equality*, and of *multiplication*. Only if he already knows these concepts can he learn the principle in the most straightforward and efficient manner.

Again let us consider the question, Is there opportunity for search and selection, for discovery, in the learning of principles? The answer is Yes, there seems to be. The reason appears to be quite simple, and perhaps it is deceptively so. When one has two or more concepts in mind, that is, in the status of ready recall, there are many possible *kinds* of combinations that may be made, and then selected or rejected. The concept 'birds' may be combined with a number of possible concepts, including fly, walk, flutter, soar, peck, and so on, whereas there are others it cannot be legitimately combined with, such as frown, bark, growl, and so on. Similarly, there are many ways that the concepts of force and mass and acceleration *might* be combined, but only a few valid ways. It is not unreasonable to suppose that a search and selection process may occur in the learning of principles. This would be a sort of 'internal trial-and-error' activity, or, as some writers might prefer to call it, a 'hypothesis selection' process. Of course, any such process must be followed by feedback, or verification, in order for the learner to complete the acquisition of the principle.

Probably everyone would agree that it is possible to learn a principle without discovery. Many examples come to mind. A scientist who is reading a technical article in his field learns a great deal from it, that is, he acquires a number of principles that are new to him. Of course, he must already know the concepts which enter into these principles in order to learn anything at all. But he does *not* discover these principles. He is told them. He engages in what Ausubel (1963) calls reception learning. If, in fact, a scientist can learn this way, and learn a tremendous number of new principles in reading his professional journals, surely a student can learn this way too. There seems to be little doubt about it—students *do* learn this way, without discovery. It is doubtless incorrect, too, as Ausubel also points out, to equate reception learning with rote learning.

There is, however, the interesting question as to whether learning principles via a discovery process is somehow better than learning them by reception. Most probably, one cannot maintain that discovery learning will be faster, since it may involve a greater number of internal trials in which hypotheses are rejected until the right one is found. How else could discovery learning of principles be 'better'? One possibility is that retention may be better, another that transferability may be greater.

There are a number of studies that bear upon this question of the value of discovery learning of principles to retention and transfer (McConnell, 1934; Thiele, 1938; Swenson, 1949; Anderson, 1949; Craig, 1956). It is not possible to review them in detail here. What may be said, though, is that it is somewhat difficult in all of these studies to be sure that only a single independent variable was being manipulated in each case. I refer again to that thoughtful critic of discovery, Ausubel (1961b), who makes a similar point. It is surely highly suggestive that advantages in retention and transfer have been found in a number of instances in which discovery was at least one of the variables being manipulated. But it is my impression that there is a strong need for a really well-controlled laboratory experiment in this area. Such an experiment should include at least the following features: (1) insure that the learners have already acquired the concepts to be combined into principles; (2) require the learning of principles, not verbal associates, or something else; (3) compare discovery with reception (that is, no discovery); and (4) apply well-designed measures of retention, transfer, or both. Surely such an experiment can be done!

There would appear to be some theoretical reasons for predicting that discovery of principles might be a more effective means of learning than the sheer reception method, if the criterion of effectiveness is either retention or transferability. First, in the process by which a second concept gets combined with a first, the selected concept is likely to be highly available in the learner's repertoire. It is recallable in all of its idiosyncratic characteristics. Such a concept, if it turns out to be the correct one, is likely to have an advantage at the very outset for both recall and for transfer. And the combination of one highly available concept with another, in the formation of a principle, is accordingly likely to possess a comparably high degree of prepotency in its retention and its transferability.

A second reason to expect advantages for discovery learning of principles derives from the nature of the process itself. As emphasized previously, it is a search-and-selection process, which means it is a *discriminative* kind of process, in which unsatisfactory combinations are rejected and successful ones confirmed. Such a process may have the effect of reducing interference with other concepts and combinations of concepts. Reduction of interference from conflicting principles may be expected to produce a result favorable to both retention and transfer.

Guidance in Learning Principles. Even after the well-designed experiment on discovery in principle learning is done, this will still leave the problem of the effects of various amounts of *guidance*. It is evident that a discovery method can be contrasted not only with a reception (or no discovery) method, but also with methods falling in between the two with respect to the degree of *independent search* they demand. The discovery of a principle defining an unknown object is progressively guided in the game of Twenty Questions, by exclusion of categories like 'animal, vegetable, or mineral.' The discovery of the principles involved in the anagram CNABO may be guided, that is, the search may be simplified, by instructions which furnish the category 'food.' One of the most carefully designed experimental studies in this field, that by Craig (1953), demonstrated large differences in transfer of a method of guided discovery versus nonguided discovery used during the original learning. A number of other studies, concerned with the learning of different principles, appear to support these findings (Kittell, 1957; and Kersh, 1958).

In the case of guided discovery, too, there is a theoretical reason why this method might be expected to be superior to unguided discovery. So far as initial learning is concerned, providing guidance should have the effect of cutting down the *search* time, and thus speeding up the act of learning. Giving the learner guidance instructions may, as

Gagné and Brown (1961) noted, make it possible for some of the wilder hypotheses to be eliminated immediately. At the same time, it may be noted, the *selection* part of the process can still occur. The learner is not told the principle, as in reception learning; the combination of concepts still takes place internally. If this is true, it may also be that the most important aspect of the discovery process is preserved, insofar as retention and transfer are concerned. Under these circumstances, highly recallable concepts are favored as the rejection of the most confusable combinations takes place. In summary, the technique of guided discovery may be successful because it cuts down the necessity for search, eliminates the most extreme wrong hypotheses, while at the same time it provides the opportunity for selection of correct combinations of concepts to occur.

Discovery in Problem Solving

A still more complex kind of learning situation within which it is appropriate to suppose that discovery may occur is called *problem solving*. In order to define this kind of learning, it is necessary to distinguish two things. First is the fact that problem solving typically requires the learner to acquire what may be called a higher-order principle, formed by putting together two or more simpler principles. In some formal sense, the drawing of conclusions in logic may represent this process. The individual already has learned the elementary principles, Birds fly, and Flying requires wings. He goes on to formulate the new higher-order principle, Birds have wings for flying. Surely this example is too simple; yet I think it is a prototype for problem solving.

The second characteristic of the problem-solving situation is a matter of method, rather than content. Problem-solving situations are usually designed to *require* discovery on the part of the learner. This is an inevitable part of their makeup; otherwise, they would probably not be called problem-solving. If I ask an individual to supply the next two numbers in the number series

$$1 \quad 2 \quad 5 \quad 14 \quad - \quad -,$$

he has a problem. If I tell him the principles, Multiply by three, and Subtract one, there is no problem. There would almost certainly be learning in this situation, but it would not be called problem solving.

By definition, then, learning which results from a situation of the sort usually considered to represent problem solving involves discovery. There is search, some of which may take place overtly, and there is selection of a higher-order principle. These features seem clearly to characterize some of the most interesting studies of problem solving, such as those of Maier (1930) and Katona (1940). In Maier's pendulum problem, for example, college students were expected to learn a complex principle involving the use of a vertical pole to wedge a horizontal stick against a ceiling, holding up two pendulums constructed from string and a weighted object. In Katona's matchstick problems, the students were learning a principle about how to open up a matchstick figure to produce fewer squares with a given number of matches.

Correct solutions to such problems as these were best achieved in both cases with considerable amounts of 'guidance.' This was delivered, in the case of Maier's study, by verbal instructions, and in the case of Katona's, by means of a blackboard demonstration. When such guidance was given, a significantly greater number of solutions was achieved than when it was omitted. Learning was thus made more probable. In Katona's study there is also the suggestion that the demonstration produced greater transfer to new matchstick problems than occurred when learners were told the higher-order principle. More evidence on this point would be welcome.

Learning to Discover

Can individuals learn how to discover the solutions of problems? The evidence just cited from Katona (1940) suggests that they can learn how to solve matchstick problems. Gagné and Brown (1961) showed that high school students were able to learn how to discover the solution to number-series problems. The work of Bruner, Goodnow, and Austin (1956) demonstrated that strategies of discovery were learned which transferred to a variety of card-coding problems. There would seem to be reasonable evidence that there is some reality to the notion of learning how to discover. But there are some extremely important limitations to this statement, which need to be carefully noted:

The strategies of discovery, the heuristics of discovery, as Bruner (1961) has called them, apparently do not have to be *learned* by discovery. Gagné and Brown's (1961) subjects learned how to discover solutions to number-series problems by several methods, and the pure discovery method was not the best. Many of Katona's subjects learned how to discover the solutions to matchstick problems when they were *told* the principles involved. Maier's subjects discovered the solutions to problems with a good deal of verbal guidance. That the criterion performance involves discovery does not automatically prove that learning this performance requires the method of discovery.

The heuristics of discovery have not been shown to be highly generalizable. People can learn to discover strategies of solving particular kinds of problems, but it is a long way from this fact to the idea that they have learned how to discover in some general sense. Critical thinking ability, as Ausubel (1961b, p. 54) avers, "can only be enhanced within the context of a specific discipline."

Summary and Conclusions

Here I have attempted to review the functions that the process of discovery might reasonably be expected to have in learning. The issues which seem to me to be in need of precise definition in relation to this question are these:

Within an act of learning, discovery may be said to occur when the performance change that is observed requires the inference of an internal process of search and selection. What is sought for and selected varies with the kind of learning that is taking place.

Discovery processes may occur as a part of most kinds of learning acts, from the relatively simple to the relatively complex. In this sense, discovery may be considered a "dimension" of learning, to use Melton's (1950) term. Usually, discovery processes occupy more time in learning than do the processes of acquiring and storing. Accordingly, methods of learning which emphasize discovery are not self-evidently more efficient than other methods.

Analyzing the role of discovery in learning requires that the kind of learning, as determined by learning conditions, be specified first. The analysis then reveals different functions of discovery for different varieties of learning. Some salient points are as follows:

The learning of simple connections (like pronouncing a strange foreign word) typically involves a process of discovery in searching for and selecting the kinesthetic part of the stimulus complex. This gives rise to a need for practice.

The learning of verbal associates may involve discovery of a mediating link between the two verbal members. Some evidence suggests that a self-generated link may be more favorable to learning and retention than a link which is externally supplied.

The learning of concepts appears to require a process of discovery in the sense that an internally generated process of representation is involved. In adults, who have available suitable verbal mediators, concept formation in a novel situation appears to be a most rapid kind of learning. Laboratory studies of effective conditions for concept learning in children seem to be singularly lacking. But the employment of a high degree of guidance, verbal or otherwise, seems to be a necessity for efficient learning.

149

Principle learning can be done with or without discovery. When discovery is introduced as a requirement, there is some evidence to suggest that the learned principle may be better retained and more readily transferable. Guided discovery may serve to cut down the time of search while maintaining the advantages of internal selection.

Problem solving, when considered as a form of learning, requires discovery, since the learner is expected to generate a novel combination of previously learned principles. In this case, too, guidance appears to have its familiar role of decreasing the time for search.

Learning to discover, or learning the heuristics of discovery, appears to be possible, according to the evidence, in an importantly restricted sense: People can learn strategies of solving particular classes of problems. How large these classes may be remains to be demonstrated. It does not, however, seem likely that this generality of content can be very great. There is no convincing evidence that one can learn to be a discoverer, in a general sense; but the question remains an open one.

What implications do these conclusions have for educational practice? First is the idea that discovery is an integral process for several varieties of learning. It is not a panacea for learning effectiveness, nor is it an essential condition for all kinds of learning. But it can be identified widely in school learning situations. Second, when discovery does occur, it is obviously dependent upon internal events generated within the learner. This means that if one is interested in promoting the occurrence of discovery to achieve some educational objective, he must somehow see to it that prerequisite capabilities have been established. In other words, there must certainly be a lot of attention to the preparation phase of instruction, if discovery is going to take place.

Chapter XI

Learning, Attention and the Issue of Discovery[1]

HAPPILY THIS ESSAY IS A LOGICAL CONTINUATION OF CRONBACH'S URG-
ing that we search for limited generalizations of the form "content
area [by] child [by] form of presentation." It is assumed, first, that we
agree that the issue of discovery versus didactic form in teaching is
too simple and overgeneralized to be discussed with profit. But it is
profitable to talk about variation in presentation of specific academic
contents to specific children at specific stages of development. Consider
a third-grade child learning the essence of multiplication. Should you
let him discover the insight that multiplication is no more than a
series of successive additions, or should you tell him this blessed idea
and let him brood about it. The core of this paper considers some issues
that must be resolved before that question can be answered. We shall
consider, first, those personological variables that affect learning in general, and then summarize the arguments pro and con the discovery
strategy.

A useful and vivid analogical model for learning in children is
the biological process of fertilization. Learning involves a change in
cognitive structures, as fertilization leads to its unique structural changes.
There are two ways to facilitate these changes. The fertilization model
implies that the sperm be made sharper or the ovum made more per-
meable. I acknowledge the advantage of each of these strategies but
vote for the latter, for altering the child's receptivity to the communication from a teacher should have a more permanent effect on future
conceptions.

The basic premise of this paper is that learning and performance
require an understanding of the interaction between cognitive skills and
motivational variables, a proposition offered by Hull over a generation

[1] This research was supported by research grant MH–8792 from the National Institute of Mental Health, U.S.P.H.S.

ago. If the child has minimal motivation to learn, manipulation of external stimulus materials may have little effect on new acquisition. There are many analogies from the natural sciences to support this view of the importance of a catalyst in creating new structures. Without the presence of an enzyme, no sugar is formed from a combination of starch and water. No structural changes occur in the starch without the proper catalyst, and motivational variables are to be viewed as catalysts. A child can be exposed to the richest possible set of material and the most exquisitely architectured schools, and experience no substantial structural changes in his cognitive life.

What are these personological variables that influence the ease of acquisition of new information? The issues are complicated, and dogmatic statements are probably not too helpful. But the advantage of this type of meeting is the license to speak with more conviction than is prudent; to make suggestions that are a bit more extreme than one believes.

The puzzlement that envelops the twin issues, What is learning? and How does it occur, is clarified by assuming that if a child attends to information he is likely to learn something about it. If attention is guaranteed, some learning is likely to occur. Many of the manipulations performed by curriculum builders begin to acquire a superstitious air, for the manipulations often become deified without realizing that the child's attention is the central process being manipulated, and there are many ways to accomplish this goal. Once this theme is assimilated, the problem of learning loses some of its mysticism. Put aside any temporary complaints to this presumptuously simple-sounding proposition, and consider the major directives suggested by the following hypothesis: inquire into the psychological variables that promote or obstruct attention to symbolic material. Let us consider some examples of the general usefulness of the concept of attention.

Many investigators have devoted much effort during the last decade to demonstrate conditioning and learning in the young infant, and many experiments came to the conclusion that the infant was not capable of learning anything during the opening weeks of life. Examination of the character of the conditioned stimulus used in these studies revealed that it was often a continuous tone of short duration. We now realize that in order to capture the young infant's attention, we must present either a tone of long duration or an intermittent tone. When these changes are made in the conditioned stimulus, learning is demonstrated with ease. When one considers the quality of the stimulus that evokes maximum attention, and shifts away from a fetish for a particular manipulation, progress is made in larger leaps. Similar examples could be found in other literatures. Elliott (1964), for example, found no relationship between a host of biological variables and performance in a reaction time task in six-year-olds. Elliott concluded that this was because the child's level of attentiveness and involvement fluctuated markedly during the experiment and influenced his heart rate, respiration, EEG, and performance in different ways.

THE CATALYSTS IN LEARNING

The learning of a new rule or a new word or a new bond between two previously unrelated elements requires, first, a certain level of prior knowledge and, second, a particular constellation of intrapsychic processes that lead to sustained attention to the material to be learned. These psychological processes, which include motives, expectancies, sources of anxiety and standards, exert primary control over the child's distribution of attention in a classroom situation. These processes lead to the initiation of mental work, and determine how long the child will persist at the learning of a new task, how difficult a task he will attempt, and how he will interpret success or failure on that task. A brief description of some of the relevant variables follows:

The motive for acceptance and positive valuation by parents and parent-surrogates. The child's desire for signs of positive evaluation from selected adults leads him to work at the learning process. Most adults issue these signs when the child invests effort in academic mastery. The child wants to obtain and retain adult praise, acceptance, nurturance and recognition, for these responses signify to the 10 year old that he is positively valued. For many preadolescent children, academic tasks are intrinsically boring. The learning of multiplication and division operations is, on the face of it, a meaningless and often monotonous procedure, but one that becomes interesting and important if it is associated with the most significant objects in the child's world—people. For most seven-year-olds, learning is primarily a socially motivated enterprise.

This conclusion may jar those who have read reports of young children enthusiastically working alone at machines to learn various skills. The writer has seen these children, and it appears that subtle social rewards are the fuel that keeps the children at work. Attractive female teachers are often present in the laboratory, and visions of accelerating mothers at home are present in the child's head. Moreover, the child's behavior is often much different when the teacher leaves the training booth and the child is working alone.

There are, of course, significant individual differences in the incentive value of adult praise and recognition. For example, praise and recognition are usually more important for girls than boys, for younger children (age five to eight) than for preadolescents and adolescents, and more relevant when the task is not directly related, in the child's purview, to previously valued instrumental skills. That is, the fuzzier the link between the task to be mastered and the skills the child values, the greater the incentive value of adult praise and recognition for task mastery.

The motivation to maximize similarity to a desirable model. A common motive among children and adults is the desire to maximize similarity to certain models who are perceived to command power, status, instrumental competence, and affection. The child wishes to be like these models who seem to possess these highly desirable resources. If these models display an active interest in intellectual mastery, the child is likely to attempt to mimic them in order to increase behavioral similarity to the model. The reward for this behavior is the strengthening of the belief that the child *is* like the model, and therefore capable of sharing vicariously in the model's more desirable attributes of power, competence and affection. Many people are prone to interpret the poor school performance of lower-class children as a result of their parents' indifference. Lower-class parents presumably do not punish poor report cards, or they fail to urge the child to do well. This belief is stereotypic and not completely valid. The writer has been in many lower-class homes where children were punished severely if they came home with poor grades. Moreover, the child is often told, "Now you'd better do good in school this week." These children perform poorly, in part, because the models to whom they are exposed daily do not reveal that intellectual mastery is a desirable activity for adults. The middle-class child learns the desirability of learning because his models convey this message directly in their behavior.

The motive for differentiation. It is a general human tendency, present in the child from six or seven years of age on, to seek to acquire attributes that differentiate him from his peers and siblings. The child attempts to acquire skills and attributes that allow him to label himself in some unique way. I recall my eight-year-old daughter pointing to the telephone book with great delight and squealing, "We're the only Kagan in the telephone book." This delight in certain kinds of uniqueness can be seen in most children, and the gratification appears to be related to a need for some degree of differentiation.

The need for differentiation is obviously important for creativity. Professor MacKinnon's (1965) work on creative architects and mathematicians indicates that a salient difference between the creative and noncreative professional is the desire of the former group to be creative, to be different from their peers. This motivation is a primary incentive for the product that society regards as creative.

Expectancy of success or failure. Children develop different degrees of expectancy of success or failure on particular intellectual tasks as early as kindergarten. The most frequent reaction to expectancy of failure in a young child is decreased involvement and subsequent withdrawal. At a stronger level of conjecture, expectancy of failure or success has a determining role in guiding preferences and motives. It is more likely that expectancies of goal attainment guide the growth of motives rather than the other way around. Children in extremely progressive school atmospheres, especially in grades one through three, may suffer from too much permissiveness in their intellectual diet. The young child is often reluctant to attempt tasks he thinks he may fail. He wants to learn to read, but questions his competence and his expectancy of failure may push him to the crayons and paints. The assumption that a six-year-old is a blossom who, if left alone, will seek the proper academic delicacies is an ingenuous and romantic view of the child. The superb school environment has the power to minimize the potential of painful humiliation that accompanies failure, but this goal is to be reached and has not been attained by most classrooms.

It is important to recognize, incidentally, that *anxiety over possible failure* is to be distinguished from *expectancy of failure*. These variables are different in meaning, although the literature speaks of 'fear of failure' as if expectancy of failure and anxiety over failure were the same constructs. It is likely that there is a curvilinear relation between these two variables. The child with extremely high or low expectancy of failure is less anxious over the possibility of failure than children who are uncertain, and where expectancies are firm (as in extreme confidence or surety of failure) anxiety should be less intense. We have tested many second- and third-grade children from lower-class homes who have been exposed to chronic failure and who behaved as if they expected failure in intellectual tasks. Nothing in their behavior reflected anxiety. There was no apprehension, and when they were incorrect and were told so, they appeared unperturbed.

Conflicts over learning. There are some specific conflicts that can obstruct the child's receptivity to learning, and we shall consider a few of them. One of the most important conflicts operative in the primary grades is related to sex-typing and sex-role values. Many young children label the school situation as a feminine activity. The reasons for this labeling are not mysterious. A child decides that objects are masculine or feminine depending on the contingencies that link these objects with either males or females in his life experience. A sailboat is masculine, a refrigerator feminine, a hammer is masculine, and a sewing machine feminine, because of the frequency with which these objects are used by males or females in the culture. The typical first-grade is led by a woman who promotes and reinforces activities like cutting, pasting, singing songs, obedience, and quiescence. These values are most congruent with the sex-role standards for girls. This double standard in the classroom may be responsible, in part, for the greater proportion of conduct and academic problems among boys than among girls. There are some data to support this conclusion. We did an experiment to demonstrate that young children label the school situation as feminine (Kagan, 1964). You cannot ask a child if a piece of chalk is more appropriate for boys or for girls. The child will laugh at the nonsensical quality of the question. But a moderate disguise seems to work. Second- and third-grade children were shown some pictures and were told, "We have some pictures here that belong to one of three groups, and we're going to call them three different crazy names. These pictures are DEP pictures, these pictures are ROV pictures, and these pictures are FAM pictures. Now you've got to guess whether the picture is a DEP, a ROV, or a FAM (the DEP pictures were masculine, the ROV pictures feminine and the FAM pictures were farm-like scenes)." The child was then shown obviously masculine, feminine, or farm-like pictures in order to teach him quickly the association between the three nonsense syllables and the three concepts. The picture contained trousers, baseballs, footballs, hammers, nails, purses, sewing machines, lipstick and so on. In five to 10 minutes the children were performing with no errors. We then inserted pictures involving academic objects, such as a blackboard, a book, and a page of arithmetic, but there were no people illustrated on these pictures. Most of the children labeled these academic objects as feminine, with one exception, and that was a picture of a map that was labeled masculine. On reflection, the map resembled those used by navigators and ship captains. However, books, pages of arthmetic, and blackboards were labeled predominantly feminine. Among third graders, the boys began to label some of these objects as masculine, because they had begun to see the link between knowledge and a masculine vocation they might choose some time in the future.

A second source of data is cross-cultural. In the United States and Western Europe, where women teach the elementary grades, the ratio of boys to girls with reading problems varies from three to one, to six to one. In Japan, the island of Hokkaido in particular, there is no excess of boys with reading problems, and half of the teachers in the elementary grades are men. Thus the link between sex-typing and school mastery is an important variable that should be attended to by psychologists and teachers.

A second conflict concerns anxiety over competitiveness, and it usually becomes intense during junior-high and high-school. Most public-school classrooms set up an implicit competitive atmosphere in which children who want very good grades must compete with their rivals in the rank-order world in which they live. It is not unlikely, therefore, that children with strong motivation to do well entertain hostile impulses toward the rivals who are competing with them for top honors. Children who have strong conflict and guilt potential over hostile motives may inhibit intense academic effort in order to attenuate the anxiety that surrounds the hostility that surrounds competitive feelings. This is one reason why preadolescent girls suddenly begin to inhibit intense motivation in school. Guilt over hostility is more intensely felt among girls than among boys, and the girl is less free to enter into intense competitive rivalry in the academic situation.

Finally, there is a special conflict, usually more intense in boys, involving assumption of a passive posture with teachers. Boys are encouraged, both by role-models and the general social environment, to be independent and autonomous, especially with respect to women. The traditional school situation, especially in the primary grades, places the young boy in a situation in which he must conform passively to the demands and requests of the female teacher. For boys for whom this is conflictful, there will be rebellion and withdrawal of involvement from the academic enterprise.

These constructs deal with some of the major motivational variables that exert control over the degree of attention and involvement in the learning of new cognitive structures. This essay continues by addressing itself to the issue of discovery. Recall the example given in the introduction: Which method of presentation is more effective in producing learning of multiplication; present the rule first and allow the child to explore the instances, or permit the child to infer the rule? The answer to that question must involve an appreciation of individual differences, not because this represents an evasion of the writer's responsibility to be specific, but because it appears to be the most valid posture to assume on this issue. It would be a mistake to promote or urge one method of presentation for all children. Individual differences in behavior are the rule rather than the exception, and there are few environmental intrusions that have the same effect on all children, regardless of the simplicity of the intrusion. Behavioral geneticists came to this conclusion years ago, and Harlow, in a personal communication, reaffirmed this view. Harlow placed rhesus monkeys individually in homogeneous black boxes for over six months. These monkeys had as homogeneous an environment as one could create. And yet, when they were placed in the Wisconsin General Test apparatus, their performances were palpably different. If individual differences in problem solving remain after this degree of environmental homogeneity, it is certainly not foolhardy to argue for interaction between method of presentation and the psychology of the school-age child. Let us consider, therefore, the pros and cons of a didactic-versus-discovery approach to the presentation of arithmetic problems.

ARGUMENTS FOR DISCOVERY LEARNING

The discovery approach requires more involvement on the part of the child and, therefore, greater attention to the component materials being presented. Studies of both animals and young children indicate that the more active involvement required of the organism, the greater the likelihood of learning. This principle is even applied to help interpret the phenomenon of imprinting. If the young chicken has to follow the decoy, imprinting is more effective, for the active following presumably leads to increased arousal and greater attention to the decoy. A major advantage of the discovery strategy is that it creates arousal, and as a result, maximal attention.

Because the discovery approach requires extra intellectual effort, the value of the task is increased. This principle is different from the first one stated above, which assumes that effort increases arousal, and subsequent involvement. This second principle is a more subtle psychological variable concerned with the value the child places upon the task. It is reasonable to assume that activities become valuable to the degree to which effort is expended in their mastery. The writer has had the experience of being more involved in a set of data collected by himself personally, than in a set of data that were more important but collected by others. One of the bases for the exhortation to scientists-administrators to spend some time in the laboratory is to guarantee that some involvement is maintained so that the value of laboratory work does not diminish below a certain threshold. A positive relation between effort expended at task-mastery and value placed upon the task is intuitively reasonable. Moreover, interesting experiments being performed in various laboratories tend to support this assumption. In the discovery approach, the child is likely to attach more value to the task because he has to exert more effort. This conclusion might be regarded as a deduction from Festinger's (1957) dissonance theory, although this theory is not necessary for this assumption.

The inferential or discovery approach is likely to increase the child's expectancy that he is able to solve different problems autonomously. One of the most important beliefs the school must teach children is the self-descriptive statement, "I am able to think autonomously." The primary aims of education are not only to teach the child a set of cognitive skills, but also to teach him confidence in his ability to think creatively about intellectual problems. The method of discovery is more likely to accomplish this end, because it requires the child to infer a major principle without excessive guidance from an external agent.

The method of discovery learning helps those children who have a passive dependency conflict with respect to the teacher. Many boys have difficulty in a traditional school setting because they have strong conflict over assuming a dependent and passive orientation with the teacher. This conflict was discussed earlier. Young boys often resist working on an academic task because it is structured as a power play between teacher and child. This discovery approach gives the child more latitude and freedom and removes him from the submissive posture ordinarily maintained between teacher and child.

These are the four advantages of the discovery method. However, there are equally compelling arguments against this method of presentation, and we shall consider them immediately.

There are many children who do not have the initial motivation to exert the necessary effort required to make inferences. The method of discovery requires a period of five, 10, or 20 minutes during which the child is attempting to tease out a simplifying rule. For children who enter the task with high motivation, this delay is not of much import. But for children with lowered motivation and usually lower IQ, the requirement of even five minutes of involvement without immediate reward is too burdensome and these children are apt to withdraw involvement from the task if some success is not immediate. Thus, the method of discovery is minimally appropriate for children who begin a problem situation with low motivation.

Young children five to seven years of age do not have a sufficient appreciation of what a problem is or what a solution is, and, therefore, the incentive value attached to discovery is fragile. I refer here to an important developmental difference in the attractiveness of making inferences. Preadolescent children have learned the joy of discovery, and for them there is an inherent incentive in the discovery method. Seven-year-olds are still in the process of acquiring this refined source of joy, and many have not even learned to appreciate what a problem is. For example, eight-year-old children usually do not remain within the constraints of a problem. Margaret Donaldson's recent book, *A Study of Children's Thinking*, illustrates this problem beautifully (Donaldson, 1964). For example, an eight-year old child is given a matching problem of the following type: There are three girls, Mary, Paula and Jean, and there are three schools, the North School, the South School and the East School. Mary goes to the North School and Jean does not go to the East School; can you tell me which school Paula goes to? The child is likely to reply that Paula goes to the East School because her girl friend Paula goes there. Or, she might say the East School is the biggest school, and Mary goes there because she is the biggest girl. The young child intrudes personal information extraneous to the problem. We first have to teach the child the meaning of a problem and what it means to solve one before we initiate discovery procedures. The tendency to confuse reality with the artificial restraints of a problem is serious when one is trying to teach principles by the discovery method.

Impulsive children are apt to settle on the wrong conclusion in the inferential method and become vulnerable to developing feelings of intellectual importance. Our research during the last four years has been concerned with an individual difference variable which is called reflection-impulsivity (Kagan et al., 1964). This variable refers to the tendency to reflect for a long time (in contrast to responding impulsively) over the differential validity of a solution hypothesis. Some children offer answers impulsively without considering their differential validity, while others tend to reflect a long time offering an answer. It is to be noted that this variable is only relevant for problem situations with response uncertainty. Decision times to questions with low response uncertainty, such as, What is an envelope? or, Who discovered Tunisia? reflect avaliability of knowledge and are not a function of the child's tendency to reflect over multiple answer possibilities. Most of the tasks used in our research involve perceptual discrimination problems in which the child is shown a standard stimulus (either a design or a familiar picture) and six highly similar variants. The child is told to pick out the one variant that is exactly like the standard. This is a problem with high response uncertainty. Some children decide very quickly, are usually wrong, and are called impulsive. Other children take a long time to decide on their first hypothesis, are usually correct, and are called reflective. There is remarkable generality for this tendency across tasks, and moderate intraindividual stability over time. As might be expected, impulsive children make more errors in learning to read and are more likely to make errors of commission.

Finally, impulsive children make more errors of inductive reasoning than reflectives. In a recently completed experiment, children matched on verbal ability and previously classified as impulsive or reflective were given reasoning items in which the child was shown three pictures that told part of a sequence and then had to select which of four alternatives was logically the next step or event. Impulsive children made significantly more errors on these items. In the classroom the impulsive child is more likely to offer the wrong answer and suffer the humiliation that so often accompanies the incorrect response. This individual-difference variable is relevant for the discovery method because discovery procedures place the impulsive child at a disadvantage. The impulsive child is likely to choose the wrong inference, experience a negative reinforcement and, over time, become discouraged about his ability to extract insightful principles.

In sum, the method of discovery is best for highly motivated, older children who might have high dependency conflict and who are prone to a reflective strategy. The method is least appropriate for younger children, especially below the age of nine, who do not have high motivation to master intellectual tasks or who are prone to be impulsive. Some aspects of these recommendations have research support, others must be tested in the laboratory. But until they are refuted by empirical test, they are reasonable propositions to defend.

SUMMARY

Educators and psychologists must begin to acknowledge the multiple interactions among content, child, and developmental level, for learning in the child is a complex phenomenon. We must begin to develop a patience for elegant answers—and a skeptical irritation toward quick and easy solutions that appear to be a panacea but derive from fragile rational grounds. The task is awesome. But excitement is high and the potential implications unlimited.

Chapter XII

Psychological Inquiry and Educational Practice

IN THE COURSE OF HIS PAPER, GAGNÉ ASSERTED THAT THE LEARNING of concepts did not generally entail a process of discovery. Students learn concepts through the use of verbal instructions while, on the other hand, young children probably acquire new concepts through discovery. The group was now led to ask for a clarification of the terms. What is an example of a new concept? Learning of a concept does not necessarily involve attaching a verbal label. It is only necessary for the learner to identify a wide variety of instances of the concept.

Another participant suggested that there is more to concepts than words. A concept is a theoretical construct, an abstraction created by the psychologist. It exists neither in imagery nor in words. A word is a package of concepts, and so is an image. There must be some way in which a perceptual input can communicate with an inner system of concepts. Some packages of concepts have phonetic things attached to them which make them pronounceable. However, any attempt to reduce conceptual thinking to the mere manipulation of words, necessarily leaves out many conceivable concepts. This is totally in keeping with our knowledge of the psychology of language.

In clarifying his use of the word *concept*, Gagné supplied the following illustration: If I teach you, as an adult, a new concept, for example, *caliche*, a term used by President Johnson in his State of the Union address, and give you a formal definition of it, as the crust of calcium carbonate that forms on top of the stony soil of arid regions, have you acquired a concept? One reply was that you have attached semantic markers to that name. It is now a bundle of concepts. You may have had the bundle of concepts before, but simply without a name. You may not be able to identify it without error even with the name, but you probably can do better than five minutes before. The

162

problem here is one of 'coding-in' the perceptual input to that particular package of concepts which you have now acquired.

Why is this called a bundle of concepts rather than a single concept? It is a single bundle! When one looks for a bundle, he looks for it in the same way that some look at the characteristics of a phoneme. The number of words in a language is finite, but the number of possible names is infinite. We put these bundles together as they are needed in referential distinctions in any particular time. We need this freedom in order to speak the language. The notion that all useful packages are preassembled and entered into the lexicon is simply unthinkable.

Gagné took the position that discovery must be regarded as an intervening process. If a student is not told an answer and finds it for himself, the intervening process must have been one of discovery. There are degrees of discovery which are probably inversely related to degrees of guidance. Guidance might take the form of supplying a large number of similar problems, all solvable by the same formula. Here you are giving a tremendous amount of guidance with the result that the amount of discovery involved in finding the formula is not large.

The topic now shifted to a consideration of what Kagan had called the paracognitive variables in the issue of learning by discovery. For example, has a child learned something different when he learns a rule inductively from what he learns by being told the rule first and then applying it? It was suggested that by allowing him to make mistakes in formulating the principle, he acquires the notion of a rule as something which is provisional, subject to later modification by experience. The rule-example method cannot lead, except by accident, to these outcomes. When the inductive method is adopted, the educational objective may be to teach children to modify and even throw away useless rules. Furthermore, when children learn by discovery, they are able to generalize their skills to solve problems that exist outside the classroom. This is similar to Cronbach's goal of intellectual independence. The teaching methods we have been calling discovery can most readily foster this kind of autonomy.

In his paper, Kagan had taken the position that for most children in the primary grades, learning is primarily a socially motivated enterprise; for many academic tasks are intrinsically boring. Social motivation is essential even though it is extrinsic to the school tasks. The discussion which followed dealt with the issue of whether the act of discovery was intrinsically motivating. Time and again, Bruner and others have maintained that there is a self-generating power to discovery. The question raised at this point was to what extent the intrinsic motivation of tasks might be fostered and used by teachers in the classroom. The answer appears related to individual differences; for any given child there must be some tasks which are intrinsically motivating. Using Kagan's categories, it appears that reflective children find tasks more intrinsically motivating than do impulsive children.

Through the course of the conference attempts were made to solve the problems of discovery in the reflected light of psychological theory. Both Gagné and Kagan attempted to generalize from their own bodies of psychological investigation to the instructional question of teaching and learning by discovery. How valid are such attempts? Can the gap between psychological and educational research be bridged? The deliberations of the discussants now centered about the following issues:

> What kinds of research strategies are most likely to generate findings relevant to the problems of developing curricula and appropriate teaching procedures?
>
> What is the status of psychological theory relative to problems of instruction?

The suggestion was made that some of the bi-fold or multi-fold methods that have been developed for looking at things like traffic flow patterns may serve as useful starting-points for a 'new look' in educational research. The traffic analyst maps out what happens and uses this map when trying to improve subsequent traffic flow. This may be a good analogy to what must be done in the field of education. This kind of approach, which one of the participants called classroom ecology, essentially suggests a modification in our over-all research strategy. We do not begin with experimental research. We try first to understand good examples of teaching and then use these as the input into subsequent experiments. Here was a position that was reiterated a number of times in the course of the conference deliberations.

How is it possible to carry out studies of sufficient complexity to meet the criteria outlined by Cronbach? Currently, in the field of psychology, there are a number of research strategies operating which show promise of converging on the basic issues at hand. These range on a continuum from the rather well-controlled studies in mathematical learning theory, computer simulation and programmed instruction, to direct observations of the classroom under grossly uncontrolled conditions. More important is the recognition that the naively simple question of discovery versus didactic teaching *per se* is really not very fruitful. Much more important are experiments to deal with such functional problems as, When do you verbalize in learning? or, How much does the instructor monitor, and how much is left for the student to check out his own verbalization? Hence, what is needed is a refurbishing of the basic paradigms utilized in curriculum research.

Further support was expressed for a practical orientation in teaching research. For example, we must attend to the structure of various pedagogical devices such as what constitute the criteria or characteristics of an effective lecture. A lecture, for example, generally provides no direct feedback for the teacher and rarely allows students to ask for clarification when they do not understand the presented material. What are the consequences of allowing questions during or after a lecture? What is the cognitive process of listening to, attending to, and understanding a lecture presentation? What really happens to the participants in a discussion class? Can subjects be trained to participate actively in the on-going process of discussion? Only with research of this practical kind can we in fact offer suggestions that have immediate pedagogical implications. We can do this only by using research strategies to better our knowledge of and appreciation for the structure of the educational system.

One member of the group raised the issue that, as a psychologist, he was much more concerned with special cases than he was with some of the more general problems being discussed by the group. He felt that the special problems were themselves already incredibly complex, and to expand the scope of our interests to these larger problems would quickly exceed the limits of our capabilities. He gave the example of an optimization scheme for paired-associate learning with which he was working. He does not really have a theory, except in the sense that meteorology has a theory. Meteorology has developed a set of useful statements for prediction purposes without any implication that these are parts of a systematic underlying theory with explanatory value. For example, we may know that certain configurations of high and low pressure areas are associated with certain weather phenomena to a high degree of probability, without suggesting that some theory of the upper atmosphere explains why this occurs. Psychology need not feel guilty about what it can only apply, but not necessarily explain. What we need is a theory on the same level as meteorology, not necessarily fitting the model of traditional psychological theories of learning.

A number of participants maintained that there was no problem of inadequate theory. Given a problem of instruction and classroom learning, it would be possible to analyze the stimuli which were input to the system of any child and the responses that constituted the output. Next, we could examine the relationships between groups of stimuli and responses. Present psychological theory was quite adequate to handle a problem of this form.

This position was opposed by another participant who felt that, although the essential problem may begin with the study of input and output, its adequate resolution goes well beyond that stage. There must be some understanding of the intervening system within the learner that transforms input into output. We must try to identify, in whatever terms will suffice, what these systems might be. Subsequently, we may try to decompose the system into components which make psychological sense. These components might be laws of association, i.e., ways of connecting Ss and Rs. In the more complex behavior studied by Piaget, what transforms the input into output is not far from statements of logic or mathematics. In fact, it appears that, for Piaget, there is not much psychology inside the child. There is really much more mathematics and logic. This participant took the position that the reason Piaget is so attractive to us today is that he is not really constructing a psychology of the child, but an epistemology instead. In terms of psychological theory, he maintained, we are bankrupt. Psychological theory as presently constituted is not built to measure these kinds of behavior. We simply do not have a psychology suitable for the teaching of a structured subject.

This position, which maintained the bankruptcy of psychological theory to handle the problem of the conference, now reiterated an earlier suggestion. The brilliant teacher is still the best instructional model available, far better than any theory. Here is where we ought to begin our research, not with theory, but with practice.

A participant now asserted that the issue had been put into either-or terms that were inappropriate and unrealistic. Since our theories are probably in bad shape for handling the more complex problems of education, we must get to work improving them as soon as possible. Meanwhile, however, we must continue to do empirical research in the classroom, even without better theories. The problem is simply too pressing to allow for any further delay. We must continue to engage in practical research without pause. A second discussant disagreed. He felt that refining our theories had priority over empirical research, for without better theories we will either find ourselves in the position of not knowing where to look for the relevant data, or of gathering quite a bit of data that will ultimately be useless.

One participant now suggested that the reason our theories were bankrupt was that psychologists, unlike meteorologists, had, throughout the history of the discipline, taken the easy way out. That is, instead of asking which questions were most critical to society and then developing techniques for dealing with these problems, psychology has preferred to remain tied to those problems which were most amenable to the safe, clean laboratory techniques that had been perfected. We turned our back on the questions that were pressing, but difficult, and instead did what we already knew how to do. Psychology has very successfully insulated itself from those essential problems of human behavior to which society has constantly been seeking answers.

Those who bemoan the sorry state of psychological theory tend to operate in a manner quite different than might be inferred from their declarations alone. We find they are still out in the classroom, engineering excitely, and gleaning all the insights they can from that very body of psychological theory whose puniness they are so quick to point out. Although they imply that education and psychology ought somehow to go their separate ways for the time-being, with psychological theories staying in the laboratory while educational research focuses on the classroom, they are surely not practicing this suggestion.

Is the issue really one of theory? We have not heretofore been in a position to gather the kinds of data in the classroom which are necessary to evaluate the relevant problems of complex human learning processes. It is this lack of a means for observing and analyzing these processes that has stymied us heretofore. However, we now have a growing computer-based technology with which we can go into classrooms and look at the problems of learning in greater detail. New techniques for teaching and studying the reading process are exemplary of this trend. As this research develops, it will have a much greater impact on the problems of education. With this observation, the discussion was brought to a close.

PART FIVE

THE CONFERENCE:
RETROSPECT AND PROSPECT

Chapter XIII

Reflections on the Conference

HOWARD H. KENDLER

IF NOTHING ELSE, THIS CONFERENCE HAS DEMONSTRATED THAT DIF-
FERENT linguistic communities, each with a different style of talking
and thinking, exist within both psychology and education. Perhaps the
intellectual distances between these communities have been exagger-
ated by all of the possible meanings that can be, and have been,
assigned to the concept of discovery, but there is no doubt that the
communities do, in fact, exist.

I will try to summarize the ideas put forth at this conference in
terms of the questions they raised. I am not completely confident that
I can report what happened, so I will protect myself by insisting that
I will report only what I think happened. This, hopefully, will be done
in a detached way without offering any value judgments—at least not
too many. Initially some remarks about the concept of discovery will
be made, then research strategy and theory will be discussed, and
finally some conclusions will be offered.

There is no disagreement that we failed to agree about the meaning of the concept of discovery. To say the least, the concept is
ambiguous. People have referred to it in a variety of ways, ranging
from phenomenal experience to a particular arrangement of a classroom situation. Perhaps most commonly discovery was equated with
some theoretical cognitive process, but the theory in which the
concept was embedded was not always crystal clear. This lack of
agreement about the meaning of discovery, although hampering communication, did not block it. When difficulties arose the participants
gracefully slipped back into common-language meanings of the term.
Although ordinary language is not the perfect vehicle for scientific
communication, it nevertheless possesses some capacity to transmit
ideas.

It was recognized that discovery cannot, and should not, be

equated with a laissez-faire educational philosophy. Students can be encouraged, prodded, and shaped to discover. In short, learning by discovery implies controlling the behavior of the student just as does the old-fashioned drill method. The only difference is the pattern of control.

One thing that I felt should have been emphasized more, although it was mentioned, is the relationship between discovery and language behavior. One of my own intuitions is that when a person discovers something, he is able to formulate it in his own language so that it fits in—that is, meshes—with his linguistic network. This allows him to retain and apply the idea he has discovered more effectively because it becomes part of a well-practiced and highly integrated habit system. On the other hand, if he is given the principle in somebody else's words, his own language system very often cannot absorb it. The idea does not really become a part of him. I know of very little research of this sort in the field of education, but I certainly think this kind of analysis might be useful.

Gagné desires to extend the concept of discovery to motor skills, a suggestion that probably surprised some participants since we think of discovery in relation to intellectual tasks that can be represented symbolically. But Gagné's idea is an interesting one, if only to focus attention upon what seems to be an apparent difference in discovering a mathematical principle and the correct way of hitting a golf ball.

Glaser offered a useful distinction between learning *by* discovery and learning *to* discover. This should help us break down the global concept of discovery into manageable components. Perhaps the distinction between discovery as assimilation and discovery as accommodation, to use Piaget's terms, will also prove useful.

The major focus of this conference was on what might be referred to as research strategy. Every scientist is, or should be, aware that every decision he makes cannot be justified by facts or logic. This is particularly true when one has to guess what kind of research problem will lead to fruitful results. If one does not want to be immobilized by doubts and fears, one must prejudge the potentialities of a research strategy in the absence of any convincing information of its ultimate worth. Differences in prejudgments is often at the root of controversy. In order to convince themselves that their prejudgments are correct, psychologists and educators often decide that only their prejudgments are appropriate; all others are misleading, sterile, and trivial. Such prejudice is unfortunate. If this conference has any positive value, some sort of tolerance and understanding of the different research strategies should develop. After this brief homily, let me now try to identify some of the different orienting attitudes that were expressed at this conference.

Differences existed about the need for operational definitions. At one end we have Hawkins, who emphasized the need to use concepts before one can actually define them. At the other extreme was the strong operational attitude of Glaser and, to the lesser extent, that of Gagné.

The participants disagreed about the relevance of experimental psychology to educational problems. Hawkins implied that it had little value as evidenced by the fact that he failed to mention any ideas or information from the traditional literature of the experimental psychology of learning except for one; the California latent-learning studies. As a person who was actively engaged in the latent-learning controversy, my advice to the philosopher Hawkins is to find a better model. The latent-learning model has a shaky empirical foundation. It is neither a clear-cut nor reliable phenomenon. It is influenced by a host of variables (e.g. swinging instead of guillotine doors in the maze) that are apparently of no relevance to learning by discovery.

Bruner also bemoaned the horrible state of experimental psychology and its inability to contribute anything of value to the classroom teacher. This has led him to get into the classroom and try to discover what, among different educational techniques, will work. Then, hopefully, the successful technique can be analyzed and its important factors can be uncovered. Bruner and Hawkins can be grouped together in their belief that the significant educational research will come from the classroom. I doubt whether Bruner accepts this principle as enthusiastically as does Hawkins, since this would mean turning his back on some of his own past efforts. At the other extreme, we find Glaser, Gagné, and Wittrock quoting data from the experimental psychology laboratory. The conflict between the Hawkins-Bruner axis and the Glaser-Gagné-Wittrock entente represents, upon analysis, a difference of opinion about the kind of behavior we should try to predict. Should we stick out our necks and try to predict 'real live' classroom behavior, or should we investigate more circumscribed educational situations and try to find the principles that govern behavior within them, and then on the basis of sophisticated intuition extend the principles to the classroom situation? I prefer the latter approach. With simple mathematical, physical, or social-science problems, the behavior of large groups of subjects in well controlled situations can be measured and analyzed, and theoretical principles formulated. But my preference is a prejudice, a prejudgment that cannot be demonstrated to be true, or even to be the most strategic.

Another basic problem raised was that of assessing educational techniques. All educational practices sooner or later should be assessed. No disagreement exists here. The problem is when and how the assessment should take place. A novel educational technique cannot get off the ground if it is obsessed initially with problems of assessment. The problem is when assessment procedures should be incorporated within an educational research program.

How should we assess educational techniques? That is, what outcome variables should we select? The discussion can begin by referring to Cronbach's list of twelve outcome variables—all of which represent to varying degrees value judgments about different forms of behavior. Kagan agreed that value judgments were involved but concluded that we educators and psychologists should make the decision. I do not disagree with him completely, but I would like society to play a larger role in the decision-making process. When psychologists are involved in establishing social values in a democracy, they should be very cautious and not confuse personal prejudices with scientific truths. I resonate to Cronbach's list but it can be used insensitively. For example, how would the final item in Cronbach's list, 'creative urge', be applied to the education of the mental retardate and the low normal. Should we try to instill in them a creative urge? Should we try to build intellectual ambitions in people who have not got the ability to achieve these goals?

Assessing educational procedures became more complicated when other factors were brought into the picture. Glaser emphasized cognitive characteristics of the student, represented in terms of stimulus-response associations, while Kagan discussed the interaction between personality variables and educational techniques. It seems that whenever an educational problem is analyzed its complexity increases.

The goals of education were also discussed. Hawkins, representing one extreme, more or less felt we should ignore them. Educate the child and the goals will be achieved. Cronbach insisted we had to be concerned with goals. As a psychologist, I think we can say with some degree of confidence, that our discipline has been successful in controlling behavior only when we know the kind of behavior we want to encourage. To put it in terms of specific examples, when we train people to be effective pilots or efficient radio code operators, we can develop techniques to select and train them. When we try to train people to be adjusted, we run into difficulty because we are uncertain what adjusted behavior is. Psychology often seems ineffective only because we are uncertain about what kind of behavior we want to encourage. Once we are sure what behavior we want to encourage, the chances of developing techniques to get people to behave in this manner improves tremendously. The effectiveness of psychology in solving educational problems will be proportional to the precision with which our educational goals are stated.

An interesting point about evaluating different educational programs was raised by Cronbach. What constitutes a control group in such assessment studies? I have become convinced that there is no such thing as a simple control group in any experimental situation. Control groups are generated by theories, and one control group is relevant to some theoretical assumptions and not to others. However, Cronbach, the pragmatist, suggests a rather interesting way of handling the problem of control groups: Limit different educational programs to the same time allotment and then see which is better. Now this seems to be a solution, but quite obviously you can have two programs which have a different effect with one time limit and have an entirely opposite effect with another time limit. How would you discover this if the two programs were compared under only one time limit? An educator can be fooled about the potential of an educational program if he limits his assessment to one arbitrary time unit.

What kind of a theory do we want? The participants differed about this issue. Bruner has a global theory. I resonate to it in spirit but not in content. I believe that everything that Bruner said could be translated into language involving habits, drives, mediational processes, and response-produced cues. He emphasized contrast effects; there are data from discrimination learning which would agree with his analysis. Gagné offers a systematic analysis within the S-R tradition, but it is obvious that it would not be acceptable to all participants. The qualities of Bruner's global theory and Gagné's theory are different, and personal preference of one over the other reflects an individual's predilection, to some extent, in favor of certain concepts and theoretical structures.

Wittrock structured the problem in terms of a theoretical formulation which distinguished independent, intervening, and dependent variables. Although I have some sympathy with this, I would like to point out that this is a model for a theory, but not necessarily the pattern for discovering the theory. I do not know what the pattern is, but I think we tend too frequently to confuse philosophy of science, or the principle of some philosophers of science, with the techniques of achieving the theory.

To me, the major theoretical problem of education is one of understanding language behavior and controlling it. I was disappointed by the limited references to language behavior at the conference. Cronbach cited the quotation that we learn not by doing, but by thinking about what we do. I interpret this to reflect the importance of language behavior on educational processes.

There is certainly no agreement about what strategy we should pursue, and to some extent this is good. In some ways it would be unfortunate if we were all doing the same thing, even though we might then have greater agreement. Can anyone have complete confidence that his research strategy will be productive? Cronbach concluded that we should be hospitable to new ideas, be skeptical, do good research, and be willing to advise the schools. Of course, quite unconsciously, no doubt, he was describing himself. Perhaps there should be some division of labor. Perhaps in addition to the solid, socially sensitive researcher we need the messiah who stirs things up, causes confusion, but nevertheless gets people to test out new ideas.

Kagan emphasized areas that are too often ignored by specialists in learning and cognitive processes. These areas are motivation and personality. Some discussion revolved about the problem of whether scholarly motives were generated in the student by other people (e.g., teacher) or by problems and ideas themselves. To me, it seems obvious that motives can emerge from both sources.

Let me conclude by making two brief points. If we emphasize the importance of identifying the behavior we wish to predict then perhaps we must get involved more in social planning. If we encourage certain kinds of behavior in schools we should be sure that these forms of behavior will be reinforced in the outside world. Otherwise we may find ourselves encouraging maladaptive responses.

No great desire was expressed among the participants to preserve the term 'discovery.' I would like to vote for its elimination. This is not a criticism of the concept of discovery. In the history of science, often concepts are extremely important until you analyze them and discover that they can be broken down into more fundamental components. I believe, with Morrisett, that this is the case here. Even though at various times Maier and others have had tremendous justification to use this term, it has become a nine-letter dirty word and we ought to eliminate it. Let us start with new words emphasizing more analytical approaches as we continue to attack the problems of education.

Chapter XIV

Further Reflections

LLOYD N. MORRISETT

HOWARD KENDLER HAS GIVEN US AN EXCELLENT REVIEW OF THE CON-ference. He accepted the responsibility to be rational and detached. As a result, I am able to be a bit irresponsible and offer some personal conclusions without necessarily being able to justify them fully.

My first conclusion is that the idea of discovery is useful for teachers and for people who are building curricula. Conversely, I doubt very much that the term has great utility for people doing research in psychology and education.

Teachers and curriculum builders may find the concept of discovery useful as a guide in the presentation of classroom materials, in the kinds of materials that they choose, and in the ways in which curriculum materials are sequenced. Discovery may thus have a place in a theory of instruction, if you conceive of a theory of instruction being useful in classroom practice.

However, even here, I think there are limits. Applying Bruner's dictum that we should sometimes push ideas to the limit to see how far they can go, I am sure we can all imagine situations in classes and curricula where discovery can be dysfunctional for learning. For example, this can happen when the discovery becomes punishing, either because the student discovers punishing information about himself or because he is led to discover something that he later finds is trivial or could have been learned more easily. In the first case the student may discover that he is slow while others are quick, or that a respected teacher's values are different from his own and his family's. It may be argued that this information can be used constructively, but to do so something must be added to discovery teaching. In the second case, a student can easily be given too little information or asked the wrong questions so that discovery becomes drudgery. This may still be called discovery, but I doubt that we would call it good teaching.

The use of discovery in teaching to build the student's confidence in his own ability to think and solve problems is certainly a highly desirable goal. As Hawkins pointed out, it may well be that in the year 1965 this is the direction in which education should be pushed, because it has been very badly overbalanced in other directions. However, other virtues that we would like to encourage through education are intellectual humility and the ability to accept the work of others. I am not sure that intellectual humility will necessarily be produced through the discovery technique. Complete reliance on discovery refutes culture.

A final comment along this line concerns the importance of knowing when to stop a line of fruitless thought or investigation. If you sort out highly creative people from those who are less creative, it is my impression that the creative person frequently stops early in an unproductive train of thought, while the less creative person takes longer to stop. How do you teach this? I do not know of any relevant studies, but I think it is important to consider the value of terminating unproductive thought sequences at the same time that we are trying to give people confidence in their intellectual abilities through the use of discovery techniques in teaching. Discovery is important, but so is knowing when to stop.

One contrast that I am trying to draw is between the usefulness of a concept in a theory of instruction, in curriculum building, and in teaching on the one hand, and in psychological and educational research on the other. So far, I think, the problem of defining the unit of behavior that is germane to a theory has not been considered at all effectively except at the level of psychological research. Here the work of Atkinson and others interested in mathematical modeling is impressive in the degree to which they have tried to specify the units of behavior to which their models will apply. A theory of instruction must also face this issue. What is to be discovered—stimuli, responses, concepts, relations, theories, or something else? Is discovery teaching equally relevant to all these goals? I think we have relatively little feeling about the definition and size of the units of behavior we are talking about when we refer to learning by discovery.

The concept of discovery is not very helpful in psychological and educational research because there is little evidence that it is useful in pointing to classes of variables that cannot be better designated by theoretically relevant names. Several papers have illustrated this. While both Glaser and Gagné were willing to talk about discovery, their papers could have been given without using the term 'discovery' at all. Glaser took somewhat of a relativistic position and said that if you wanted to call it discovery, this is the way he would talk about it. Gagné said that he would talk about some things that involve discovery, but if you leave discovery out we can still talk about those same things.

The concept of discovery seems to refer, at different times, to motivational effects, reinforcing effects, and heuristic or mediating effects of sequences of behavior. The first two, need little comment. The process of discovery can be highly involving and sustain task-relevant behavior. A discovery can also, quite obviously, be personally satisfying and tend to increase the probability that similar behavior will recur. In some areas of intellective performance, useful problem solving heuristics are known and can be taught. In other areas, however, teachable heuristics are not well known. Several speakers have made the point that discovery teaching may allow students to invent their own heuristics when recognized teachable heuristics are not available. Intuition and other important but poorly defined abilities may well involve the use of indiosyncratic heuristics, and these modes of thought may be encouraged by discovery teaching.

The second main conclusion that I have drawn as I listened to the discussion, is that research on the topic of discovery, as judged by both Wittrock's review and our discussions, is relatively impoverished. It is impoverished first in the range of variables that have been considered. Cronbach's, Kagan's, and Bruner's papers all pointed toward the conclusion that the main things we know about learning by discovery have also been found important in other areas of psychological research. This may be because the range of variables being studied has been restricted and that attention to the interaction of learning by discovery with personality variables, previous experience, and teacher behavior will reveal new knowledge. If not, this becomes further justification for discarding learning by discovery as a research topic.

A second kind of impoverishment in this research is the impoverishment of the subject matters that have been studied. We talk as if learning by discovery was a generally interesting phenomena, but the work is almost entirely in mathematics and the sciences. This is a serious deficit both to educational research and to the utility of discovery in teaching. I wonder if learning by discovery, as we have been discussing it, is thought to be useful in building curricula in the humanities and arts. Perhaps so, but the meaning of learning by discovery will probably change when we move from mathematics, through the sciences, to the humanities and arts.

I conclude with a very general comment on the kinds of statements that have been made throughout the conference regarding values and educational philosophy. One of the beliefs most commonly shared by scientists is that application of rational thought will lead to human progress. This theme has been a *leitmotif* in our conference. This is very natural, for, as research scientists and psychologists, this is a necessary part of our value system—necessary in order that we engage ourselves in research effectively. As we have talked about learning by discovery, we have implied that this method of learning will necessarily lead people to rational decisions and better lives. Is this, however, any more of a panacea than any other educational method? Educational statistics show higher percentages of age groups in high-school and college. More people than ever before are being exposed to education. Good, bad, or indifferent, I suspect that increased education increases rationality, the ability to be critical, and the ability to learn by discovery. I wonder, however, if this education is inclining people to build a better society. Do people make the right choices? As Kagan asked, Have we made the value commitments that lead students to the right choices? Do they learn about the good and the beautiful and things of enduring value, or do they discover things of less worth? No education is value-free, and a commitment to rational discovery as a method of learning may ignore issues that we cannot afford to turn aside.

Chapter XV

The Problem of Discovery: Conference in Retrospect

EVAN R. KEISLAR
LEE S. SHULMAN

THE CONTROVERSY OVER LEARNING BY DISCOVERY EXISTS SIMULTANEOUS-
ly at a number of levels. These levels include those of classroom instruction, curriculum development, psychological studies of learning, and
research strategy. Hence, in order to deal with this issue in some
meaningful fashion, it becomes necessary to distinguish among these
levels of discourse and to specify at which level we are operating at any
given moment.

At the level of classroom instruction, the question to be studied
is, As I teach Johnny, should I give him a wide variety of examples and
expect him to infer the underlying rule, or should I tell him what the
rule is while he applies it to examples?

At the level of curriculum development, the question involves
something like the following: To what extent ought the order of subjects into which the students inquire be determined by us, and to what
extent should this order be determined by the students themselves?

At the level of psychological investigations of learning, the question becomes, What is the transfer value of statements of principles
given to a subject, as contrasted with individually-derived principles?

At the level of research strategy, the issue takes on a very different,
yet parallel form: What is the most fruitful way to investigate the
nature of instruction?

It is the purpose of this chapter to reexamine the contributions of
the conference members within the framework just described. One of
the difficulties is that the participants tended to shift back and forth
among levels. We will thus distinguish among the levels of discourse
implicity or explicitly utilized by contributors, and will examine the
extent to which consensus or disagreement resulted. We will also attempt to outline the important questions, as we see them, remaining at

each of these levels. Thus, though this chapter is, in fact, a view of the conference in retrospect, it might also be seen as a prospectus for further dialogues.

THE LEVEL OF CLASSROOM INSTRUCTION

When we explore the meaning of the learning-by-discovery issue for classroom teachers, we need to ask what the statements on this question will lead teachers to do. Sentences which are worded in the form of clear specific suggestions are likely to elicit greater uniformity in teacher practice than statements where the referents are unclear. However, since teachers relate to their pupils in a highly complex fashion, even phrases which have vague denotations may have profound and varied effects on teaching styles. Instructions such as Help the child to discover the solutions by himself, might lead some teachers to undertake a most productive lesson; conversely, this same statement might lead other teachers, with the best of intentions, to let many pupils flounder entirely too long.

When the assertion was made at the conference that research studies had not yet produced evidence to support the hypothesis of learning by discovery, concern was expressed that the publication of this statement could have ill effects on teacher behavior. It was hinted that some teachers might go back to a learning-by-rote approach to teaching if it were implied that learning by discovery had been discredited. While no one at the conference perceived the issue in terms of this dichotomy, the importance of examining the kind of statements made to teachers cannot be ignored.

One way of posing the issue, therefore, is in terms of teacher behavior: How much and what kind of guidance should the teacher provide? Attempts to offer answers to this question have usually been expressed at a common-sense level, such as that found in the following selections from *Theory and Practice of Teaching:*

> It is always a very difficult question for the teacher to settle, 'How far shall I help the pupil and how far shall the pupil be required to help himself?' . . . That the pupil should be taught mainly to depend on his own resources . . . is the teaching of common sense. Whatever is learned, should be so thoroughly learned, that the next and higher step may be comparatively easy. And the teacher should always inquire, when he is about to dismiss one subject, whether the class understands it so well that they can go on to the next. He may, indeed, sometimes give a word of suggestion during the preparation of a lesson, and by a

seasonable hint, save the scholar the needless loss of much time. But it is a very greater evil if the pupils acquire the habit of running to the teacher as soon as a slight difficulty presents itself, to request him to remove it. . . . The inquirer should never be frowned upon; this will diminish his self-reliance without enlightening him; for whatever is done for a scholar without his having studied closely upon it himself, makes but a feeble impression upon him, and is soon forgotten. The true way is, neither to discourage inquiry nor answer the question. Converse with the scholar a little as to the principles involved in the question; refer him to principles which he has before learned, or has now lost sight of; perhaps call his attention to some rule or explanation before given to the class; go just so far as to enlighten him a little and *put him on the scent,* then leave him to achieve the victory himself (Page, 1885).

This excerpt, first written in 1847, dramatizes how little what is said to the average classroom teacher has changed over the past century. The quotation might easily have been taken from an article written for teachers today.

How did the conference deal with this problem of specifying the nature and amount of guidance to be supplied by the classroom teacher? There was general agreement among the conference participants that the degree of guidance by the teacher varies from time to time along a continuum, with almost complete direction of what the pupil must do at one extreme to practically no direction at the other. This was illustrated in both of the examples of teaching presented by Cronbach and Davis. We may here add a third illustration. A teacher introduces a group of students to a totally new subject-matter area, for example, surveying, simply by arranging a wide variety of materials such as instruments, maps, and so forth, across the classroom. There is no overt guidance here from the teacher in the form of clear-cut distinctions between correct and incorrect student responses. Hence, there is little probability of behavior that could be called 'error' on the part of the students.

Subsequently, the teacher might shift to a second phase wherein she provides almost full guidance for the students. They are given very careful practice in using the surveying instruments and in recording their observations. After they have acquired some of the basic skills, the teacher might demonstrate how certain kinds of problems are handled in surveying flat land. When the students have understood some of these possible applications, she then poses the question of surveying other types of terrain. Students would be expected to arrive at a number of possible solutions to these general questions with little guidance from the teacher.

As the class progresses, the teacher may thus provide sometimes more and sometimes less guidance, depending on her objectives and the performance of the students. Here, in a period of a few days, a teacher may have manifested behavior that ranged from little guidance to full guidance and it would seem patently absurd in this context to ask the question of which degree of guidance was best. This question can only be asked in terms of the specific situation in which a decision about guidance must be made. Clearly, it is more relevant to ask, specifically, Given the subject matter, the kind of students in the class, the objectives to be attained, and what the students have previously learned, what kind and how much guidance is best?

The conference brought out the distinction between what the teacher might do during a given lesson when she, for example, is helping the students to induce a rule, and what she might do during the days and weeks and months prior to that event to prepare the students to profit from this learning experience. The period of preparation, for Hawkins, would involve experiences of exploration during which a student learned the lay of the land for the subject to be mastered. It would require teacher planning, selection, and arrangement of materials, so that related objects could be seen together and compared by the learner. This form of guidance does differ from guided instruction with respect to the scope of sequential decisions left to the students and to the student's perception of the extent to which he is being directed. For example, the student makes his own decisions on such questions as, What should I look at first?

While this period of antecedent criss-crossing of a field may be considered as undirected by the teacher, it depends upon careful teacher planning and is as profound in its effects as directed instruction. For example, the teacher should thoughtfully arrange the materials in a classroom so that the exploration is likely to be most profitable. What the student will look at first may be determined, for example, by placing the object to be noted in an eye-catching location. While the student is clearly making his own decisions in these explorations, the range of alternatives available to him has been somewhat constrained and directed by the teacher's preparation of the situation.

In his paper, Bruner suggested six ways in which teachers may prepare pupils for discovery. He would include such devices as having pupils learn strategies and heuristics for attacking problems, teaching them to select and use information, helping them make full use of their own self-cues, and cultivating appropriate motives. So prepared, children would not have to resort to blind trial-and-error in order to discover. Teachers' guidance would also involve helping children locate and master the essential information they need; no one suggests that children should discover all facts anew.

Is it possible to *prepare* a student to learn by discovery, using a direct program of guidance? A sequence of learning activities, based on an hierarchical analysis of the task, might be highly effective by assuring competency in the prerequisite abilities for the inductive experience. Gagné reported one study to support such a possibility but the evidence still is fragmentary.

What can be said about the particular lesson in which a teacher expects her pupils to learn inductively? The guidance she provides at this point can take many different forms. She may set the stage for the desired behavior by posing a problem, revealing a paradox, or directing the learner's attention to a problem-filled situation. She may need to supply broad general instructions to direct the learner's attention somewhat more appropriately. She will, presumably, have structured the environment so that the student will obtain relevant information as a consequence of his own efforts. She may even provide general hints or indirect clues affording further guidance; but she does not, of course, provide the solution directly. It is thus clear that there are many dimensions along which the amount of guidance may be considered.

The conference also examined the dilemma of meeting individual differences when the inductive teaching method is used with a group. If the questions are posed for group discussion, the most competent pupils in the class are likely to make all of the discoveries. It was pointed out that in such a class situation there is heightened activity on the part of all members because of competition, demand for social approval, and so forth. A critical question involves what is learned by that large portion of the class which does not participate actively but simply listens to the few discoverers. Is their learning indistinguishable from that of students who have been taught the same material didactically? Is there some additional advantage to having been a participant, albeit vicariously, in an inductive learning experience? These are pivotal questions in the learning-by-discovery controversy which appear quite amenable to empirical study.

How can the teacher tell whether she has provided the right amount and kind of guidance during a lesson? One alternative is to ask herself, Has the student discovered? and proceed to get evidence as to whether or not the act of discovery has occurred. On the other hand, she may turn her attention directly to the outcomes of the experience and ask whether students demonstrate new abilities and values without reference to the hidden act of discovery. In either case, she must ultimately see if the learner is now able to deal effectively with a broader class of problems as a consequence of her instruction. The teacher may or may not find it helpful to use the language of discovery for this purpose.

Whether one chooses to talk about the effects of guidance in terms of an inferred internal act or its observable consequences is a reflection of one's point-of-view about instructional goals. In the former case, it is assumed that the inferred, covert event of 'discovery' is to be sought, in and of itself, as a major objective. In the second case, the observable outcomes are the primary criteria; less attention is paid to the intervening events. Which way is best? This question is a reflection of the issue of 'process' versus 'product,' and will be examined in the following section.

In any event, two conclusions for classroom instruction are clear: (1) There is no useful way of posing a broad question regarding how much and what kind of guidance the teacher should supply. The question should always be formulated for a specific context including the type of subject, the maturity of the pupils, prior learning experiences and so on. (2) Regardless of which way of talking about learning by discovery is adopted, no single teaching method is likely to accomplish the wide range of cognitive and affective objectives discussed at the conference.

THE LEVEL OF CURRICULUM DEVELOPMENT

At the level of curriculum, two kinds of decisions are made. One deals with the 'oughts' of education: What objectives do we choose as the goals of our teaching? The other decision reflects the general organization and patterning of subject areas and topics, 'scope and sequence,' in the language of the curriculum-writers: How do we organize a subject matter and identify the order in which it is taught?

At the conference, the questions which dealt with the identification of goals for education took two forms: (1) What is the role of the psychologist in making value judgments which influence the activity of educational institutions? (2) What form is most appropriate for the statement of educational objectives?

The first of these two questions created more consternation than possibly any other raised at the conference. It was generally agreed that psychology is a science which deals with the description, prediction, and, ultimately, control of human behavior. Does this then provide the psychologist with uniquely relevant insights concerning the most fruitful directions in which to modify that behavior? Participants seemed to divide into three camps. Some felt that, as scientists of human behavior, they are obliged to extrapolate their understanding into objectives for education. Others felt that, considerations of psychology aside, they have this obligation as individual private citizens who happen to be psychologists. A third group reflected the position that psychologists must actively avoid involving themselves in such controversies, because of the necessity for continually emphasizing that science deals with the description of nature and not with the manner in which it ought to be modified. This was a deep-seated disagreement for which no hint of resolution was forthcoming at the conference.

On the second question, the form in which objectives must be stated, discussions were somewhat more fruitful. Concerning the topic, the arguments pivoted around the question of whether statements of educational objectives ought to be made in operational terms which identify in detail the behaviors to be acquired. On those occasions when clear-cut descriptions of desired behaviors have been employed, psychologists have often been successful in producing the desired outcomes. Yet, to some participants, the notion of discovery in learning connoted the very antithesis of such behavioral control. Discovery implies diversity; teaching for specified objectives suggests conformity to a model. Discovery implies novelty and unpredictability; instruction for predetermined goals suggests imitation and constraint. At times, these participants seemed to be defining themselves out of business. They implied that true discovery behavior cannot be defined a priori, or it is not discovery. Their goal was to 'open up' the pupil, and they maintained that attempts to define this outcome behaviorally constrain the young scholar. Yet, the dual function of stated objectives is to suggest courses of action on the one hand, and, on the other, to provide a set of standards for evaluating the consequences of action. If one's goal statements are not specific and subject to subsequent evaluation, how do they differ from a vague poetic set of pious pronouncements?

As we read between the lines of controversy, one possible interpretation emerges. A good deal of what semanticists call 'bypassing' was occurring in these dialogues. Participants disagreed to a great extent because they were focusing on different aspects of learning behavior. Those favoring goal-directed teaching were concerned with 'what' questions—What is to be learned, and What methods are most appropriate to that end? Those favoring open-ended teaching were also concerned

187

with what is to be learned, but they give a higher priority to the question, of How is it to be learned? In many ways, the old distinction between process and product in psychology is reflected in these disagreements. At present, and for the foreseeable future, psychologists can make far more precise and communicable statements about product variables and their control than they can about the more ephemeral range of intervening process variables. We simply lack a reliable language for discussing processes, and the ambiguity of the term discovery as a process-referent is a case in point. Does open-endedness deny the importance of clear-cut objectives? We doubt it. On the other hand, does goal-directedness imply that openness and autonomy are unacceptable human goals? Probably not. The emphasis is simply upon the present inaccessibility of such constructs to scientific explication and investigation.

Those supporting open-ended teaching correctly insist that psychologists attend to the multi-level complexity of the learning process, i.e., that the child who learns a new concept is simultaneously, if incidentally, learning ways to understand future concepts, ideas about the stability or tentativeness of concepts in general, as well as some perceptions about himself as a conceiver. Yet, in focusing upon these important processes, they too often ignore or pay too little attention to the specific learning task from which the others are derived. We not only wish students to discover as an end in itself; we wish them to discover something which will contribute to their further growth, and thus serve as a basis for new learning.

Participants favoring goal-directed teaching were accused of saying, If you can't measure it, don't try to teach it. It appears likely that some participants, while rejecting such a statement, in practice reflect the narrowness implied by the comment; they give little attention to broadening the range of outcomes measured in education. While progress in bringing 'fuzzy' goals within the purview of measurement will not alter the basic issue, at the practical level it can alter the importance given to it.

We may now move briefly to the questions of scope and sequence in the curriculum. By overemphasis upon the process of discovery, one group of participants tended to denigrate the engineering of learning, i.e., the careful planning of sequences of activities through which students will attain desired objectives. Hawkins called attention to Tolman's finding that rats presumably benefit from unreinforced and, hence, undirected, exploration. In contrast, those who speak in terms of the careful planning or programming of learning sequences seem to ignore the possible educative consequences of relatively unguided exploratory activity.

We would direct both groups to the wisdom of Dewey's *Experience and Education*. The first position reflects the folly of Progressive Education (as distinct from progressive) which sacrificed necessary *experience* to momentary *experiencing*. The second position resembles Traditional Education (again in Dewey's sense) which used the subject-matter to be learned as the starting point and too often treated the pupil as a learning machine.

The different emphases on process and product may be seen in another light. Those who favored stressing the act of discovery did not regard such events necessarily to be beyond the scope of evaluation in terms of outcomes. They objected to the premature application of external criteria to such a method. This point of view essentially was saying, Let us focus our attention on how to teach children to discover more effectively as a way of learning; later on we can find out the relationship between this process of learning and overall outcomes. To some extent, but probably not entirely, the disagreement reflected a difference in strategy, rather than a fundamental divergence in value systems.

Another way in which the curriculum problem has been posed is whether the activities of students studying a subject matter ought to parallel the activities of the practitioners of the discipline themselves or whether the learning of a subject content, e.g., physics, demands a structure quite different from that of the discipline qua object of inquiry. The implication is that the activity of scientists is discovery, in contrast to the traditional activity of students, reception learning. This, however, is much too facile, and resembles a verbalism more than a viable distinction.

Quite clearly, scientists do not spend all their time discovering. They exhibit a broad range of activities, from hypothesis-generation and model-building to listening to lectures and reading journal articles reporting someone else's research. Hence, justification of curriculum development which stresses inductive teaching on the grounds that induction is the *sine qua non* of scientific behavior is a half-truth, at best. Scientists do discover, it is true. That they also engage in a wealth of additional activities is also true. That many of these are didactic or receptive in nature is apparent. It is further clear that whether a scientist induces, deduces, plays hunches, or looks up answers in trade books, is contingent not upon the values of those processes in themselves, but on what he intends to accomplish in a given situation. If one wishes to emphasize the analogy of the scientist to the student, one cannot ignore that in science, decisions about means are dictated by goals.

What then can be said about the issue of learning by discovery and the area of curriculum development? First, unless some consensus can be reached about the statement of objectives, there is little reason to continue dialogues regarding methods of teaching. The question of the superiority of one curriculum over another is moot if the objectives of each are stated in mutually incompatible terms. One approach would be the extension of present efforts in educational measurement to develop procedures which assess far more complex behaviors than has been done up to now. We need more adequate measures of the kinds of outcomes in Cronbach's list, such as 'creative urge,' and 'openness.' As long as our present objective criteria are deemed utterly inadequate, debate concerning the general question of process versus product will remain clouded.

Second, process and product variables are not inexorably labeled as such, but are definable only in terms of the other variables to which they are referred. Thus, problem-solving can be a process variable in one context and a product variable in another.

Third, the activities of scientists vary too greatly from day to day and man to man to be used as the model justifying any single curricular strategy based on discovery.

Fourth, a curriculum refers to the organization and sequence of a subject matter in which statements about that subject, methods of teaching, and the activities of the learners are intricately interrelated to form a single entity. Research at this level, as distinct from the level of specific acts of instruction or general psychological processes, should include the study of the consequences of the curriculum as a whole. The effects of a particular segment of a curriculum may be quite different *in vivo* than they are when studied in isolation from the rest of that curriculum. If research is to be relevant to curriculum development and evaluation, the research must be conducted at the same level of abstraction as are the decision-alternatives which confront the curriculum workers. This does not exclude the possibility of using such overall evaluation in a diagnostic sense, to throw light, for example, on those aspects of the curriculum which need improvement. But the issue of learning by discovery will not be adequately assessed until we can obtain a broad evaluative base to assess the effectiveness of the curriculum.

THE LEVEL OF PSYCHOLOGICAL INVESTIGATIONS OF LEARNING

One of the major questions posed for this conference was the following: What conclusions can be drawn from the research evidence to date regarding the effectiveness of the method of learning by discovery?

Examination of both the exhaustive reviews of the literature and deliberations of the conference lead to an inescapable conclusion: The question as stated is not amenable to research solutions because the implied experimental treatment, the discovery method, is far too ambiguous and imprecise to be used meaningfully in an experimental investigation. Where investigators have spelled out learning by discovery in terms of a set of educational procedures, the results have been equivocal. For example, there is no evidence that supports the proposition that having students encounter a series of examples of a generalization and then requiring them to induce the rule is superior to teaching the rule first and asking the students to apply it to a wide variety of examples.

Wittrock's review indicated that research has not yet done justice to the magnitude and complexity of the problem. One basic difficulty is that of precise description of procedures. Studies purportedly designed to assess this question have used the same term to apply to a wide variety of instructional activities. In some experiments the name 'rote learning' is applied to a treatment which other investigations call 'discovery.' Unfortunately, not enough information is supplied to enable the reader to identify the precise procedures under either label.

Instead of debating whether or not to call a treatment by the label 'discovery,' we should insist that published reports include a clear description of the events which comprise the treatment or lesson, as well as a few typical examples of each of the instructional procedures being contrasted. In some studies, a complete record might be made available in the form of a program, a tapescript, a film, or a typed record which would be available on request. When such details are available to experimenters, reanalysis and replication of studies is possible. For example, the conference members generally agreed that the filmed demonstration lesson shown by Davis was excellent group teaching, even though the interpretations of what was happening in those filmed lessons differed widely.

A fundamental question from which much of this disagreement derived was related to the nature and the role of unobservable mediating events in learning. The participants who treated discovery as an internal event considered it to be different from the processes that characterize reception or didactic learning. How can one know when such a covert act of discovery has occurred? This hidden event is always an inference based on several kinds of evidence, among which the following are minimal criteria:

1) Although the learner may have access to a good deal of information prior to solving a problem, the identification of the solutions themselves must never be part of the information he is given.

2) The learner must be able to generalize the solution to other situations. If no such transfer is evident, the successful first solution is considered an accident and not a discovery.

There were four different approaches represented at the conference, differing with respect to the value of internal events, the use of the word 'discovery' to apply to these events, and the importance of the act of discovery as a goal.

The first group of participants discarded the whole issue of covert mediational mechanisms as having no practical relevance. They maintained the researcher should focus directly on the relationship between the environmental changes a teacher introduces (the input variable) and what a student consequently learns to do (the output variable); the language of mediation is excess baggage.

Most of the participants in the conference, however, took the position that a discussion of mediating mechanisms is necessary for any fruitful investigation of learning by discovery. Of this number, a second group felt that the mediating mechanisms of language play a central role in the educational process. In his reflections on the conference, Kendler regretted that greater attention had not been given to a discussion of language. He felt that investigators should study the ways in which students can be helped to incorporate new experiences into preexisting linguistic structures so as to produce optimal learning in subsequent situations. Thus, the second group recognized the value of talking about internal events, but felt that this could be done more efficiently if the centrality of language for these mediating processes were emphasized.

A third group, represented by Gagné, used the term, 'discovery', in an exceedingly broad sense. Gagné maintained that a learner is discovering if he is engaged in any process involving search and selection. This would include the acquisition of many motor skills (such as learning to hit a golf ball), simple verbal learning (such as paired-associates, for which appropriate mediators might be found), as well as more complex verbal learning (such as concept formation, or the derivation of rules for solving various classes of problems).

A fourth group of participants limited the use of the word discovery to cognitive areas of learning. Some members of this group saw the critical process as one wherein the student by himself sought a match between models he had stored in his own head and objects, sets of objects, or events experienced about him. This process could be seen as operating at different levels of discovery. Finding a stored model to fit the problem event exactly, e.g., seeing that all words in an anagram task were coded by being written backwards, was an example of a little-d discovery. On the other hand, big-D discoveries were involved in cases where the stored models themselves had to be restructured or recombined in order to make a fit, as might be the case when a student constructs a general principle under which he can subsume and integrate a series of isolated rules previously learned in a somewhat mechanical fashion.

For this last group, the internal process of search and selection, this act of discovery, was seen as the essence of what the student is learning. Bruner, for example, was more concerned with devising procedures to foster this act of discovery than he was with evaluating the valuable consequences of the act itself. Such evaluation, he felt, could come later. It is this emphasis on the act of discovery, per se, which distinguishes the fourth group from the other three. For the rest of the participants, regardless of how they differed concerning the value of talking about mediating mechanisms, there was greater interest in measurable progress with respect to educational outcomes.

The conference gave some attention to the frameworks within which research on this topic might proceed. There was disagreement, however, regarding the usefulness of psychological theory as a basis for deriving questions and launching new studies. Several participants felt that psychological concepts and tools were ill-suited for the complexities of classroom endeavors, and Hawkins suggested that the practitioner's common-sense way of talking might be more valuable than scientific language. On the other hand, as we noted earlier, Kendler and others emphasized that more precise terms are exactly what we need.

A large number of promising suggestions for future research were presented during the conference. The previous papers have described in detail these proposed directions. In particular, both the critical reviews of Wittrock and Cronbach offered specific as well as general suggestions for the improvement of research investigations concerning this problem. Cronbach, for example, advocated focusing on a narrow problem under limited circumstances with a well-defined population rather than attempting definitive tests of the overall hypothesis of learning by discovery. Other suggestions involved important features of experimental design such as the use of multiple criteria as dependent variables, the handling of the problem of time differences in instructional treatments, and the disposition of subjects who fail to discover. Research studies were generally criticized for failing to pose questions relevant to education. It was suggested that investigators should pay greater attention to tasks growing out of classroom learning situations.

Participants suggested other possible approaches to this research area such as the application of information theory, mathematical models, and computer simulation. Research in education might also be seen as an engineering task, involving, tryout, revision, and evaluation, until an adequate educational program has been developed.

Another promising approach, with implications for the issues of the conference, is the development of computer-based instruction. Because of the flexibility continuously afforded during instruction, the use of such a research program permits the presentation of task and guidance in almost any way desired. It is possible, therefore, to study, under controlled situations, a wide diversity of sequences to answer questions involving instructional decisions concerning the amount and kind of help teachers should offer.

At the level of psychological investigations of learning, the discussions of the conference reflected an underlying parallel between statements made about the process of education and pronouncements by the same individuals about the process of scientific inquiry. It appeared that often the image of what constitutes the most fruitful approach to teaching was a reflection of the same participants' position concerning the best kind of research strategy for scientific investigation. Quite clearly, adjective pairs such as controlled-open, precise-global and logical-intuitive are equally applicable within the domains of both research and instruction. Hence, the two questions of, How should the teaching of a given subject be conducted? and How should research on teaching be conducted? were inexorably interwoven.

Those who took the position that the best kind of teaching opened up the child and insisted that the demand for operational statements of objectives was instructionally constricting, took a similar position with reference to the practice of research. They advocated the discarding, or at least the temporary suspension, of the classical hypothesis-testing model of experimental psychology and recommended in its place a more general exploratory approach to the problems. They have usually found their research approaches most fruitful when applied to forms of human behavior that are difficult to identify reliably and measure accurately, and their formulations concerning education have tended to reflect the degree of precision that is typical of their objects of research.

In contrast, those who maintained that the best instruction occurs when objectives are carefully specified also felt that systematic experimental studies with precisely stated goals and procedures showed the most promise leading to knowledge about teaching. Those with this goal-directed research orientation have been most successful in dealing with situations where the individual parameters can be reliably identified and systematically varied. Hence, in studying educational problems, they too have been drawn to those situations which best fit their own model. As Dewey observed repeatedly, the processes of education and of scientific inquiry are remarkably similar. It should be no surprise that men are found to hold parallel positions about the 'best' form of each activity. It is to a consideration of these strategies of inquiry that we now turn.

THE LEVEL OF RESEARCH STRATEGY

There is an oft-related story of the drunk who was crawling on his hands and knees under a lamppost when he was accosted by a policeman. The policeman asked the drunk what he was doing. "Looking for my wallet," was the drunk's reply. The policeman offered to help him find his wallet and asked him where he had lost it. The drunk thought for a moment and answered "About half a block down, in the alley." The policeman asked, with a mixture of curiosity and sarcasm, "Why in the world don't you look for your wallet where you lost it?" The drunk quickly responded, "It's much too dark to look for it there."

Controversies over research strategies reflect much of this drunk's dilemma. Do we look where the visibility is good, but where the probability of finding what we seek is low; or do we venture forth into the dark where the answers frequently lie, but probably in some form so obscured by their surroundings that they will not be visible to us?

The problem of strategy may be posed in the following fashion: Is it better to begin a research program by asking highly limited questions in an area where precise answers are possible, and then gradually extend the scope of inquiry so that ultimately precise answers are possible to broad questions? Or is it better to start by posing general questions which, although loosely formulated, deal with a large section of the field, and subsequently to attempt to increase the precision of the statements made?

It is unfortunate that precision and generality, both important research goals, are usually incompatible. If a line of research deals with a series of closely related but precise experiments, inevitably the scope must be restricted. The experimenter's findings, although precise, may well be irrelevant with respect to many interesting problems. Hopefully, of course, the researcher will gradually, in a small-step program of development, extend his sphere of precise description and control to include more and more general questions.

On the other hand, a research strategy which deals broadly and comprehensively with issues in a, field may produce statements which appear to be relevant to important issues; however, these generalizations are so lacking in definition that they are of no greater value than the gross over-extrapolations obtained under the first strategy. Here the need is to make the vague formulations more precise so that statements made about a large class of phenomena are more meaningful.

Thus, the dilemma remains. The strategy of beginning with narrowly focused and well controlled studies may not yield the expected base for broadening the scope. Yet, the findings of the global approach may be so inadequate to cope with the problems posed that the researcher finds himself able to state only tenuous formulations which he offers hopefully to others as a general guide.

But there is another alternative. Cronbach has suggested that perhaps an intermediate strategy is desirable. First, the tasks used for the experiments would represent the mastery of some phase of the subjects actually being taught in the school. Second, the duration of the instructional treatment would be long enough to produce cumulative learnings, without becoming so long as to be unwieldy and undefinable; experiments lasting two to twenty weeks might provide an appropriate compromise. As has been previously suggested (Keislar and Mace, 1965), generalizing from a two-month experiment to a two-year curriculum may involve over-extrapolation but at least it seems more reasonable than to base one's judgment on data collected from a 50 minute laboratory session on the same problem.

Third, with an experimental treatment a few weeks in length, it is possible to use standardized instruction, carefully prepared lessons which are manageable in terms of time and money. Under such controlled conditions, the problems of teacher variability and adequate monitoring of instructional events are minimized. Fourth, where instructional treatments last for many weeks, the total testing time can be increased to permit the assessment of a wide diversity of outcomes which may take several sessions for testing alone.

It is always satisfying to recommend a golden mean as the solution to a confrontation of opposites. The middle way has time and again demonstrated its durability in a wide range of circumstances and over a broad array of controversies. There is yet another form of middle way, which can be identified by using Schwab's (1960) term, the "grand strategy."

Since different approaches to research in themselves can highlight only parts of a total object of inquiry, a possibility could be, in Schwab's ords, "that some particular order of different strategies, constituting a grand strategy, may be better than all other orders." That is, instead of committing himself to a single orientation, whether polar or intermediate in our framework, the investigator would shift among strategies as he reformulated his questions and refocussed his inquiry. Thus, for example, it is not uncommon for psychologists to combine correlational, descriptive, and experimental designs into the same program of research. Similarly, the investigator might pose his research questions in a sequence of different ways, very much like the teacher who utilizes different instructional procedures.

The grand strategy is probably best reflected in the history of psychological studies of learning. Individual investigations, growing out of contrasting or conflicting orientations, reflect a long-term dialectic of strategies. As one set of approaches has asserted its superiority for dealing with some psychological issue, some other group has inevitably proposed an alternative to it. Frequently, these confrontations have fostered productive restatements of important issues. Yet, the resulting rhetoric of claim and counter-claim has too often led to an unfortunate overemphasis upon differences in theory, leading to research involving the examination of otherwise trivial problems. The advantage of a grand strategy for an individual worker is that he may be able to retain the flexibility of alternating among strategies while avoiding the pitfalls of conflict among them.[1]

However, such a broad approach may require the coordinated efforts of a group of specialists; few individual investigators are likely to possess the temperament and the diversity of high-level skills required. The currently rapid growth of centers of research in education

---

[1] The authors of this chapter are fully aware that the positing of these intermediate and grand strategies does not exhaust the range of alternatives available. As participants in the conference themselves, they can lay no greater claim to omniscience than any other participants. It was, in fact, with some amusement that they simultaneously recognized that the two solution strategies outlined above represented extensions of their respective research styles.

may foster the development of research programs which reflect such grand strategies. Yet, the frequent emphasis upon *inter*disciplinary research in these settings, though clearly not objectionable in themselves, may obscure an important alternative. There is great value in gathering together members of the same discipline who reflect highly contrasting investigatory styles, thus constituting an *intra*disciplinary research approach. In this way, the development of centers of research may encourage a continuing dialogue among advocates of various strategies and thus permit a fruitful restatement of a question in the early stages of a research enterprise before conflicting points of view become vested interests.

THE STATE OF THE ISSUE

This volume has attempted, from many vantage points, to deal with a major issue in education and psychology. We have described the past history of the issue and its present status. What lies ahead for the controversy over learning by discovery?

John Dewey (1910a), in his essay on "The Influence of Darwinism on Philosophy," wrote:

> . . . the conviction persists—though history shows it to be a hallucination— that all the questions that the human mind has asked are questions that can be answered in terms of the alternatives that the questions themselves present. But in fact, intellectual progress usually occurs through sheer abandonment of questions together with both of the alternatives they assume—an abandonment that results from their decreasing vitality and a change of urgent interest. We do not solve them: We get over them. Old questions are solved by disappearing, evaporating, while new questions corresponding to the changed attitude of endeavor and preference take their place.

Dewey maintained that controversies are resolved through redefinition and reformulation, rather than through victory of one side over another. We have seen in this volume a recurrent call for this very kind of reformulation of the present issue. Throughout the history of psychology, similar issues have arisen and, though not resolved in the same terms in which they were set, have nevertheless disappeared. Such questions have included nature versus nurture, insight versus trial-and-error and imageless versus image-full thinking; in not too many years, we will probably add to that list such burning questions as incremental versus all-or-none learning and learning by discovery versus guided learning.

Dewey has observed that "old ideas give way slowly, for they are more than abstract logical forms and categories. They are habits, predispositions, deeply engrained attitudes of aversion and preference." This is particularly true of the terms in which we couch those compelling controversies of which this volume is characteristic. These terms have become part of the 'familiar furniture of the mind,' and the resolution of the issue lies not in the moving of this furniture about, but in refurnishing with new terms, and perhaps, coming up with new oppositions.

It is the hope of the authors of this chapter that a highlighting of the terms of the controversy will hasten the process of reformulation rather than impede it.

Bibliography

Numbers in square brackets refer to pages in this volume where reference is cited. A number of references which were not cited directly have been included because of their general relevance to the topic.

Adams, J. K. Laboratory studies of behavior without awareness. *Psychol. Bull.*, 1957, 54, 383–405. [67]

Anderson, G. L. Quantitative thinking as developed under connectionist and field theories of learning. In Swenson, Esther J. et al, *Learning theory in school situations.* Minneapolis: University of Minnesota Press, 1949. Pp. 40–73. [48–49, 145]

Atkin, J. M., and Karplus, R. Discovery or invention? *Sci. Teacher*, 1962, 29 (5), 45–51.

Ausubel, D. P. In defense of verbal learning. *Educ. Theor.*, 1961a, 11, (1), 15–25.

Ausubel, D. P. Learning by discovery: rationale and mystique. *Bull. nat. Assoc. sec. sch. Princ.*, 1961b, 45, 18–58. [145, 149]

Ausubel, D. P. *The psychology of meaningful verbal learning.* New York: Grune and Stratton, 1963. [45, 145]

Baddeley, A. D. A Zeigarnik-like effect in the recall of anagram solutions. *Quart. J. exp. Psychol.*, 1963, 15, 63–64. [83–84]

Barnes, J. M., and Underwood, B. J. "Fate" of first-list associations in transfer theory. *J. exp. Psychol.*, 1959, 58, 97–105. [139]

Beberman, M. An emerging program of secondary school mathematics. In R. W. Heath (Ed.), *New curricula.* New York: Harper and Row, 1964. Pp. 9–34. [38]

Boole, M. E. *The preparation of the child for science.* Oxford: Clarendon Press, 1904.

Bower, G. H. An association model for response and training variables in paired-associate learning. *Psychol. Rev.,* 1962, *69,* 34–53. [20]

Breland, K., and Breland, M. The misbehavior of organisms. *Amer. Psychologist,* 1961, *16,* 681–684. [137]

Brown, R., and Fraser, C. The acquisition of syntax. In C. N. Cofer and Barbara S. Musgrave (Eds.), *Verbal behavior and learning.* New York: McGraw-Hill, 1963. Pp. 158–197. [144]

Bruner, J. S. Learning and thinking. *Harvard educ. Rev.,* 1959, *29,* 184–192. [34–35]

Bruner, J. S. *The process of education.* Cambridge: Harvard University Press, 1960.

Bruner, J. S. The act of discovery. *Harvard educ. Rev.,* 1961, *31,* 21–32. [33–34, 54, 140, 148]

Bruner, J. S. The course of cognitive growth. *Amer. Psychologist,* 1964a, *19,* 1–15.

Bruner, J. S. Some theorems on instruction illustrated with reference to mathematics. In *Sixty-third yearb. nat. Soc. Stud. Educ.,* 1964b, 306–335, Part 1. [55]

Bruner, J. S., Goodnow, Jacqueline J., and Austin, G. A. *A study of thinking.* New York: Wiley, 1956. [148]

Bugelski, B. R., and Scharlock, D. P. An experimental demonstration of unconscious mediated association. *J. exp. Psychol.,* 1952, *44,* 334–338. [67]

Burke, C. J., Estes, W. K., and Hellyer, S. Rate of verbal conditioning in relation to stimulus variability. *J. exp. Psychol.,* 1954, *48,* 153–161. [20]

Campbell, J. A. CHEM Study—an approach to chemistry based on experiments. In R. W. Heath (Ed.), *New curricula,* New York: Harper and Row, 1964. Pp. 82–93. [39]

Carroll, J. B. A model of school learning. *Teachers Coll. Rec.,* 1963, *64,* 723–733. [86, 89]

Clarkson, D. M. Taxicab geometry, rabbits, and Pascal's triangle—discoveries in a sixth-grade classroom. *The Arithmetic Teacher,* 1962, *9,* 308–313.

Corman, B. R. The effect of varying amounts and kinds of information as guidance in problem solving. *Psychol. Monogr.,* 1957, *71,* No. 2 (Whole No. 431). [59–61, 85, 88]

Craig, R. C. *The transfer value of guided learning.* New York: Teacher's College, Columbia University, 1953. [57–58, 61–62, 146]

Craig, R. C. Directed versus independent discovery of established relations. *J. Educ. Psychol.*, 1956, 47, 223–234. [57–59, 61–62, 145]

Cronbach, L. J. *Educational psychology*, 2nd edition. New York: Harcourt, Brace and World, Inc., 1963. [76]

Cronbach, L. J. Evaluation for course improvement. In R. W. Heath (Ed.), *New curricula.* New York: Harper and Row, 1964. Pp. 231–248.

Croobach, L. J. Issues current in educational psychology. In Morrisett, L. N., and Vinsonhaler, J. F. Mathematical learning. *Monog. Soc. Res. Child Develpm.*, (Serial No. 99), 1965. Pp. 109–126.

Crutchfield, R. S., and Covington, M. V. Facilitation of creative thinking and problem solving in school children. Paper presented in Symposium on Learning Research Pertinent to Educational Improvement, American Association for the Advancement of Science, Cleveland, 1963.

Davis, R. B. Mathematical thought and the nature of learning: The Madison project view. *Frontiers of education.* Report of the Twenty-Seventh Educational Conference Sponsored by the Educational Records Bureau. American Council on Education, Educational Records Bureau. 21 Audubon Ave., New York 32, New York. 1963. Pp. 79–83.

Davis, R. B. *Discovery in mathematics: A text for teachers.* Reading, Massachusetts: Addison-Wesley Publishing Co., 1964.

Davis, R. B. The Madison project's approach to a theory of instruction. *J. res. sci. Teaching*, 1964, 2, 146–162.

de Charms, R., Carpenter, Virginia, and Kuperman, A. The 'origin-pawn' variable in person perception. *Sociometry.* In press. [126]

Deese, J. From the isolated verbal unit to connected discourse. In C. N. Cofer (Ed.), *Verbal learning and verbal behavior.* New York: McGraw-Hill, 1961. PP. 11–31. [140]

Della-Piana, G., and Eldredge, G. M. Discovery learning in programmed instruction. Paper read at the Second Annual Convention of the National Society for Programmed Instruction, San Antonio, Texas, 1964. [54, 70, 72]

Dewey, J. *How we think.* Boston: Heath, 1910. [41–42]

Dewey, J. The influence of Darwinism on philosophy. In *The influence of Darwinism on philosophy and other essays in contemporary thought*. New York: Henry Holt and Co., 1901a. [198]

Dienes, Z. P. *The power of mathematics*. London: Hutchinson Educational Lte., 1964.

Dietze, Doris. The facilitating effect of words on discrimination and generalization. *J. exp. Psychol.*, 1955, 50, 255–260.

Donaldson, Margaret. *A study of children's thinking*. New York: Humanities Press, 1964. [160]

Duncan, C. P. Recent research on human problem solving. *Psychol. Bull.*, 1959, 56, 397–429. [71]

Duncan, C. P. Effect of instructions and information on problem solving. *J. exp. Psychol.*, 1963, 65, 321–327.

Duncan. C. P. Learning to learn in response-discovery and in paired-associate lists. *Amer. J. Psychol.*, 1964, 77, 367–379. [79, 86]

Elliott, R. Physiological activity and performance: A comparison of kindergarten children with young adults. *Psychol. Monogr.*, 1964, 78, No. 10 (Whole No. 587). [153]

Ervin, Susan M. Transfer effects of learning a verbal generalization. *Child Develpm.*, 1960, 31, 537–554.

Estes, W. K. The statistical approach to learning theory. In S. Koch (Ed.), *Psychology: A study of a science; Vol. 2., General systematic formulations, learning, and special processes*. New York: McGraw-Hill, 1959. Pp. 380–491. [137]

Evans, J. L., Homme, L. E., and Glaser, R. The ruleg system for the construction of programmed verbal learning sequences. *J. educ. Res.*, 1962, 55, 513–518. [15–16]

Ewert, P. H., and Lambert, J. F. Part II: The effect of verbal instructions upon the formation of a concept. *J. gen. Psychol.*, 1932, 6, 400–413. [66, 67]

Farber, I. E. The things people say to themselves. *Amer. Psychologist*, 1963, 18, 185–197.

Festinger, L. *A theory of cognitive dissonance*. Evanston, Ill.: Row, Peterson, 1957. [159]

Finlay, G. C. Secondary school physics: The physical science study committee, *American J. Physics*, 1960, 28, 286–293.

Forgus, R. H., and Schwartz, R. J. Efficient retention and transfer as affected by learning method. *J. Psychol.*, 1957, 43, 135–139. [49, 82]

Fowler, H. *Curiosity and exploratory behavior.* New York: Macmillan, 1965. [25–26]

Gagné, R. M. The acquisition of knowledge. *Psychol. Rev.,* 1962, 69, 355–365. [55, 68–69]

Gagné, R. M. Problem solving. In A. W. Melton (Ed.), *Categories of human learning.* New York: Academic Press, 1964. Pp. 293–317. [56]

Gagné, R. M. *The conditions of learning.* New York: Holt, Rinehart and Winston, Inc., 1965. [139, 143]

Gagné, R. M., and Brown, L. T. Some factors in the programming of conceptual learning. *J. exp. Psychol.,* 1961. 62, 313–321. [52–54, 71, 79–81, 84–85, 88–89, 146–148]

Gagné, R. M., and Paradise, N.E. Abilities and learning sets in knowledge acquisition. *Psychol. Monogr.,* 1961, 75, No. 14 (Whole No. 518). [69]

Gagné, R. M., and Smith, E. C., Jr. A study of the effects of verbalization on problem solving. *J. exp. Psychol.,* 1962, 63, 12–18. [67, 85]

Gagné, R. M., Foster, Harriet, and Crowley, Miriam E. The measurement of transfer of training. *Psychol. Bull.,* 1948, 45, 97–130. [72]

Gagné, R. M., Mayor, J. R., Garstens, H. L., and Paradise, N. E. Factors in acquiring knowledge of a mathematical task. *Psychol. Monogr.,* 1962. 76, No. 7 (Whole No. 526).

Gibson, J. J. A critical review of the concepts of set in contemporary experimental psychology. *Psychol. Bull.,* 1941, 38, 781–817. [135–136]

Gilbert, T. F. An approximation to principles of programming continuous discourse, self-instructional materials. A report to the Bell Telephone Laboratories, September, 1958. (Unpublished paper, mimeo). Abstracted in Lumsdaine, A. A. and Glaser, R. (Eds.) *Teaching machines and programmed learning.* Washington: National Education Association, 1960. Pp. 630–635. [22–23]

Glaser, R. Instructional technology and the measurement of learning outcomes: Some questions. *Amer. Psychologist,* 1963, 18, 519–521. [72]

Glaser, R., Klaus, D. J., and Egerman, K. Increasing team proficiency through training. II. The acquisition and extinction of a team response. Pittsburgh: American Inst. for Res., 1962. [86]

Glass, B. Renascent biology: A report on the AIBS biological sciences curriculum study. In R. W. Heath (Ed.), *New curricula*. New York: Harper and Row, 1964. Pp. 94–119.

Goldstein, M., and Weber, R. J. Contingent discrimination in humans. *Percept. and Mot. Skills*, 1965, 21, 171–176. [142]

Grote, C. N. A comparison of the relative effectiveness of direct-detailed and directed discovery methods of teaching selected principles of mechanics in the area of physics. Unpublished doctoral dissertation. Urbana, Ill., University of Illinois, 1960. [63]

Hanson, N. R. *Patterns of discovery*. New York: Cambridge University Press, 1958. [78]

Harlow, H. F. The formation of learning sets. *Psychol. Rev.*, 1949, 56, 51–65. [140–142]

Harlow, H. F. Learning set and error factor theory. In Sigmund Koch (Ed.), *Psychology: A study of science*. Vol. 2. New York: McGraw-Hill. 1959. Pp. 492–537. [20]

Haslerud, G. M., and Meyers, Shirley. The transfer value of given and individually derived principles. *J. educ. Psychol.*, 1958, 49, 293–298. [62, 67, 79, 82–83]

Hawkins. D. On living in trees. Karl Muenzinger Memorial Lecture, University of Colorado, 1964.

Hendrix, Gertrude. A new clue to transfer of training. *Elem. sch. J.*, 1947, 48, 197–208. [44–45, 49–50]

Hendrix, Gertrude. Prerequisite to meaning. *Math. Teacher*, 1950, 43, 334–339. [49]

Hendrix, Gertrude. Learning by discovery. *Math. Teacher*, 1961, 54, 290–299. [49]

Hilgard, E. R., Edgren, R. D., and Irvine, R. P. Errors in transfer following learning with understanding: Further studies with Katona's card-trick experiments. *J. exp. Psychol.*, 1954, 47, 457–464. [85]

Hilgard, E. R., Irvine, R. P., and Whipple, J. E. Rote memorization, understanding, and transfer: An extension of Katona's card-trick experiments. *J. exp. Psychol.*, 1953, 46, 288–292. [80–81, 89]

Hunter, W. S. The delayed reaction in animals and children. *Behav. Monogr.*, 1913, 2, No. 1. [141]

Jeffrey, W. E. The effects of verbal and nonverbal responses in mediating an instrumental act. *J. exp. Psychol.*, 1953, 45, 327–333.

Jenkins, J. J. Mediated associations: Paradigms and situations. In C. N. Cofer and Barbara S. Musgrave (Eds.), *Verbal behavior and learning.* New York: McGraw-Hill, 1963. Pp. 210–245. [139–140]

Judd, C. H. The relation of special training to general intelligence. *Edu. Rev.,* 1908, 36, 28–42. [57]

Judson, A. J., and Cofer, C. N. A study of direction in problem solution. *Amer. Psychologist,* 1950, 5, 274. (abstract)

Kagan, J. The child's sex role classification of school objects. *Child Develpm.,* 1964, 35, 1051–1056. [156]

Kagan, J., Rosman, Bernice L., Day, D., Albert, J., and Phillips, W. Information processing in the child: Significance of analytic and reflective attitudes. *Psychol. Monogr.,* 1964, 78, No. 1 (Whole No. 578). [160]

Katona, G. *Organizing and memorizing.* New York: Columbia University Press, 1940. [67, 147–148]

Keislar, E. R., and Mace, L. Sequence of speaking and listening training in beginning French. In J. Krumboltz (Ed.) *Learning and the educational process.* Chicago: Rand McNally & Co., 1965. [196]

Keller, F. S., and Schoenfeld, W. N. *Principles of psychology.* New York: Appleton-Century-Crofts, 1950. [19]

Kendler, Tracy S., and Kendler, H. H. Reversal and nonreversal shifts in kindergarten children. *J. exp. Psychol.,* 1959, 58, 56–60.

Kendler, H. H., and Kendler, Tracy S. Effect of verbalization on reversal shifts in children. *Science,* 1961, 134, (3490), 1619–1620. (abstract) [141–143]

Kendler, H. H., and Kendler, Tracy S. Vertical and horizontal processes in problem solving. *Psychol. Rev.,* 1962, 69, 1–16.

Kersh, B. Y. The adequacy of "meaning" as an explanation for superiority of learning by independent discovery. *J. educ. Psychol.,* 1958, 49, 282–292. [50–51, 71, 84, 87–89, 146]

Kersh, B. Y. The motivating effect of learning by directed discovery. *J. educ. Psychol.,* 1962, 53, 65–71. [50–52, 88]

Kersh, B. Y. Directed discovery vs. programmed instruction, a test of a theoretical position involving educational technology. Final Report, NDEA Title VII. Project Number 907, Grant Number 7-47-0000-165, Oregon State System of Higher Education, 1964. [86, 88–89]

Kersh, B. Y. Learning by discovery: what is learned? *The Arithmetic Teacher*, 1964, 11, 226–232. [86, 88–89]

Kersh, B. Y., and Wittrock, M. C. Learning by discovery: An interpretation of recent research. *J. teacher Educ.*, 1962, 13, 461–468. [45]

Kittle, J. E. An experimental study of the effect of external direction during learning on transfer and retention of principles. *J. educ. Psychol.*, 1957, 48, 391–405. [57–58, 61–62, 146]

Kuenne, Margaret. Experimental investigation of the relation of language to transposition behavior in young children. *J. exp. Psychol.*, 1946, 36, 471–490. [141]

Lawrence, D. H. The evaluation of training and transfer programs in terms of efficiency measures. *J. Psychol.*, 1954, 38, 367–382. [84]

Lewis, B. N., and Pask, G. The theory and practice of adaptive teaching systems. In R. Glaser (Ed.), *Teaching machines and programmed learning. II: Data and directions.* Washington: National Educational Association. 1965. [20–21]

Lorge, I., Fox, D., Davitz, J., and Brenner, M. A survey of studies contrasting the quality of group performance and individual performance, 1920–1957. *Psychol. Bull.*, 1958, 55, 337–372. [86]

Luchins, A. S. Mechanization in problem solving: The effect of Einstellung. *Psychol. Monogr.*, 1942, 54, No. 6 (Whole No. 248). [66]

Luria, A. R. *The role of speech in the regulation of normal and abnormal behavior.* New York: Liveright Publishing Corporation, 1961.

McConnell, T. R. Discovery vs. authoritative identification in the learning of children. *Stud. Educ.*, 1934, 9, (5), 13–60. [81–82, 86, 89, 145]

MacKinnon, D. W. Personality and the realization of creative potential. *Amer. Psychologist*, 1965, 20, 273–81. [155]

Mackworth, N. H. Originality. *Amer. Psychologist*, 1965, 20, 51–66. [78]

Maier, N. R. F. Reasoning in humans I: On direction. *J. comp. Psychol.*, 1930, 10, 115–143. [65–66, 147–148]

Mandler, G. From association to structure. *Psychol. Rev.*, 1962, 69, 415–427. [55]

Mechner, F. *Programming for automated instruction.* New York: Basic Systems, 1961. (Mimeo) [16–18]

Mechner, F. Science education and behavioral technology. In R. Glaser (Ed.), *Teaching machines and programmed learning. II: Data and directions.* Washington: National Educational Association, 1965. [23–24]

Melton, A. W. Learning. In W. S. Monroe (Ed.), *Encyclopedia of educational research.* (rev. ed.). New York: Macmillan Company, 1950. Pp. 668–690. [138, 149]

Montessori, Maria. *The Montessori method.* New York: Frederick A. Stokes Company, 1912. [40]

Montessori, Maria. *The advanced Montessori method: Spontaneous activity in education.* New York: Frederick A. Stokes Co., 1917. [40–41]

Moss, J., Jr. An experimental study of the relative effectiveness of the direct-detailed and the directed discovery methods of teaching letterpress imposition. Unpublished doctoral dissertation. Urbana, Ill.: University of Illinois, 1960. [63]

Mowrer, O. H. *Learning theory and behavior.* New York: Wiley and Sons, Inc., 1960. [136]

Noble, C. E. Meaningfulness and familiarity. In C. N. Cofer and Barbara S. Musgrave (Eds.), *Verbal behavior and learning.* New York: McGraw-Hill, 1963. Pp. 76–119. [139]

Olson, D. R. Note on Haslerud and Meyers' transfer-of-principles experiment. *J. educ. Psychol.,* 1965, 56, 107–108. [82–83]

Orata, P. T. Recent research studies on transfer of training with implications for the curriculum, guidance, and personnel work. *J. educ. Res.,* 1941, 35, 81–101.

Osgood, C. E. *Method and theory in experimental psychology.* New York: Oxford University Press, 1953. [55]

Osgood, C. E., Suci, G. J., and Tannenbaum, P. H. *The measurement of meaning.* Urbana, Illinois: University of Illinois Press, 1957. [55]

Osler, Sonia F., and Fivel, Myrna W. Concept attainment: I. The role of age and intelligence in concept attainment by induction. *J. exp. Psychol.,* 1961, 62, 1–8. [90]

Osler, Sonia F., and Trautman, Grace. Concept attainment: II. Effect of stimulus complexity upon concept attainment at two levels of intelligence. *J. exp. Psychol.,* 1961, 62, 9–13. [90]

Page, D. P. *Theory and practice of teaching.* New York: A. S. Barnes and Company, 1885. [183]

Pincus, M. An adventure in discovery. *The Arithmetic Teacher,* 1964, 11, 28–29.

Postman, L. The present status of interference theory. In C. N. Cofer (Ed.), *Verbal learning and verbal behavior.* New York: McGraw-Hill, 1961. Pp. 152–179. [139]

Postman, L. Short-term memory and incidental learning. In A. W. Melton (Ed.), *Categories of human learning.* New York: Academic Press, 1964. Pp. 145–201. [67]

Postman, L., and Sassenrath, J. The automatic action of verbal rewards and punishments. *J. gen. Psychol.,* 1961, 65, 109–136. [67]

Ray, W. E. Pupil discovery vs. direct instruction. *J. exp. Educ.,* 1961, 29, 271–280. [63, 88]

Reed, H. B. The learning and retention of concepts: II. The influence of length of series: III. The origin of concepts. *J. exp. Psychol.,* 1946a, 36, 166–179. [66]

Reed, H. B. The learning and retention of concepts. IV. The influence of the complexity of the stimuli. *J. exp. Psychol.,* 1946b, 36, 252–261.

Ripple, R. E., and Rockcastle, V. N. (Eds.), Piaget rediscovered. *J. res. sci. teaching,* 1964, 2, (3). And as a separate, Cornell University, 1964. [79]

Rowlett, J. D. An experimental comparison of direct-detailed and directed discovery methods of teaching orthographic projection principles and skills. Unpublished doctoral dissertation. Urbana, Ill.: University of Illinois, 1960. [63]

Russell, W. A. Purpose and the problem of associative selectivity. In C. N. Cofer and Barbara S. Musgrave (Eds.), *Verbal behavior and learning.* New York: McGraw-Hill, 1963. Pp. 258–271. [139]

Sassenrath, J. M. Transfer of learning without awareness. *Psychol. Rep.,* 1962, 10, 411–420. [67]

Saugstad, P. Problem-solving as dependent on availability of functions. *Brit. J. Psychol.,* 1955, 46, 191–198. [66]

Saugstad, P., and Raaheim, K. Problem-solving, past experience and availability of functions. *Brit. J. Psychol.,* 1960, 51, 97–104.

Schlosberg, H., and Solomon, R. L. Latency of response in a choice discrimination. *J. exp. Psychol.,* 1943, 33, 22–39. [19]

Schultz, R. W. Problem solving behavior and transfer. *Harvard educ. Rev.*, 1960, 30, (1), 61–77. [71]

Schwab, J. J. What do scientists do? *Behavorial Sci.*, 1960, 5, 1–27. [197]

Schwab, J. J., and Brandwein, P. F. *The Teaching of Science.* Cambridge: Harvard University Press, 1962.

Simon, H. A., and Newell, A. Information processing in computer and man. *Amer. Scientist*, 1964, 52, 281–300. [24]

Simon, H. A., and Simon, P. A. Trial and error search in solving difficult problems: Evidence from the game of chess. *Behavioral Sci.*, 1962, 7, 425–429. [24–25]

Smedslund, Jan. The acquisition of conservation of substance and weight in children. III. Extinction of conservation of weight acquired 'normally' and by means of empirical controls on a balance. *Scand. J. Psychol.*, 1961, 2, 85–87. [89]

Snyder, H. D. An impromptu discovery lesson in algebra. *The mathematics teacher*, 1964, 57, 415–416.

Spence, K. W. The differential response in animals to stimuli varying within a single dimension. *Psychol. Rev.*, 1937, *44*, 430–444. [141]

Staats, A. W., and Staats, Carolyn K. *Complex human behavior.* New York: Holt, Rinehart and Winston, 1963. [139]

Stacey, C. L. The law of effect in retained situation with meaningful material. In Swenson, Esther *J. et al, Learning theory in school situations.* University of Minnesota Studies in Education. Minneapolis: University of Minnesota Press, 1949. Pp. 74–103. [57–58, 79]

Stanley, J. C., Jr. The role of instruction, discovery, and revision in early learning. *Elem. sch. J.*, 1949, *49*, 455–458.

Stolurow, L. M., and Bergum, B. Learning diagnostic information-effects of direction of association and of prose versus paired-associate presentation. Air Force Personnel and Training Research Center, Technical Documentary Report Series, AFPTRC-TN57-12, ASTIA Document Number 113052, 1957. [69–70]

Suchman, J. R. Inquiry training in the elementary school. *Sci. Teacher*, 1960, 27, (7), 42–47.

Suchman, J. R. Inquiry training: Building skills for autonomous discovery. *Merrill-Palmer Quart. Behav. Develpm.*, 1961, 7, 147–169. [37–38]

Suchman, J. R. The child and the inquiry process. In A. H. Passow (Ed.), *Intellectual development: Another Look*. Washington, D. C.: Association for Supervision and Curriculum Development, 1964. [124]

Suppes, P., and Ginsberg, Rose. Application of a stimulus sampling model to children's concept formation with and without overt correction responses. *J. exp. Psychol.*, 1962, 63, 330–336. [20]

Swenson, Esther J. Organization and generalization as factors in learning, transfer, and retroactive inhibition. In Swenson, Esther J. et al, *Learning theory in school situations*. Minneapolis: University of Minnesota Press, 1949. Pp. 9–39. [46–48, 145]

Taba, Hilda. Learning by discovery: Psychological and educational rationale. Paper presented to the American Educational Research Association, Atlantic City, N. J., February, 1962.

Terrace, H. S. Discrimination learning with and without "errors." *J. exp. anal. Behav.*, 1963a, 6, (1), 1–27. [19]

Terrace, H. S. Errorless transfer of a discrimination across two continua. *J. exp. anal. Behav.*, 1963b, 6, (2), 223–232. [19]

Thiele, C. L. *The contribution of generalization to the learning of addition facts*. New York: Teachers College, Columbia University, 1938. [49, 81–82, 145]

Thorndike, E. L. Animal intelligence. An experimental study of the associative processes in animals. *Psychol. rev. monogr. Suppl.*, 1898, 2, No. 4 (Whole No. 8). [137]

Thorndike, E. L. *The psychology of wants, interests, and attitudes*. New York: Appleton-Century, 1935. [46]

Tolman, E. C. Cognitive maps in rats and men. *Psychol. Rev.*, 1948, 55, 189–208. [11, 97, 173]

Tomlinson, R. M. A comparison of four methods of presentation for teaching complex technical material. Unpublished doctoral dissertation. Urbana, Ill.: University of Illinois, 1962. [63]

Toulmin, S. *The philosophy of science*. London: Hutchison's University Library, 1953. [9–10]

Travers, R. M. W. *An introduction to educational research* (2nd ed.), New York: Macmillan, 1964. [83]

Underwood, B. J., and Richardson, J. Verbal concept learning as a function of instructions and dominance level. *J. exp. Psychol.*, 1956, 51, 229–238. [66–67]

Underwood, B. J., and Schulz, R. W. *Meaningfulness and verbal learning.* Chicago: Lippincott, 1960. [56, 139]

Underwood, B. J. Stimulus selection in verbal learning. In C. N. Cofer and Barbara S. Musgrave (Eds.), *Verbal behavior and learning.* New York: McGraw-Hill, 1963. Pp. 33–48. [139]

Underwood, B. J. The representativeness of rote verbal learning. In A. W. Melton (Ed.), *Categories of human learning.* New York: Academic Press, 1964. Pp. 47–78. [139]

White, R. W. Motivation reconsidered: The concept of competence. *Psychol. Rev.,* 1959, 66, 297–333. [53, 107]

Wickelgren, W. A. Cues that elicit analytic-deductive methods in concept attainment. *Brit. J. Psychol.,* 1964, 55, 143–154. [85]

Wittrock, M. C. Set applied to student teaching. *J. educ. Psychol.,* 1962, 53, 175–180. [66]

Wittrock, M. C. Effect of certain sets upon complex verbal learning. *J. educ. Psychol.,* 1963a, 54, 85–88. [62–63, 66]

Wittrock, M. C. Set to learn and proactive inhibition. *J. educ. Res.,* 1963b, 57, 72–75. [66]

Wittrock, M. C. Verbal stimuli in concept formation: Learning by discovery. *J. educ. Psychol.,* 1963c, 54, 183–190. [45]

Wittrock, M. C., Keislar, E. R., and Stern, Carolyn. Verbal cues in concept identification. *J. educ. Psychol.,* 1964, 55, 195–200. [63–65, 79]

Wittrock, M. C., and Keislar, E. R. Verbal cues in the transfer of concepts. *J. educ. Psychol.,* 1965, 56, 16–21. [64–65]

Wooten, W. The history and status of the school mathematics study group. In R. W. Heath (Ed.), *New curricula.* New York: Harper and Row, 1964. Pp. 35–53. [39]

Index

213

Discrimination, 18-19
effects of reward and punishment, 19
sensory, 13
use in concept learning, 18-19
without intervention of teacher, 40
(see also Learning, discrimination)
Discussion:
compared to lectures, 165
unequal participation of all students in, 129, 164
(see also Group instruction)
Discussions:
manner of summarizing for this volume, viii-ix
Dissonance theory, 159

Education:
as cultural transmission, 76, 101-102
distinguished from training, 127-128
as engineering, 94
fads, 91
as growth, 76
Socratic, 86, 94
(see also Objectives, educational)
Educational design, 13-14, 77
Educational goals:
(see Objectives, educational)
Educational objectives:
(see Objectives, educational)
Educational procedure:
as a system, 84-85
Educational research:
as investigative art, 3
preparation, 6
techniques:
analysis of, 173-174
assessment of, 174
interaction with personality variables, 174
Educational researchers:
should look like teachers not laboratory scientists, 6
Einstein, A., 10
Eskimos, 106
Error, 46
amount of, 22
condition for discrimination, 19-20
and correction, 96
definition, 19
as function of objectives, 96-97
as function of subject matter, 96-97, 183
minimization of:
(see Error minimization)
probability of occurrence in discovery sequences, 15
use, 17, 96-97
(see also Errorful learning)
Error factor theory (Harlow), 20
Error minimization, 19-21
effect in discovery sequence, 19-21
lack of investigation of effects, 20-22
overt correction:
in young children, 20-21
in programmed instruction, 19
rationale for, 16-17, 20-21
frustration and emotional effects, 20
lack of control over the learning process, 20
richer association learning, 20

Error minimization—*Cont.*
value of, 20
Errorful learning, 15, 18-21
differential usefulness depending upon goals, 21-23
function in discovery sequence, 19-20
Evaluation:
of behavioral results of mediating events, 55-56
of discovery learning, 36, 193
in educational design, 14
of educational programs, 175
of processes or product, 189
Expectancy of success or failure, 155
and anxiety, 155
Experimental analysis of behavior, 13-14, 83
Experimental design:
inadequacy of theory for, 113
problems in:
assignment of experimental subjects failing to discover, 83, 194
training subjects to criterion versus equating time, 83-84, 194
types of:
transfer, 96
Experimental psychology:
relevance to educational problems, 5, 173
of California latent learning studies, 11, 97, 173
Experimental tasks:
(see Tasks, experimental)
Exploration:
(see Preparation and exploration)

Field theory:
(see Learning, theory of, field theory)

Goals:
(See Objectives, educational)
Goal directed teaching:
contrasted with open-ended teaching, 187-188
Group instruction:
differences from individual instruction, 86, 131
(see also Discussion)
Guidance:
amount, 51, 53, 77
and kind of students, 184
and nature of objectives, 184
in problem solving, 148
and subject matter, 184
(see also Guidance, degrees of)
character:
didactic teaching of algorithms, 85
hints, use, 85
by classroom teacher, 183-185
decreasing time for search, 150
degrees, 85, 130, 149, 163, 182-183
amount of independent search demanded, 146
full guidance, 142-143, 183
guided discovery, 142-143, 183
(see also Guided discovery)
no guidance, 142-143
shifting, 183-184
(see also Guidance, amount of)
in educational design, 14

Printed in U.S.A.